The Triangle Strike and Fire

The Triangle Strike and Fire

John F. McClymer
Assumption College

HARCOURT BRACE COLLEGE PUBLISHERS

Fort Worth   Philadelphia   San Diego   New York   Orlando   Austin   San Antonio
Toronto   Montreal   London   Sydney   Tokyo

PUBLISHER	Christopher P. Klein
ACQUISITIONS EDITOR	David Tatom
PRODUCT MANAGER	Steve Drummond
DEVELOPMENTAL EDITOR	Margaret McAndrew Beasley
PROJECT EDITOR	Andrea Wright
ART DIRECTOR	Scott Baker
PRODUCTION MANAGER	Linda McMillan

Cover Image: Victor Joseph Gatto, *Triangle Fire*, March 25, 1911. Oil on canvas, 19″ × 28″. Museum of the City of New York, Gift of Mrs. Henry L. Moses.

ISBN: 0-15-503818-4

Library of Congress Catalog Card Number: 97-73494

Address for orders:
Harcourt Brace College Publishers
6277 Sea Harbor Drive
Orlando, FL 32887-6777
1-800-782-4479

Address for editorial correspondence:
Harcourt Brace College Publishers
301 Commerce Street, Suite 3700
Fort Worth, TX 76102

Web site address: http://www.hbcollege.com

Printed in the United States of America
7 8 9 0 1 2 3 4 5 6   039   9 8 7 6 5 4 3 2 1

To Joan

The Story behind the Series

On April 23, 1911—only one month after the Triangle Fire claimed the lives of 146 textile factory workers in New York City—another industrial disaster, another fire, claimed more lives. This fire was at the Gypsy Grove mine near Scranton, Pennsylvania. A locomotive was hauling coal to the top of the breaker, the several-story structure where the coal was "broken" into baseball-sized lumps, when a spark from its smokestack leaped onto some paper. Within seconds the fire spread to the coal-dust-saturated wooden frame of the breaker which went up, in the words of the only survivor, "like a giant kitchen match." One of those killed was the checkweigh man, the union official who certified the tonnage credited to each miner. His name was John Earley. As the flames enveloped him, he cried out "Mary!"—the name of his five-year-old daughter.

More than three decades later, Mary McClymer, née Mary Earley, gave birth to a son whom she called John. What she sought in giving me her father's name—what we all seek when we inscribe births, deaths, and marriages so carefully into family Bibles or save photographs of our grandparents to show our grandchildren—was to affirm that our lives extend backward to people we have never seen and forward to people who will never see us but will know that we lived and that our living mattered. She sought what we all seek: meaning in the stories of history.

The American Stories Series

American Stories is a series of documentary readers, each devoted to some salient event in American history. Each brings together evidence about some of those people whose lives mattered in the making of our common story. In each story, the goal is to enable students to use the evidence gathered to construct their own version of that story, to determine what happened, to decide who did what and why, and, most of all, to enable them to see for themselves why and how those lives mattered. The goal is to enable students to discover the fascination of "doing" history.

The Triangle Strike and Fire

The Triangle Strike and Fire is the first volume in this series. Like volumes to follow—on the Mississippi Freedom Summer of 1964 and the First Woman's Rights Convention of 1850—*The Triangle Strike and Fire* is concerned with events which represent intersections of several major themes in the American story. *Triangle* tells of the first successful strike of women workers, the "Uprising of the Twenty Thousand," and of one of the worst industrial disasters of our century. It tells of sorority, of the joining together of immigrant workers, college-educated "New Women," society grandes dames, and suffrage activists in an improbable alliance. It tells too of that coalition's unraveling along class, ethnic, and ideological divides and then, in the post-fire campaign for factory safety legislation, of its brief but triumphant re-emergence. It tells the story of the beginnings of a new reform partnership linking labor unions, middle-class reform organizations, and big city machines like New York's Tammany Hall. And it tells the stories of some of the many individuals whose struggles changed the history of their time and continue to shape ours.

Historians, like other scholars, divide as they conquer, developing specializations in labor history, cultural studies, women's history, ethnic history, "new" political and social histories, and so on almost ad infinitum. But, as the Triangle story reminds us, these are all dimensions of a single past. And because this story pulls all of these themes and approaches together, instructors can give their students the opportunity to "do" real history without sacrificing breadth of coverage.

Triangle brings together the stories of the strike and the fire, stories usually (inexplicably) studied separately. It brings together women's history and political history, ethnic history and cultural studies, business history, and urban history. It also integrates the fine and popular arts into the story. The graphic images in this book do not so much illustrate as propel the story. John Sloan's cartoons, for instance, grew out of his resolve that his art should change the world about him, not simply capture or comment upon some aspect of the passing scene.

Acknowledgments

Many people have helped bring this project to fruition, starting with Drake Bush, then history acquisitions editor at Harcourt Brace College Publishers, whose support, tact, and friendship were invaluable. Only slightly less important was the tireless energy of Michele Roy, an undergraduate student at Assumption College, who spent the summer of 1996 working as my research assistant, and who contributed to this book in more ways than I can enumerate. I also want to thank Carol Maksian, the chief research librarian at Assumption College, and her staff, particularly Amanda Nelson and Larry Spongberg. Nancy Gaudette, of the Worcester Public Library, also went well out of her way to help me locate materials. Once I had put a draft together, I benefited mightily from the suggestions of my friend, Gerd Korman, professor emeritus of history at Cornell University. I would also like to thank the following reviewers whose comments on the manuscript did much to improve it: Debra Barth, San Jose City College; and Michael Mayer, University of Montana. Thanks as well to David Tatom, acquisitions editor, and Margaret Beasley, developmental editor at Harcourt Brace, for their many helpful suggestions and support. Finally, I would like to thank my students in History 113: Women in the American Experience, upon whom I tested an early version of this book, and the many students at schools across the country who visited my Triangle Web site, asked questions, offered suggestions, and proved, by their enthusiasm, that nothing makes history come alive like a compelling story.

Contents

Preface   vii

Frontispiece   xvi

Prologue   xviii

New York *World* Account of the Triangle Fire, March 26, 1911   xviii

1   The "Working Girl"   1

Introduction: "Who Will Protect the 'Working Girl'?"   1

Portfolio I   1

    Notes   9

"Working Girls" in Their Own Words   12

    "The Story of a Sweatshop Girl" and "A Cap Maker's Story"   12

       "The Story of a Sweatshop Girl," Sadie Frowne, *The Independent* 54
       (September 25, 1902)   13

       "A Cap Maker's Story," Rose Schneiderman, *The Independent* 58
       (March 20, 1905)   17

2   The Strike: The "Uprising of the Twenty Thousand"   20

Portfolio II   21

Chronology of the Strike   22

    Rules for Pickets, circular issued by Local 25 of the International
    Ladies Waist Makers Union   24

News Accounts of the Strike   26

    "Arrest Strikers for Being Assaulted," *New York Times,*
    November 5, 1909   27

    "The Strike of the Shirtwaist Makers," *The World Today*
    (March 1910)   28

    "Girl Strikers Well Treated"   29

    "Girl Strikers Well Treated, Says Baker," *New York Times,*
    November 6, 1909   29

    Cooper Union Meeting   31

    "40,000 Called Out in Women's Strike," *New York Times,*
    November 23, 1909   32

    "The Shirtwaist Makers' Strike," *The Survey,*
    December 18, 1909   33

First Day of General Strike   33

"Waist Strike On; 18,000 Women Out," *New York Times*,
November 24, 1909   34

"Waist Strike Grows"   35

"Waist Strike Grows," *New York Times*,
November 25, 1909   36

"Girl Strikers Riot"   36

"Girl Strikers Riot; Quelled by Police," *New York Times*,
November 27, 1909   37

"Girl Strikers Go to the City Hall"   38

"Girl Strikers Go to the City Hall," *New York Times*,
December 4, 1909   38

The Hippodrome Meeting   41

"Throng Cheers on the Girl Strikers," *New York Times*,
December 6, 1909   41

Colony Club Meeting   42

"Girl Strikers Tell the Rich Their Woes," *New York Times*,
December 16, 1909   43

Violet Pike Arrest   44

"Arrest Suffragist Talker," *New York Times*,
December 19, 1909   45

"Police Break Up Strikers' Meeting," *New York Times*,
December 22, 19.09   45

Reception for Strikers Released from Workhouse   46

"Pickets from Prison are Guests of Honor," *New York Times*,
December 23, 1909   47

Strikers Reject Arbitration Agreement   48

"Shirtwaist Strike Peace Plan Fails," *New York Times*,
December 28, 1909   49

Carnegie Hall Meeting   49

"The Rich Out to Aid Girl Waistmakers," *New York Times*,
January 3, 1910   50

Postscript to New Accounts   51

"Mrs. Belmont Holds Stock in Union Shop,"
New York Times, January 15, 1910   52

Strike Participants' Accounts   52

"The Spirit of the Girl Strikers"   52

"The Spirit of the Girl Strikers," Miriam Finn Scott,
The Outlook 94 (February 19, 1910)   53

Natalya Perovskaya's "Tale of Adventure"   57

"The Shirt-Waist Makers' Strike"   58
  By Sue Ainsley Clark and Edith Wyatt from *Making Both
  Ends Meet: The Income and Outlay of New York Working Girls*
  (New York: Macmillan, 1911)   58
  "The Spirit of the Strikers"   67
    "The Spirit of the Strikers," Mary Brown Sumner,
    The Survey 23 (January 22, 1910)   68
  All for One   70
Excerpts from *All For One*   71
  By Rose Schneiderman (with Lucy Goldthwaite)
  (New York: Paul S. Eriksson, 1967)   71
Contemporary Assessments   74
  "The Hygienic Aspects of the Shirtwaist Strike"   74
    "The Hygienic Aspects of the Shirtwaist Strike," Woods
    Hutchinson, M.D., *The Survey* 23 (January 22, 1910) 75
  An "Ally" Views the Strike   78
    "A Woman's Strike—An Appreciation of the Shirtwaist
    Makers of New York," Helen Marot, *Proceedings of the
    Academy of Political Science of the City of New York* 1
    (October 1910)   79

3 The Triangle Fire   84
Portfolio III   85
Chronology of the Fire   86
The Fire and Its Immediate Aftermath   88
  "The Washington Place Fire"   88
    "The Washington Place Fire," Rosey Safran,
    The Independent 70 (April 20, 1911)   89
  "Partners' Account of the Disaster"   90
    "Partners' Account of the Disaster," *New York Times*,
    March 26, 1911   91
  "Scenes at the Morgue"   94
    "Scenes at the Morgue," *New York Times*,
    March 26, 1911   94
  Shirtwaist Makers' Union Memorial Meeting   96
    "Faint in a Frenzy over Tales of Fire," *New York Times*,
    March 30, 1911   98
  Rose Schneiderman's Speech at the Metropolitan Opera   99
    "Mass Meeting Calls for New Fire Laws,"
    New York Times, April 4, 1911   101

"120,000 Pay Tribute to the Fire Victims"   102

"120,000 Pay Tribute to the Fire Victims,"
New York Times, April 6, 1911   103

Red Cross Relief Efforts   104

"The Factory Fire and the Red Cross," *The Survey* 28
(May 25, 1912)   105

"Budgets of the Triangle Fire Victims,"
Elizabeth Dutcher, *Life and Labor* (September 1912)   107

"Lives at $75"   109

"Lives at $75," *The Literary Digest* 48 (March 28, 1914)   109

Assaying Responsibility   110

Trial Accounts   110

"Enraged Women Mob Triangle Waist Men,"
New York Times, December 6, 1911   112

"Jury Hears of Locked Door," *New York Times*,
December 7, 1911   113

"Fatal Lock Let in Triangle Fire Case," *New York Times*,
December 16, 1911   114

Cross Examination of Kate Alterman by Defense Attorney,
Max D. Steuer *(The People v. Harris & Blanck*, 1911)   115

"Triangle Owners Acquitted by Jury," *New York Times*,
December 28, 1911   126

"One of Them"   127

Excerpt from "One of Them": A chapter from *A Passionate
Autobiography*   128

By Elizabeth Hasanovitz, (Boston and New York:
Houghton Mifflin Co., 1918)   128

"Fire and the Skyscraper"   132

"Fire and the Skyscraper: The Problem of Protecting
the Workers in New York's Tower Factories,"
Arthur E. McFarlane, *McClure's Magazine* 37
(September 1911)   134

Protecting "Working Girls": New York Factory Investigating
Commission Hearings (from Preliminary Reports II and III,
October–December, 1911)   139

Abram I. Elkus, Opening Statement   139

Opening Statement: Abram I. Elkus, Counsel to
the Commission   140

William L. Beers Testimony [former fire marshal,
New York City]   142

Testimony of William L. Beers   143

  G. I. Harmon Testimony [factory inspector, NYS
    Department of Labor]   145

Testimony of G. I. Harmon   146

  Henry Bruere Testimony [director, Bureau of
    Municipal Research, NYC]   149

Testimony of Henry Bruere   150

  Rose Schneiderman Testimony [East Side organizer,
    Women's Trade Union League]   151

Testimony of Rose Schneiderman   152

  Alfred R. Conkling Testimony [factory owner and former
    state legislator]   154

Testimony of Alfred R. Conkling   154

  Dr. Antonio Stella Testimony [physician, expert on
    tuberculosis, officer in several Italian-American
    organizations]   156

Testimony of Dr. Antonio Stella   157

  Melinda Scott Testimony [Women's Trade Union
    League organizer]   158

Testimony of Melinda Scott   159

  Florence Kelley Testimony [general secretary, National
    Consumers' League]   161

Testimony of Florence Kelley   162

Tammany Hall and the Politics of Reform   163

  The Roosevelt I Knew   163

Excerpt from *The Roosevelt I Knew*   165

  By Frances Perkins, (New York: Harper & Row, 1964
    reprint of 1946 Viking Press edition)   165

Excerpt from "One of Them": Chapters from *A Passionate
Autobiography*   168

  By Elizabeth Hasanovitz, (Boston and New York:
    Houghton Mifflin Co., 1918)   168

Postscript   171

  The "General Strike" of 1916   171

Index   181

Charles Dana Gibson's drawings defined the ideal woman of the late nineteenth and early twentieth centuries. She was tall, with regal bearing, regular features, and long hair that she wore piled on her head. Gibson often drew her in an evening dress and occasionally in a swimsuit. But her daytime uniform was a long skirt and shirtwaist. This latter was a long-sleeved, high-necked blouse fitted very snugly ("tucked") at the waist. With all the "Gibson Girl" rage, the "waist" became a staple of every woman's wardrobe. The extent of Gibson's influence can be glimpsed in Jacob Epstein's *Intensely Serious*, a drawing of a young Jewish woman of the early twentieth century. Epstein, who later achieved fame as one of the foremost sculptors of his day, did not draw in the manner of Gibson, but his model reflected the power of the "Gibson Girl" as the ideal American woman in her dress and figure even as her pose called that ideal into question.

INTENSELY SERIOUS

New York *World* Account of the Triangle Fire
March 26, 1911

When the fire started at the Triangle Shirtwaist Company on the eighth floor of the Asch Building in lower Manhattan late Saturday afternoon, March 25, 1911, William Shepherd, a reporter for the United Press, happened to be across the street. He rushed to a nearby telephone, called his office, and dictated an eyewitness account of the disaster that appeared in newspapers across the country. The New York *World's* follow-up on the following day, excerpted here, is factually more complete but draws heavily on Shepherd's initial story for dramatic detail.

At 4:35 o'clock yesterday afternoon fire springing from a source that may never be positively identified was discovered in the rear of the eighth floor of the ten-story building at the northwest corner of Washington Place and Greene Street, the first of three floors occupied as a factory of the Triangle Shirtwaist Company.

• • •

It was the most appalling horror since the Slocum disaster and the Iroquois Theater fire in Chicago. Every available ambulance in Manhattan was called upon to cart the dead to the morgue—bodies charred to unrecognizable blackness or reddened to a sickly hue—as was to be seen by shoulders or limbs protruding through flame-eaten clothing. Men and women, boys and girls were of the dead that littered the street; that is actually the condition—the streets were littered.

The fire began in the eighth story. The flames licked and shot their way up through the other two stories. All three floors were occupied by the Triangle Waist Company. The estimate of the number of employees at work is made by Chief Croker at

about 1,000. The proprietors of the company say 700 men and girls were in their place. . . .

Before smoke or flame gave signs from the windows, the loss of life was fully under way. The first signs that persons in the street knew that these three top stories had turned into red furnaces in which human creatures were being caught and incinerated was when screaming men and women and boys and girls crowded out on the many window ledges and threw themselves into the streets far below.

They jumped with their clothing ablaze. The hair of some of the girls streamed up aflame as they leaped. Thud after thud sounded on the pavements. It is a ghastly fact that on both the Greene Street and Washington Place sides of the building there grew mounds of the dead and dying.

And the worst horror of all was that in this heap of the dead now and then there stirred a limb or sounded a moan.

• • •

Shivering at the chasm below them, scorched by the fire behind, there were some that still held positions on the window sills when the first squad of firemen arrived.

The New York *World*, March 26, 1911.

(continued)

The nets were spread below with all promptness. Citizens were commandeered into service, as the firemen necessarily gave their attention to the one engine and hose of the force that first arrived.

The catapult force that the bodies gathered in the long plunges made the nets utterly without avail. Screaming girls and men, as they fell, tore the nets from the grasp of the holders, and the bodies struck the sidewalks and lay just as they fell.

• • •

It was a fireproof building in which this enormous tragedy occurred. Save for the three stories of blackened windows at the top, you would scarcely have been able to tell where the fire had happened.

• • •

On the ledge of a ninth-story window two girls stood silently watching the arrival of the first fire apparatus. Twice one of the girls made a move to jump. The other restrained her, tottering in her foothold as she did so. They watched firemen rig the ladders up against the wall. They saw the last ladder lifted and pushed in place. They saw that it reached only the seventh floor.

For the third time, the more frightened girl tried to leap. The bells of arriving fire wagons must have risen to them. The other girl gesticulated in the direction of the sounds. But she talked to ears that could no longer hear. Scarcely turning, her companion dived head first into the street.

The other girl drew herself erect. The crowds in the street were stretching their arms up at her shouting and imploring her not to leap. She made a steady gesture, looking down as if to assure them she would remain brave. But a thin flame shot out of the window at her back and touched her hair. In an instant her head was aflame. She tore at her burning hair, lost her balance, and came shooting down upon the mound of bodies below.

From opposite windows spectators saw again and again pitiable companionships formed in the instant of death—girls who placed their arms around each other as they leaped.

• • •

By eight o'clock the available supply of coffins had been exhausted, and those that had already been used began to come back from the morgue.

The "Working Girl"

Introduction: "Who Will Protect the 'Working Girl'?"

Some shirtwaists were very simple, but many featured quite intricate stitchwork. Manufacturers competed with each other to put out inexpensive versions of high-fashion waists as the advertisement from *Harper's Bazar* for January 1908 illustrates. It also shows the immense popularity of the look associated with Charles Dana Gibson's "Gibson Girl."

The following are two representations of young women, probably garment workers. The first is by Jacob Epstein for Hutchins Hapgood's 1902 book, *The Spirit of the Ghetto*. Epstein's workers are dressed in the basic uniform of the working women of the early twentieth century: long skirt, shirtwaist, and short fitted jacket. Epstein's picture suggests something of the seriousness of purpose of young working women. In the drawing by John Sloan, *The Return from Toil*, they are not wearing jackets because it is summertime. Sloan, one of the founders of the Philadelphia School of Social Realism in American Art and one of the most important painters of his generation, sought to capture a different dimension of life on the Lower East Side. He described his subjects as "a bevy of boisterous girls with plenty of energy left after a hard day's work."* His drawing appeared in a radical magazine, *The Masses*, in July 1913.

---

* Sloan returned to this scene in 1915 when he turned it into an etching. His comment appears in *John Sloan, New York Etchings* (1905–1949) (New York: Dover Publications, Inc., 1978).

Late in the afternoon of March 25, 1911, just as the workers at the Triangle Shirtwaist Company in New York City were getting ready to quit work, a fire broke out near a pile of rags. The building housing the factory was fireproof, but oil from the long rows of sewing machines had soaked through the work tables and wooden flooring. Scraps of highly flammable cotton cloth lay all about. The fire quickly enveloped the top three floors. Most workers got out; 146 did not.

History is replete with catastrophes. So rapidly do they rush at us that we scarcely have time to register the magnitude of a given disaster before another demands our attention. Yet some have the power to haunt our imaginations, their horror as palpable to us as to those who lived through them. The Triangle fire is such an event. Almost a century later we can still see the young immigrant women crawling out onto the narrow ledge nine stories above the Manhattan pavement as firemen clambered up ladders that did not reach as far as the eighth floor and pointed hoses at the flames they could not reach because the necessary water pressure was lacking. We picture the flames jumping through the open windows toward the desperate figures on the ledge. Their dresses begin to smolder in our mind's eye, and we watch as a few jump toward the firemen, who reach out and almost manage to catch them. But the women have already fallen three stories, and their momentum wrenches them from rescuing arms. Firemen on the ground, aided by volunteers drawn from the crowd of horrified spectators, stretch out nets in the hope of catching others. The nets do not hold. The force of the falling bodies rips them from the hands of their would-be rescuers, and the victims crash to the street. Those left on the ledge, knowing hope is gone, hold hands or embrace as they step off into eternity. One young man gently holds co-workers, perhaps afraid to take the fatal plunge, over the edge and lets them drop.

We can imagine them still. Why? After almost a century of even worse tragedies whose victims number in the millions, why does this particular event still replay itself in our reveries? In part it is the sheer awfulness of their deaths. In part it is the youth of the victims. The vast majority were in their teens and twenties. Their lives should have been in front of them. The death of the young is often hardest to bear.[1] In addition, the fact that almost all were immigrants makes their deaths the more poignant, the sacrifices they made in leaving homes and relatives to embark on a journey to what they hoped would be a "land of opportunity" add unwonted irony to inexpressible pain.

Then there is gender. In the years immediately preceding the disaster, contemporaries fretted endlessly over the rapid increase in the number of working women. They worried about the welfare of the women themselves, but they also pondered what women's entry into the labor market portended for the new urban, industrial, pluralistic society the United States was becoming. "Who will protect the working girl?" became the question of the hour precisely because she epitomized many of the most troubling developments of the new America that was emerging with the new century. The "land of Lincoln," the America of only a generation before, had been agricultural; but this new America was industrial. It was urban. Earlier Americans had grown up on farms or in small towns. Those Americans had been Protestants, indeed had thought of the Revolution as a continuation of the Reformation even as they had ratified the First Amendment, which prohibited the establishment of a state church. In the new America Protestants were still a majority, but each year Catholics and Jews became more numerous. The old America had drawn its citizens from the descendants of colonists and slaves. In the new America they were joined by a host of other groups from Europe and Asia. The cumulative impact of these changes daunted—and also exhilarated— those who lived through them. Would their country be able to adjust to such a rapid and profound transformation? Would they?

The "working girl," often an immigrant, frequently Catholic or Jewish, often living alone or in a family without a father in a big city, embodied the changes that were transforming the country. Further, her independence, limited as it was by her paltry wages and the family responsibilities she so often shouldered, made her a sister to the "New Woman" of the late nineteenth and early twentieth centuries, the college-educated, middle- or upper-class woman entering new professions like social work or old ones like medicine or law, determined to play a more active role in the life of her times. All of this made the "working girl" a major national preoccupation even before the fire realized everyone's worst fears.

That "the working girl" needed protecting was only too clear. Studies examining her situation proliferated as "New Women," some of whom helped invent the field of investigative journalism, took jobs as factory workers, shop girls, cashiers, and the like and then wrote exposés for *McClure's* and other mass-circulation magazines detailing the grim conditions they encountered. Others, who largely pioneered the new fields of settlement house and social work, undertook related studies in which they compiled typical budgets for women workers, analyzed their diets, and described the tenements and boarding-houses they lived in. The findings of the muckraking journalist and the practitioner of the new helping professions were all of a piece: Wages were too low, hours too long, working conditions too dangerous, employers and foremen too likely to demand sexual favors in return for hiring or keeping a girl on. These new professional women discovered that the "working girl," despite the widespread belief that she worked only to earn "pin money," that is, cash to enable her to buy fancier clothes or other discretionary items, was often the main support of her family. Because she earned less than men, she often skipped meals or walked to work or went without a decent winter coat so that younger brothers or sisters could stay in school or a widowed mother could pay the rent. What little relief she found from the tedium of work, the investigators discovered to their dismay, often came from attending dance halls where, unchaperoned, she sought excitement and romance.[2]

It wasn't just the "working girl" who needed protecting, however. Elizabeth Beardsley Butler, assistant secretary of the Socialist party's Rand School in New York City, was one of many who argued that the greatest danger was not to the "girls" but to "racial vitality" in the form of "nervous exhaustion." She noted that "where there is such nervous loss its cost is not borne by industry." These "girls" typically began work in their early teens and "most . . . marry at twenty or twenty-one, just at the time when their [working] speed breaks." The "cost," as a result, "is borne by the homes into which they go." Such homes were "unfit," Butler claimed, because the children of these women were "undervitalized."[3]

Butler's Darwinian language—her references to race, survival of the "fit," "undervitalized" children, the implied risk of extinction—marked her as an exponent of new ideas.[4] So did her socialist leanings. Yet the combination led her to emphasize the most traditional of women's roles—motherhood. In this she was not atypical. Many who thought of themselves as "progressives" committed to the rational redesign of society shared Butler's preoccupation with the working "girl" as the future "mother" of the race. As Butler exemplified, even professional women, busy carving out new careers for themselves and eager to advance the cause of suffrage, accepted the notion that they were members of the "weaker sex." Most did not question that their sisters, if not they themselves, needed the protection of a man, or of the state.[5]

Society, students of the issue almost universally agreed, had to do more to protect the "working girl" because harm done to her was passed on to the next generation. Woods Hutchinson, a pioneer in the field of public health, made the standard "progressive" argument in forceful terms:

> It is believed that the community is not merely interested in knowing, but has the right to know, what are the wages received, the hours worked, the sanitary conditions under which the work is done, in . . . any industry, for the simple reason that if these wages and these hours and conditions impair the health or stunt the development of the workers, these ultimately become . . . dependents upon the private or public charity of the community.
>
> . . . The interest of the community becomes all the keener and its right to know and interfere the stronger, when these workers happen to be young and particularly when they are of the sex who will become the mothers of the future generation. The right therefore of the employer, to declare that "it's nobody's damn business what I pay my employes" or that of the employe that it is none of the public's affair for what wages or under what conditions he is willing to work, both belong to the dark ages, and no longer exist in communities calling themselves civilized and progressive.[6]

Here is one of the building blocks of the culture's notorious "double standard." Progressives were beginning to challenge the long-accepted belief that young men frequently had to risk their lives. Indeed, despite their best efforts, the popular culture of the day continued to glorify soldiers, gunfighters, and big-game hunters precisely because they seemed to court danger.[7] But part of the glorification of male risk-taking was the notion that the men who put their own lives in danger were thereby protecting women. In contrast, women who risked their lives jeopardized the future of "the race."[8] One hundred forty-six male deaths, in a coal mine cave-in would have been a terrible but bearable tragedy. But the fact that so many women died in the Triangle fire suggested a social universe spinning out of control.

Contemporaries, however, did not think of the "working girl" only in terms of frailty and/or motherhood. She also symbolized for them a contrary possibility, the self-sufficient "New Woman," confidently exploring new possibilities and assuming new responsibilities. None fit this image better than the shirtwaist workers, as evidenced by the one thought that flashed through the minds of almost everyone who heard of the fire, starting with John Sloan, several of whose drawings inspired by the fire are reproduced here: "These girls made the successful strike of last year!"

The "Uprising of the Twenty Thousand" of New York's shirtwaist workers was the largest strike involving women workers in the industrial world to that date and led to the formation of the first successful trade union of women workers in the United States, the International Ladies Garment Workers Union (ILGWU). Upward of forty thousand walked out. Half or more were back at work within a week because small producers—most employed fewer than fifty—could not afford to remain idle for more than a few days and hastily agreed to the union's terms. The bigger manufacturers formed an association and proclaimed their willingness to starve their workers into submission. As a result, the "Uprising" dragged on for months. Police harassed strikers and arrested fifteen- and sixteen-year-old pickets for assault when they tried to defend themselves against thugs hired by the employers' association. Police court judges railroaded defendants off to jail while affluent sympathizers, many connected to the suffrage movement, held rallies on their behalf to raise bail money. All of New York and then all of the nation watched as, against all odds, the strikers forced one employer after another—but not Triangle and several other large firms—to settle.[9] By winning even this partial victory the shirtwaist workers gave a different answer to the question of who would protect the "working girl": "We can protect ourselves," they proclaimed. "Our union makes us strong."

The fire's victims were not anonymous. They were the strikers, emblems of American society's conflicting, still to be resolved, hopes and fears. They were "working girls" in need of protection and young women of proven mettle; they were the future mothers whose long hours in the shops threatened the "vitality" of their unborn children, and they were the heroines who had battled police and strikebreakers on the picket lines.

By a curious twist of fate, the strike had started at Triangle and one other shirtwaist manufacturer. Further, Triangle's owners led the handful of large producers who had held out against the union. Had they accepted the union's demands, no one would have been in the building on the afternoon of the fire because one of the terms of the new contract was a half day on Saturday. The fire haunted contemporaries, in short, not just because of how the victims died but also because of who they were.

The fire haunts us today because of the impact that both strike and fire had upon the rest of American society. Not only did the "Uprising" mark the advent of women in the labor movement, but it also transformed, for a few months, the women's movement as a whole by bringing to life a true "sisterhood" that spanned class, ethnic, religious, and political divides. Middle- and upper-class Yankees closed ranks with Russian Jewish and Italian Catholic immigrant workers. Anne Morgan, daughter of banker J. P. Morgan, invited strikers like the sixteen-year-old Rose Perr to the Colony Club to tell their story to the wealthy members whose previous dealings with immigrants and working women had been limited to their own servants. Wellesley and Vassar students flocked to hear Rose Schneiderman, a union organizer only a few years older than themselves, tell of the valor of the strikers and then pledged to buy only union-made clothes. Mrs. August Belmont, reputedly the second-wealthiest woman in the country and a leader in the campaign for women's suffrage, put up her Manhattan town house to raise bail for jailed strikers.[10]

Perhaps most remarkably, the strike brought to life the dream of two sisters, Mary and Margaret Dreier, daughters of a well-to-do German immigrant merchant, who had founded a few years before the Women's Trade Union League (WTUL), an organization that sought to bring together affluent and working-class women on a basis that approached equality. It was the WTUL that helped the fledgling International Ladies Garment Workers organize the strike. WTUL volunteers rented halls for strikers to meet in, kept membership records, provided liaison with the English-language newspapers, and recruited other middle- and upper-class volunteers. For a brief moment the strike called forth a genuine sorority.[11] And this suggested still another answer to the question of the day: Women, banding together, could protect each other.

Because the victims were the strikers, the demand that their deaths not be in vain was deafening. The New York State legislature responded by creating a Factory Investigating Commission around whose work another remarkable coalition gathered. Some of the coalition's members were union activists like Rose Schneiderman, who signed on as a staff investigator. Others were young professionals like Frances Perkins, later secretary of labor in Franklin Roosevelt's administration, the first woman to hold cabinet rank in American history. Perkins supervised much of the staff work. Still other "New Women," experts in such emerging fields as public health, scientific management, factory safety, and social work, joined the staff. The other key participants were the two state legislators who chaired the commission. Both were products of New York City's notorious Tammany Hall

political machine, and their appointment had initially driven most reformers to despair because Tammany had historically thrown its influence against measures designed to limit the freedom of employers.
Both legislators had well-deserved reputations for voting as Tammany
boss Charlie Murphy wished. Progressives, for their part, thought of
Tammany as epitomizing everything that needed changing in American politics.[12]

To the surprise and delight of the reformers, however, the two
"pols" threw themselves heart and soul into the work of the commission. Not only did they make sure the investigation was thorough and
entirely aboveboard, but they also drafted all of the staff's key recommendations and then pushed the legislation through. The bills were
copied in state after state, so that it is not too much to say that the
work of the commission helped change the relationship between the
citizen and the state in modern America by enlarging the powers of
the government to "protect" its citizens. One of these two Tammany
"pols" was Robert Wagner, then president of the state Senate. He
would go on to become a U.S. senator and sponsor of much of the New
Deal legislation during the 1930s.[13] The other, then speaker of the
state Assembly, was Al Smith. Smith would, as governor, pioneer many
of the social programs that Franklin Roosevelt later introduced on the
national level. In addition, as the Democratic presidential candidate in
1928—the first Catholic to run for the White House as the nominee
of a major party—Smith would further cement the political alliance of
urban machines and expert reformers that formed a key element of
the Roosevelt coalition.[14]

By virtue of the success of their work, the "pols" and the "New
Women" staff members on the commission helped shape a most important, and deeply troubling, answer to the question of protecting the
"working girl": The state's admitted authority to act to protect the
welfare of its children justifies its acting to protect women as well.
This is a position known as "social feminism," and it led to laws that
"protected" women but also, by creating a double standard based on
gender, barred them from many forms of employment.[15]

Contemporaries were right to think of the "Uprising," the Triangle fire, and the Factory Investigating Commission's work as three
acts in a single drama. It was a drama in which some of the central issues of their time were played out. It showed that women would take
more active roles in and out of the labor force and in and out of the
labor movement. It showed, too, that women could come together

across class, religious, and ethnic lines even as it demonstrated how difficult such a "sisterhood" was to sustain. It foreshadowed a new political coalition that would later reinvent American government. It proved that the state could act decisively and effectively to address social problems even as it furnished a textbook example of how one generation's solutions—-limits on the number of hours women could work, for example—could become another's problems. We do well to remember the Triangle fire.

Notes

1. It is perhaps for this reason that Anne Frank is the best-known victim of the Holocaust and Emmet Till the most famous of the thousands of African-Americans murdered in the South.

2. For examples, see Rheta Childe Dorr, *A Woman of Fifty* (New York: Funk & Wagnalls, 1924), in which she recounted her experiences posing as a "working girl" for *Everybody's* magazine; Anne Steele Richardson, *The Girl Who Earns Her Own Living* (New York: B.W. Dodge & Co., 1909), a cheery how-to series originally published in *The Woman's Home Companion* magazine in 1905; Maud Younger, "Diary of an Amateur Waitress: An Industrial Problem from the Worker's Point of View," *McClure's* (March 1907): 543–552; and Sue Ainslie Clark and Edith Wyatt, *Making Both Ends Meet: The Income and Outlay of New York Working Girls* (New York: Macmillan, 1911), a work that contains a gripping narrative of the shirt-waist workers' strike excerpted here.

3. Elizabeth Beardsley Butler, *Women and the Trades* (New York, 1909), 95–96. This was one of the volumes of the Pittsburgh Survey, a pioneering investigation of the nation's greatest industrial center. It was reprinted by the University of Pittsburgh Press in 1984 with an introduction by Maurine Weiner Greenwald.

4. Historians, following Richard Hofstadter, often refer to this set of ideas as "reform" Darwinism to distinguish it from the "social" Darwinism of William Graham Sumner. Reform Darwinists believed that the survival of the "race" required state intervention to promote healthy families; social Darwinists instead believed that such intervention stymied the basic working out of evolution by "unnaturally" permitting the "less fit" to

reproduce. Richard Hofstadter, *Social Darwinism in American Thought,* revised edition (Boston, 1955), especially pp. 51–84.

5.   See the testimony of such reformers as Florence Kelley before the New York State Factory Investigating Commission reprinted here. An excellent recent case study is Nancy K. Bristow, *Making Men Moral: Social Engineering during the Great War* (New York: New York University Press, 1996), 91–130.

6.   Woods Hutchinson, M.D., "The Hygienic Aspects of the Shirtwaist Strike, *The Survey* (January 22, 1910): 541. This essay is reprinted here.

7.   Richard Slotkin, *Regeneration through Violence: The Mythology of the American Frontier, 1600–1860* (Middletown, Conn.: Wesleyan University Press, 1973), is a pioneering study in what has become of late a crowded field of scholarly endeavor. Recent works include Gail Bederman, *Manliness & Civilization: A Cultural History of Gender and Race in the United States, 1880–1917* (Chicago: University of Chicago Press, 1995); and Michael A. Bellesîles, "The Origins of Gun Culture in the United States, 1760–1865," *Journal of American History* 83 (September 1996): 425–455.

8.   The Supreme Court adopted this view in *Muller v. Oregon* (1908) by ruling that a state could use its police power to restrict the number of hours that women could legally work even though it could not restrict those of men. A useful recent study is Nancy Woloch, *Muller v. Oregon: A Brief History with Documents* (Boston and New York: Bedford Books of St. Martin's Press, 1996).

9.   Not every fire victim participated in the strike. Turnover in the shirtwaist industry was very high, perhaps approaching 100 percent per year. As a result, many Triangle employees had started working in the trade only after the strike was over. There are several excellent accounts of the strike. Perhaps the best is the earliest, Louis Levine (Lewis Levitzski Lotwin), *The Women's Garment Workers: A History of the International Ladies' Garment Workers Union* (New York: B.W. Huebsch, Inc., 1924), 144–167. This was the "official" history commissioned by the union.

10.   See the strike documents included here.

11.   The coalition did not outlast the struggle that called it into being. Within months working-class women were accusing wealthy suffragists of attempting to "use" the strike for their own purposes, and Anne Morgan was accusing socialists in the trade union movement of putting revolutionary

ideology ahead of practical politics. Within a few years even the WTUL would split over the issue of recruiting foreign-born women, and Rose Schneiderman, a Russian Jewish immigrant, would lose an election for the New York branch's presidency precisely because she insisted that the league honor its own traditions. Even before that, the WTUL would have a falling-out with the leadership of the International Ladies Garment Workers. See the documents reprinted here. Nonetheless, the fact that the Dreiers' dream did live for however brief a time has had profound import for present-day feminist scholars. See Nancy Schrom Dye, *As Equals and As Sisters: Feminism, Unionism and the Woman's Trade Union League of New York* (Columbia: University of Missouri Press, 1980), and Elizabeth Anne Payne, *Reform, Labor, and Feminism: Margaret Dreier Robins and the Women's Trade Union League* (Urbana: University of Illinois Press, 1988).

12. See my 'Of 'Mornin' Glories' and 'Fine Old Oaks': John Purroy Mitchel, Al Smith, and Reform as an Expression of Irish American Aspiration," in *The New York Irish*, edited by Ronald H. Bayor and Timothy J. Meagher (Baltimore: Johns Hopkins University Press, 1996), 374–394, for an analysis of the strength of anti-Tammany Hall sentiment among the reformers who ultimately made common cause with Smith. Frances Perkins's account of Tammany's decision to back reform is reprinted here.

13. The Wagner act of 1935, which guaranteed unions' rights to organize and strike, is often called labor's Magna Carta. See J. Joseph Huthmacher, *Senator Robert F. Wagner and the Rise of Urban Liberalism* (New York, 1968).

14. For Smith's continuing connections with "New Women," see Elisabeth Israels Perry, *Belle Moskowitz: Feminine Politics and the Exercise of Power in the Age of Alfred E. Smith* (New York: Oxford University Press, 1987). Moskowitz was by Smith's own account his "closest advisor in connection with my two national campaigns." "My closest Advisor: Belle Moskowitz As I Knew Her," *Jewish Chronicle*, February 17, 1933, as reprinted in Perry, 220–221.

15. Theda Skocpol, *Protecting Soldiers and Mothers: The Political Origins of Social Policy in the United States* (New York: Cambridge University Press, 1994); Susan Lehrer, *Origins of Protective Labor Legislation for Women, 1905–1925* (Albany: State University of New York Press, 1987); Diane Kirby, "'The Wage-Earning Woman and the State': The Women's Trade Union League and Protective Labor Legislation, 1903–1928," *Labor History* 28 (1987): 54–74; and Ulla Wikander, Alice Kessler-Harris, and Jane Lewis, eds., *Protecting Women: Labor Legislation in Europe, the United States, and Australia, 1880–1920* (Urbana: University of Illinois Press, 1995).

"The Story of a Sweatshop Girl" and "A Cap Maker's Story"

Between 1902 and 1907 Hamilton Holt, publisher of *The Independent*, a popular magazine, ran a series of short autobiographies of "undistinguished" Americans that he called "lifelets." The goal was to provide his largely middle-class readers with first-person accounts of, in Jacob Riis's celebrated phrase, "how the other half lives." Sadie Frowne's story was one of the first to appear.[1] Hers was, Holt claimed, a common story. She had been born in Poland, came to the United States with her widowed mother to escape persecution and poverty, and found herself, after her mother's death, fending for herself while still in her middle teens. Rose Schneiderman, subject of the second of the accounts reprinted here, was also a young Jewish immigrant employed in the needle trades.

Frowne epitomized the exuberance of Sloan's young "girls with plenty of energy left after a hard day's work." Schneiderman could have sat for Epstein's "Intensely Serious." Whereas Frowne spent some of her free time going to dance halls with a steady "beau," Schneiderman devoted her leisure hours to public meetings and earnest conversations about the plight of the working class. Frowne, still in her teens, wanted to have "fun." Schneiderman, only twenty, wanted to change the world. Little is known of Frowne's subsequent life; Schneiderman, on the other hand, did not long remain "undistinguished." She became a union organizer, played an important role in the great shirtwaist workers' strike of 1909–1910, worked as an investigator for the New York Factory Investigating Commission created in the wake of the Triangle fire, became the president of the New York branch of the Women's Trade Union League, worked for Al Smith, one of the co-chairs of the commission, when he was governor of New York, and served in Franklin Roosevelt's gubernatorial and presidential

---

[1] Holt collected some, including Frowne's, in *The Life Stories of Undistinguished Americans: As Told by Themselves* (New York: James Pott & Co., 1906). The volume, with several additional "lifelets," was reprinted by Routledge in 1990 with an introduction by Werner Sollors.

administrations. Several of these activities can be followed in materials reprinted next. She wrote an autobiography, *All for One*, in 1967 with Lucy Goldthwaite.[2]

---

[2] It provides a somewhat different account of her early family life. An interesting discussion of the differences is Ellen Condliffe Lagemann, *A Generation of Women: Education in the Lives of Progressive Reformers* (Cambridge: Harvard University Press, 1979), 115–137

THE STORY OF A SWEATSHOP GIRL

BY SADIE FROWNE

[Miss Frowne is little more than sixteen years of age, and her story was consequently dictated to a representative of THE INDEPENDENT. It was afterward read over to herself and relatives and pronounced accurate in all respects. Save for slight alterations of her language there is no deviation from the narrative. Brownsville is the Hebrew sweatshop quarter of Brooklyn, New York—EDITOR]

My mother was a tall, handsome, dark complexioned woman with red cheeks, large brown eyes and a great quantity of jet black, wavy hair. She was well educated, being able to talk in Russian, German, Polish and French, and even to read English print, tho, of course, she did not know what it meant. She kept a little grocer's shop in the little village where we lived at first. That was in Poland, somewhere on the frontier, and mother had charge of a gate between the countries, so that everybody who came through the gate had to show her a pass. She was much looked up to by the people, who used to come and ask her for advice. Her word was like law among them.

She had a wagon in which she used to drive about the country, selling her groceries, and sometimes she worked in the fields with my father.

The grocer's shop was only one story high, and had one window, with very small panes of glass. We had two rooms behind it, and were happy while my father lived, altho we had to work very hard. By the time I was six years of age I was able to wash dishes and scrub floors, and by the time I was eight I attended to the shop while my mother was away driving her wagon or working in the fields with my father. She was strong and could work like a man.

When I was a little more than ten years of age my father died. He was a good man and a steady worker, and we never knew what it was to be hungry while he lived. After he died troubles began, for the rent of our shop was about $6 a month and then there were food and clothes to provide. We needed little, it is true, but even soup, black bread and onions we could not always get.

We struggled along till I was nearly thirteen years of age and quite handy at housework and shop keeping, so far as I could learn them there. But we fell behind in the rent and mother kept thinking more and more that we should have to leave Poland and go across the sea to America where we heard it was much easier to make money. Mother wrote to Aunt Fanny, who lived in New York, and told her how hard it was to live in Poland, and Aunt Fanny advised her to come and bring me. I was out at service at this time and mother thought she would leave me—as I had a good place—and come to this country alone, sending for me afterward. But Aunt Fanny would not hear of this. She said we should both come at once, and she went around among our relatives in New York and took up a subscription for our passage.

We came by steerage on a steamship in a very dark place that smelt dreadfully. There were hundreds of other people packed in with us, men,

Sadie Frowne, "The Story of a Sweatshop Girl," *The Independent* 54 (September 25, 1902), 2279–82.

(continued)

women and children, and almost all of them were sick. It took us twelve days to cross the sea, and we thought we should die, but at last the voyage was over, and we came up and saw the beautiful bay and the big woman with the spikes on her head and the lamp that is lighted at night in her hand (Goddess of Liberty).

Aunt Fanny and her husband met us at the gate of this country and were very good to us, and soon I had a place to live out (domestic servant), while my mother got work in a factory making white goods.

I was only a little over thirteen years of age and a greenhorn, so I received $9 a month and board and lodging, which I thought was doing well. Mother, who, as I have said, was very clever, made $9 a week on white goods, which means all sorts of underclothing, and is high class work.

But mother had a very gay disposition. She liked to go around and see everything, and friends took her about New York at night and she caught a bad cold and coughed and coughed. She really had hasty consumption, but she didn't know it, and I didn't know it, and she tried to keep on working, but it was no use. She had not the strength. Two doctors attended her, but they could do nothing, and at last she died and I was left alone. I had saved money while out at service, but mother's sickness and funeral swept it all away and now I had to begin all over again.

Aunt Fanny had always been anxious for me to get an education, as I did not know how to read or write, and she thought that was wrong. Schools are different in Poland from what they are in this country, and I was always too busy to learn to read and write. So when mother died I thought I would try to learn a trade and then I could go to school at night and learn to speak the English language well.

So I went to work in Allen street (Manhattan) in what they call a sweatshop, making skirts by machine. I was new at the work and the foreman scolded me a great deal.

"Now then," he would say, "this place is not for you to be looking around in. Attend to your work. That is what you have to do."

I did not know at first that you must not look around and talk, and I made many mistakes with the sewing, so that I was often called a "stupid animal." But I made $4 a week by working six days in the week. For there are two Sabbaths here—our own Sabbath, that comes on a Saturday, and the Christian Sabbath that comes on Sunday. It is against our law to work on our own Sabbath, so we work on their Sabbath.

In Poland I and my father and mother used to go to the synagogue on the Sabbath, but here the women don't go to the synagogue much, tho the men do. They are shut up working hard all the week long and when the Sabbath comes they like to sleep long in bed and afterward they must go out where they can breathe the air. The rabbis are strict here, but not so strict as in the old country.

I lived at this time with a girl named Ella, who worked in the same factory and made $5 a week. We had the room all to ourselves, paying $1.50 a week for it, and doing light housekeeping. It was in Allen street, and the window looked out of the back, which was good, because there was an elevated railroad in front, and in summer time a great deal of dust and dirt came in at the front windows. We were on the fourth story and could see all that was going on in the back rooms of the houses behind us, and early in the morning the sun used to come in our window.

We did our cooking on an oil stove, and lived well, as this list of our expenses for one week will show:

ELLA AND SADIE FOR FOOD (ONE WEEK).

Tea	$0.06
Cocoa	.10
Bread and rolls	.40
Canned vegetables	.20
Potatoes	.10
Milk	.21
Fruit	.20
Butter	.15
Meat	.60
Fish	.15
Laundry	.25
Total	$2.42
Add rent	1.50
Grand total	$3.92

Of course, we could have lived cheaper, but we are both fond of good things and felt that we could afford them.

We paid 18 cents for a half pound of tea so as to get it good, and it lasted us three weeks, because we had cocoa for breakfast. We paid 5 cents for six rolls and 5 cents a loaf for bread, which was the best quality. Oatmeal cost us 10 cents for three and one-half pounds, and we often had it in the morning, or Indian meal porridge in the place of it, costing about the same. Half a dozen eggs cost about 13 cents on an average, and we could get all the meat we wanted for a good hearty meal for 20 cents—two pounds of chops, or a steak, or a bit of veal, or a neck of lamb—something like that. Fish included butter fish, porgies, codfish and smelts, averaging about 8 cents a pound.

(continued)

Some people who buy at the last of the market, when the men with the carts want to go home, can get things very cheap, but they are likely to be stale, and we did not often do that with fish, fresh vegetables, fruit, milk or meat. Things that kept well we did buy that way and got good bargains. I got thirty potatoes for 10 cents one time, tho generally I could not get more than 15 of them for that amount. Tomatoes, onions and cabbages, too, we bought that way and did well, and we found a factory where we could buy the finest broken crackers for 3 cents a pound, and another place where we got broken candy for 10 cents a pound. Our cooking was done on an oil stove, and the oil for the stove and the lamp cost us 10 cents a week.

It cost me $2 a week to live, and I had a dollar a week to spend on clothing and pleasure, and saved the other dollar. I went to night school, but it was hard work learning at first as I did not know much English.

Two years ago I came to this place, Brownsville, where so many of my people are, and where I have friends. I got work in a factory making underskirts—all sorts of cheap underskirts, like cotton and calico for the summer and woolen for the winter, but never the silk, satin or velvet underskirts. I earned $4.50 a week and lived on $2 a week, the same as before.

I got a room in the house of some friends who lived near the factory. I pay $1 a week for the room and am allowed to do light housekeeping—that is, cook my meals in it. I get my own breakfast in the morning, just a cup of coffee and a roll, and at noon time I come home to dinner and take a plate of soup and a slice of bread with the lady of the house. My food for a week costs a dollar, just as it did in Allen street, and I have the rest of my money to do as I like with. I am earning $5.50 a week now, and will probably get another increase soon.

It isn't piecework in our factory, but one is paid by the amount of work done just the same. So it is like piecework. All the hands get different amounts, some as low as $3.50 and some of the men as high as $16 a week. The factory is in the third story of a brick building. It is in a room twenty feet long and fourteen broad. There are fourteen machines in it. I and the daughter of the people with whom I live work two of these machines. The other operators are all men, some young and some old.

At first a few of the young men were rude. When they passed me they would touch my hair and talk about my eyes and my red cheeks, and make jokes. I cried and said that if they did not stop I would leave the place. The boss said that that should not be, that no one must annoy me. Some of the other men stood up for me, too,

especially Henry, who said two or three times that he wanted to fight. Now the men all treat me very nicely. It was just that some of them did not know better, not being educated.

Henry is tall and dark, and he has a small mustache. His eyes are brown and large. He is pale and much educated, having been to school. He knows a great many things and has some money saved. I think nearly $400. He is not going to be in a sweatshop all the time, but will soon be in the real estate business, for a lawyer that knows him well has promised to open an office and pay him to manage it.

Henry has seen me home every night for a long time and makes love to me. He wants me to marry him, but I am not seventeen yet, and I think that is too young. He is only nineteen, so we can wait.

I have been to the fortune teller's three or four times, and she always tells me that tho I have had such a lot of trouble I am to be very rich and happy. I believe her because she has told so many things that have come true. So I will keep on working in the factory for a time. Of course it is hard, but I would have to work hard even if I was married.

I get up at half-past five o'clock every morning and make myself a cup of coffee on the oil stove. I eat a bit of bread and perhaps some fruit and then go to work. Often I get there soon after six o'clock so as to be in good time, tho the factory does not open till seven. I have heard that there is a sort of clock that calls you at the very time you want to get up, but I can't believe that because I don't see how the clock would know.

At seven o'clock we all sit down to our machines and the boss brings to each one the pile of work that he or she is to finish during the day, what they call in English their "stint." This pile is put down beside the machine and as soon as a skirt is done it is laid on the other side of the machine. Sometimes the work is not all finished by six o'clock and then the one who is behind must work overtime. Sometimes one is finished ahead of time and gets away at four or five o'clock, but generally we are not done till six o'clock.

The machines go like mad all day, because the faster you work the more money you get. Sometimes in my haste I get my finger caught and the needle goes right through it. It goes so quick, tho, that it does not hurt much. I bind the finger up with a piece of cotton and go on working. We all have accidents like that. Where the needle goes through the nail it makes a sore finger, or where it splinters a bone it does much harm. Sometimes a finger has to come off. Generally, tho, one can be cured by a salve.

(continued)

All the time we are working the boss walks about examining the finished garments and making us do them over again if they are not just right. So we have to be careful as well as swift. But I am getting so good at the work that within a year I will be making $7 a week, and then I can save at least $3.50 a week. I have over $200 saved now.

The machines are all run by foot power, and at the end of the day one feels so weak that there is a great temptation to lie right down and sleep. But you must go out and get air, and have some pleasure. So instead of lying down I go out, generally with Henry. Sometimes we go to Coney Island, where there are good dancing places, and sometimes we go to Ulmer Park to picnics. I am very fond of dancing, and, in fact, all sorts of pleasure. I go to the theater quite often, and like those plays that make you cry a great deal. "The Two Orphans" is good. Last time I saw it I cried all night because of the hard times that the children had in the play. I am going to see it again when it comes here.

For the last two winters I have been going to night school at Public School 84 on Glenmore Avenue. I have learned reading, writing and arithmetic. I can read quite well in English now and I look at the newspapers every day. I read English books, too, sometimes. The last one that I read was "A Mad Marriage," by Charlotte Braeme. She's a grand writer and makes things just like real to you. You feel as if you were the poor girl yourself going to get married to a rich duke.

I am going back to night school again this winter. Plenty of my friends go there. Some of the women in my class are more than forty years of age. Like me, they did not have a chance to learn anything in the old country. It is good to have an education; it makes you feel higher. Ignorant people are all low. People say now that I am clever and fine in conversation.

We have just finished a strike in our business. It spread all over and the United Brotherhood of Garment Workers was in it. That takes in the cloakmakers, coatmakers, and all the others. We struck for shorter hours, and after being out four weeks won the fight. We only have to work nine and a half hours a day and we get the same pay as before. So the union does good after all in spite of what some people say against it—that it just takes our money and does nothing.

I pay 25 cents a month to the union, but I do not begrudge that because it is for our benefit. The next strike is going to be for a raise of wages, which we all ought to have. But tho I belong to the Union I am not a Socialist or an Anarchist. I don't know exactly what those things mean. There is a little expense for charity, too. If any worker is injured or sick we all give money to help.

Some of the women blame me very much because I spend so much money on clothes. They say that instead of a dollar a week I ought not to spend more than twenty-five cents a week on clothes, and that I should save the rest. But a girl must have clothes if she is to go into high society at Ulmer Park or Coney Island or the theater. Those who blame me are the old country people who have old-fashioned notions, but the people who have been here a long time know better. A girl who does not dress well is stuck in a corner, even if she is pretty, and Aunt Fanny says that I do just right to put on plenty of style.

I have many friends and we often have jolly parties. Many of the young men like to talk to me, but I don't go out with any except Henry.

Lately he has been urging me more and more to get married—but I think I'll wait.

BROOKLYN, N.Y.

A CAP MAKER'S STORY

BY ROSE SCHNEIDERMAN

[Miss Schneiderman led the women capmakers in their recent successful strike for the union shop. She is a small, quiet, serious, good looking young woman of twenty years, already a member of the National Board, and fast rising in the labor world.—EDITOR.]

My name is Rose Schneiderman, and I was born in some small city of Russian Poland. I don't know the name of the city, and have no memory of that part of my childhood. When I was about five years of age my parents brought me to this country and we settled in New York.

So my earliest recollections are of living in a crowded street among the East Side Jews, for we also are Jews.

My father got work as a tailor, and we lived in two rooms on Eldridge Street, and did very well, though not so well as in Russia, because mother and father both earned money, and here father alone earned the money, while mother attended to the house. There were then two other children besides me, a boy of three and one of five.

I went to school until I was nine years old, enjoying it thoroughly and making great progress; but then my father died of brain fever and mother was left with three children and another one coming. So I had to stay at home to help her and she went out to look for work.

A month later the baby was born, and mother got work in a fur house, earning about $6 a week and afterward $8 a week, for she was clever and steady.

I was the house worker, preparing the meals and looking after the other children—the baby, a little girl of six years, and a boy of nine. I managed very well, tho the meals were not very elaborate. I could cook simple things like porridge, coffee and eggs, and mother used to prepare the meat before she went away in the morning, so that all I had to do was to put it in the pan at night.

The children were not more troublesome than others, but this was a hard part of my life with few bright spots in it. I was a serious child, and cared little for children's play, and I knew nothing about the country, so it was not so bad for me as it might have been for another. Yet it was bad, tho I did get some pleasure from reading, of which I was very fond; and now and then, as a change from the home, I took a walk in the crowded street.

Mother was absent from half-past seven o'clock in the morning till half-past six o'clock in the evening.

I was finally released by my little sister being taken by an aunt, and the two boys going to the Hebrew Orphan Asylum, which is a splendid institution, and turns out good men. One of these brothers is now a student in the City College, and the other is a page in the Stock Exchange.

When the other children were sent away mother was able to send me back to school, and I stayed in this school (Houston Street Grammar) till I had reached the Sixth Grammar Grade.

Then I had to leave in order to help support the family. I got a place in Hearn's as cash girl, and after working there three weeks changed to Ridley's where I remained for two and a half years. I finally left because the pay was so very poor and there did not seem to be any chance of advancement, and a friend told me that I could do better making caps.

So I got a place in the factory of Hein & Fox. The hours were from 8 a.m. to 6 p.m., and we made all sorts of linings—or, rather, we stitched in the linings—golf caps, yachting caps, etc. It was piece work, and we received from $3\frac{1}{2}$ cents to 10 cents a dozen, according to the different grades. By working hard we could make an average of about $5 a week. We would have made more but had to provide our own machines, which cost us $45, we paying for them on the installment plan. We paid $5 down and $1 a month after that.

I learned the business in about two months, and then made as much as the others, and was consequently doing quite well when the factory burned down, destroying all our machines—150 of them. This was very hard on the girls who had paid for their machines. It was not so bad for me, as I had only paid a little of what I owed.

The bosses got $500,000 insurance, so I heard, but they never gave the girls a cent to help

Rose Schneiderman, "A Cap Maker's Story," *The Independent* 58 (March 20, 1905), 935–38.

(continued)

them bear their losses. I think they might have given them $10, anyway.

Soon work went on again in four lofts, and a little later I became assistant sample maker. This is a position which, tho coveted by many, pays better in glory than in cash. It was still piece work, and tho the pay per dozen was better the work demanded was of a higher quality, and one could not rush through samples as through the other caps. So I still could average only about $5 per week.

After I had been working as a cap maker for three years it began to dawn on me that we girls needed an organization. The men had organized already, and had gained some advantages, but the bosses had lost nothing, as they took it out of us.

We were helpless; no one girl dare stand up for anything alone. Matters kept getting worse. The bosses kept making reductions in our pay, half a cent a dozen at a time. It did not sound important, but at the end of the week we found a difference.

We didn't complain to the bosses; we didn't say anything except to each other. There was no use. The bosses would not pay any attention unless we were like the men and could make them attend.

One girl would say that she didn't think she could make caps for the new price, but another would say that she thought she could make up for the reduction by working a little harder, and then the first would tell herself:

"If she can do it, why can't I?"

They didn't think how they were wasting their strength.

A new girl from another shop got in among us. She was Miss Bessie Brout, and she talked organization as a remedy for our ills. She was radical and progressive, and she stimulated thoughts which were already in our minds before she came.

Finally Miss Brout and I and another girl went to the National Board of United Cloth Hat and Cap Makers when it was in session, and asked them to organize the girls.

They asked us:

"How many of you are there willing to be organized?"

"In the first place about twelve," we said, We argued that the union label would force the bosses to organize their girls, and if there was a girls' union in existence the bosses could not use the union label unless their girls belonged to the union.

We were told to come to the next meeting of the National Board, which we did, and then received a favorable answer, and were asked to bring all the girls who were willing to be organized to the next meeting, and at the next meeting, accordingly, we were there twelve strong and were organized.

When Fox found out what had happened he discharged Miss Brout, and probably would have discharged me but that I was a sample maker and not so easy to replace. In a few weeks we had all the girls in the organization, because the men told the girls that they must enter the union or they would not be allowed to work in the shop.

Then came a big strike. Price lists for the coming season were given in to the bosses, to which they did not agree. After some wrangling a strike was declared in five of the biggest factories. There are 30 factories in the city. About 100 girls went out.

The result was a victory, which netted us—I mean the girls—$2 increase in our wages on the average.

All the time our union was progressing very nicely. There were lectures to make us understand what trades unionism is and our real position in the labor movement. I read upon the subject and grew more and more interested, and after a time I became a member of the National Board, and had duties and responsibilities that kept me busy after my day's work was done.

But all was not lovely by any means, for the bosses were not at all pleased with their beating and had determined to fight us again.

They agreed among themselves that after the 26th of December, 1904, they would run their shops on the "open" system.

This agreement was reached last fall, and soon notices, reading as follows, were hung in the various shops:

NOTICE

"After the 26th of December, 1904, this shop will be run on the open shop system, the bosses having the right to engage and discharge employees as they see fit, whether the latter are union or nonunion."

Of course, we knew that this meant an attack on the union. The bosses intended gradually to get rid of us, employing in our place child labor and raw immigrant girls who would work for next to nothing.

On December 22nd the above notice appeared, and the National Board, which had known about it all along, went into session prepared for action.

Our people were very restive, saying that they could not sit under that notice, and that if the National Board did not call them out soon they would go out of themselves.

At last word was sent out, and at 2.30 o'clock all the workers stopped, and, laying down their scissors and other tools, marched out, some of them singing the "Marseillaise."

(continued)

We were out for thirteen weeks, and the girls established their reputation. They were on picket duty from seven o'clock in the morning till six o'clock in the evening, and gained over many of the nonunion workers by appeals to them to quit working against us.

Our theory was that if properly approached and talked to few would be found who would resist our offer to take them into our organization. No right thinking person desires to injure another. We did not believe in violence and never employed it.

During this strike period we girls each received $3 a week; single men $3 a week, and married men $5 a week. This was paid us by the National Board.

We were greatly helped by the other unions, because the open shop issue was a tremendous one, and this was the second fight which the bosses had conducted for it.

Their first was with the tailors, whom they beat. If they now could beat us the outlook for unionism would be bad.

Some were aided and we stuck out, and won a glorious victory all along the line. That was only last week. The shops are open now for all union hands and for them only.

• • •

The bosses try to represent this open shop issue as tho they were fighting a battle for the public, but really it is nothing of the sort. The open shop is a weapon to break the unions and set men once more cutting each other's throats by individual competition.

• • •

The shops are open now for all union people, and all nonunion people can join the union. In order to take in newcome foreigners we have for them cut the initiation fees down to one-half what we Americans have to pay, and we trust them till they get work and their wages.

• • •

Our trade is well organized, we have won two victories and are not going backward.

But there is much to be done in other directions. The shop girls certainly need organization, and I think that they ought to be easy to organize, as their duties are simple and regular and they have a regular scale of wages.

Many saleswomen on Grand and Division streets, and, in fact, all over the East Side, work from 8 a.m. til 9 p.m. week days, and one-half a day on Sundays for $5 and $6 a week; so they certainly need organization.

The waitresses also could easily be organized, and perhaps the domestic servants. I don't know about stenographers. I have not come in contact with them.

Women have proved in the late strike that they can be faithful to an organization and to each other. The men give us the credit of winning the strike.

Certainly our organization constantly grows stronger, and the Woman's Trade Union League makes progress.

The girls and women by their meetings and discussions come to understand and sympathize with each other, and more and more easily they act together.

It is the only way in which they can hope to hold what they now have or better present conditions.

Certainly there is no hope from the mercy of the bosses.

Each boss does the best he can for himself with no thought of the other bosses, and that compels each to gouge and squeeze his hands to the last penny in order to make a profit.

So we must stand together to resist, for we will get what we can take—just that and no more.

New York, March 20, 1905.

The Strike: The "Uprising of the Twenty Thousand"

When contemporaries thought about the "girl strikers" of the shirtwaist strike, they were most likely to think of Rose Schneiderman (left) or Clara Lemlich. Both were young, still in their twenties. Both appeared to be physically frail but demonstrated a fierce dedication to the union and dauntless courage that belied their size.

Schneiderman was, by 1909, no longer a garment worker but a paid organizer for the Women's Trade Union League. After the New York branch of the WTUL decided to put its resources at the disposal of the strikers, Schneiderman helped organize meetings, negotiated contracts with the hundreds of manufacturers affected, and, perhaps most critically, raised money. Lemlich was a union activist, an officer of the Local that called the strike that grew into the "Uprising of the Twenty Thousand." It was she who gave the fiery speech at Cooper Union that led to the vote for a general strike. And she continued to play a leading role throughout. In addition to helping organize the thousands who flocked into the union, she gave a series of highly publicized speeches describing the plight of the workers, and, like Schneiderman, helped raise money so that the union could pay benefits to its members.

Jacob Epstein might have used either Schneiderman or Lemlich as the model for *Intensely Serious*, his depiction of the young woman of the Lower East Side, and the workers photographed in "Going out for better conditions" display some of the exuberance John Sloan sought to capture in *The Return from Toil*. As several commentators on the strike noted, including the not entirely sympathetic reporter for the *New York Times*, for many shirtwaist workers the strike was an

Going out for better conditions

adventure. Not only did it offer a break from the relentless pace and repetitive nature of work in the factories, but it also offered hope of a new life. Strikers felt that this was their chance to take charge of their own lives.

CHRONOLOGY OF THE STRIKE

1909

September 27: Local 25 of the International Ladies Garment Workers Union, declaring that the Triangle Shirtwaist Company had locked out its workers, declared a strike against the company. Workers at the Leiserson Company were already on strike.

October 21: General meeting of membership of Local 25 voted in favor of a "general [i.e., industrywide] strike"; appointed "committee of five" to plan it.

October 23: Margaret Johnson, a member of the Women's Trade Union League, was arrested for picketing in front of the Leiserson shop.

October 29: Management of the Triangle company started the Employers' Mutual Protective Association (later called the Waist and Dressmakers Manufacturers' Association).

November 4: Mary E. Dreier, president of the New York WTUL, was arrested for picketing in front of the Triangle company. Triangle co-owner Max Blanck denied that his company had locked out its workers or that the workers were on strike.

November 15: "Committee of five" called a mass meeting for November 22 at Cooper Union to vote on general strike.

November 18: Workers at the Diamond Waist Company struck rather than do work contracted from the Triangle company; fliers in English, Yiddish, and Italian announcing the November 22 meeting were distributed throughout the East Side.

November 22: Mass meeting at Cooper Union (overflow crowds met in Beethoven Hall, Manhattan Lyceum, and other venues) heard Samuel Gompers, president of the American Federation of Labor, Mary E. Dreier, and other speakers discuss advisability of a strike. Climactic moment was the "Philippic in Yiddish" from Clara Lemlich, striker against the Leiserson Company and member of the executive committee of Local 25. The strike officially began when Lemlich's motion was passed by acclamation, and all present took "ancient Hebrew oath" to keep faith.

November 23–30: Upward of forty thousand shirtwaist workers (according to the *New York Times*) from hundreds of shops walked off the job. WTUL volunteers helped enroll strikers in the union, walk picket duty, supply bail for strikers arrested while picketing, and provide publicity. The Socialist party appointed a committee to help the union organize the strike, as did its Italian branch and the United Hebrew Trades Union. Many sympathetic individuals also volunteered their services.

November 25: Formation of the Waist and Dressmakers Manufacturers' Association announced; pickets and "scabs" clashed on Greene Street—seventeen strikers arrested.

November 30: Several small manufacturers yielded to ILGWU demands, establishing a pattern of small firms settling individually over the next two months while large companies held out.

December 3: Protest march to City Hall against police mistreatment of pickets, led by WTUL president Mary Dreier and several strikers who had been arrested; met with Mayor George B. McClellan.

December 5: Mass meeting at Hippodrome (eight thousand in attendance) held under the auspices of the Political Equality Association, a women's suffrage organization headed by socialite Mrs. O. H. P. Belmont. Speakers included union activist Leonora O'Reilly, a member of the WTUL.

December 5: Markus Marks, president of the Clothiers' Association, an employers' association, and John Mitchell, former president of the United Mine Workers union, proposed that strike issues be arbitrated.

December 6: Associated Waist and Dress Manufacturers accepted the offer of arbitration in the name of the employers. After unsuccessfully demanding union recognition as a precondition, the ILGWU followed suit.

December 10: Initial efforts at arbitration foundered over employers' refusal to consider question of union recognition.

December 15: Mary Dreier, Rose Schneiderman (WTUL member and union activist), and several strikers met with 150 members of the exclusive Colony Club in New York City at the invitation of Mrs. Belmont, Anne Morgan (daughter of banker J. P. Morgan), and other affluent supporters; raised $1,300 for the strike.

December 18: Suffrage activist and WTUL member Violet L. Pike arrested for making pro-strike speech on street without a permit.

December 19: Mrs. Belmont put up her town house as bail for four strikers.

December 20: Seven thousand Philadelphia shirtwaist workers, protesting that New York manufacturers were seeking to break the strike by contracting work to their employers, struck in solidarity with the New York strikers.

December 21: Police raided strike headquarters to arrest eight pickets accused of assaulting two "scabs"; several strikers jailed.

December 22: Strikers hosted dance for compatriots just released from workhouse; arrests of pickets continued.

December 23: New arbitration efforts eventuated in an eight-point proposal endorsed by the manufacturers' association.

December 27: Strikers overwhelmingly rejected the arbitration offer over the issue of the "open" shop, that is, the right of the employer to hire nonunion workers.

December 29: Special issue of *New York Call* (socialist newspaper) with proceeds going to strike fund.

1910

January 2: Meeting at Carnegie Hall to protest police mistreatment of pickets.

January 6: Special issue of *New York Evening Journal* (published by William Randolph Hearst); proceeds of sale of first fifty thousand copies donated to the strike fund.

January 9: Four strikers arrested in Brooklyn for assaulting nonunion workers.

January 11: ILGWU called for renewed arbitration; manufacturers' association refused.

January 14: Mass meeting to protest police harassment of pickets.

January 16: Smith College students voted to boycott nonunion waists and dresses.

January 19: Wellesley College students donated $1,000 to strike.

January 24: Mrs. Belmont and others established "model" shirtwaist factory; police arrested more strikers.

February 6: Philadelphia shirtwaist makers voted to accept arbitration offer and end strike.

February 15: ILGWU declared the strike officially over; by then 339 manufacturing firms had reached agreements with the union; thirteen firms, including Triangle, with eleven hundred workers did not settle.

December 21: One thousand New York City shirtwaist makers struck eleven firms over refusal to renew union contracts.

December 24: Local 25, with over ten thousand members, set January 6, 1911, as date for general strike unless companies agreed to renew contracts.

Rules for Pickets

Crucial to the success of the "Uprising," limited as it proved to be, was what Paul U. Kellogg, editor of *The Survey* magazine, one of the most influential outlets for "progressive" ideas of the day, called the "extraordinary sympathy" the strike received. There were several reasons why it attracted so much sympathy, not least of which was the strong-arm tactics of the employers who, as a *New York Times* story reprinted here reported, hired "thugs" to break up picket lines and bribed ("sugared") police to look the other way. Kellogg spoke for many who considered themselves "progressive." Sympathy, he wrote, "is the burning, penetrating ray of light which alone can pierce the fogs and clouds of prejudice, bigotry, ignorance and misunderstanding." It was, therefore, "a good thing"

> . . . that policemen and magistrates should have been thought to be unduly severe in suppressing picketing; that girls whose disorderly conduct consists of attempting to persuade other girls not to take the place of strikers should have been put into prison in the enforced company of women whose disorderly conduct is that of the common prostitute; and that all of this should have occurred in the center of Manhattan island, where women of wealth and social position, and college women whose minds are already aflame with the current ideas of social responsibility and solidarity, could easily come into personal touch with it, under the

eye, moreover, of newspaper reporters, and affording a natural topic for continuous editorial discussion.[1]

RULES FOR PICKETS

Don't walk in groups of more than two or three

Don't stand in front of the shop; Walk up and down the block.

Don't stop the person you wish to talk to; Walk alongside of him.

Don't get exited and shout when you are talking

Don't put your hand on the person you are speaking to. Don't touch his sleeve or button. This may be construed as a "technical assault".

Don't call any one "scab" or use abusive language of any kind.

Plead, persuade, appeal, but do not threaten.

If a policeman arrest you and you are sure that you have committed no offence, take down his number and give it to your union officers.

רולס פיר פיקעטס

CIRCULAR ISSUED BY THE STRIKERS.

"Rules for Pickets," circular issued by Local 25 of the International Ladies Waist Makers Union as reprinted in William Mailly, "The Working Girls' Strike," *The Independent* 67 (December 23, 1909), 1417.

[1] Paul U. Kellogg, "The Shirtwaist Workers' Strike," *Survey* 23 (January 15, 1910): 505–506.

Crucial to the rise of this sympathy were the repeated reassurances in many newspapers and magazines that the strikers did not have any recourse to violence or in any way initiate the incidents leading to their arrests. Instead these accounts routinely described the strikers as faithfully obeying their union's "Rules for Pickets," reprinted here from *The Independent* for December 23, 1909. As other materials included here make clear, however, the strikers did not always follow the "Rules."

NEWS ACCOUNTS OF THE STRIKE

Except where noted, the following excerpts come from the *New York Times*. Editorially, the *Times* spoke out against the strikers' demand for the union shop, that is, their insistence that employers hire only those willing to belong to the union. This lack of sympathy for the strikers' cause, combined with the paper's determination to present the views of all parties to the dispute, particularly the employers', makes the *Times's* account especially valuable when used in conjunction with the strikers' and their supporters' account of events.

Its coverage began on November 5, 1909, weeks after the workers at Leiserson's and Triangle first walked out. The *Times*, like the rest of the New York press with the exceptions of the socialist *Call* and the Yiddish-language *Forward*, did not notice the strike until police arrested Mary Dreier, president of the New York Women's Trade Union League. Following the *Times's* version of that story is that of Mary Clark Barnes, "The Strike of the Shirtwaist Makers," in the March 1910 issue of *The World Today* (pp. 266–267), which illustrates how quickly certain strike events such as Dreier's arrest achieved mythic status. Much of the historical literature on the strike follows Barnes's account and retells the story of the flustered magistrate eager to hustle Dreier out of court. Of more moment is the way Dreier's own account of her arrest, as recounted in the *Times*, launched the campaign for "sympathy" that proved so crucial in the final outcome of the strike.

ARREST STRIKERS FOR BEING ASSAULTED

New York Times, November 5, 1909

Policeman Joseph De Cantillon of the Mercer Street Station—the "Penitentiary Precinct" of the Police Department—arrested yesterday morning Miss Mary Dreier, President of the Women's Trade Union League, a wealthy champion of laboring women in this city, because she advised a young woman operative, hurrying to the lofts of the Triangle Waist Company of 29 Washington Place, that there was a strike there, and urged her not to be a strikebreaker.

This, however, Miss Dreier said last night was only the latest of a series of outrages which had been perpetrated by men of the "penitentiary precinct" for months. Miss Dreier asserted that upon every occasion the police have taken the part of the shop owners in Washington Place and the surrounding neighborhood where there have been strikes of women operatives in the last few months. The police, said Miss Dreier, always arrest the pickets put out by the striking girls, even when the pickets have been beaten, in the presence of the police, by strike-breakers, both men and women.

• • •

At the station Lieut. Von Derzelsky told her that her arrest had been a mistake and that she was at liberty to go.

• • •

Just why the police have so openly sided with the employers as Miss Dreier charged, she declared she did not know, but among the employes in many of the shops the reason was boldly stated to be that the employers had "sugared" the police. This charge is being made upon every side.

Miss Dreier, who is a frail young woman and speaks with a foreign accent, said that about 150 girls were on strike. The Woman's Trades Union League, of which she is the President, is backing them in their fight against Harris & Blanck, owners of the Triangle Waist Company. The strike, she said, began about five weeks ago. The girls were "locked out," the owners of the factory giving as a reason that they had no work for them to do.

• • •

"The Woman's Trades Union League became interested in the matter, and a committee in charge of Miss Violet Pike was named to take charge of the picketing. Policemen were sent to the place, some of them in plain clothes, and from the first they have all apparently been in sympathy with the employers. They have arrested many of the girls, and have been telling us we were doing wrong when we talked to the strikebreaking girls about what they were doing, despite the fact that, as we all know, moral suasion in such matters is legal.

WAS KEEPING WITHIN THE LAW.

"Whenever we spoke to the girls the police would come up and gruffly order us to stop talking, and when we asserted our legal rights in the matter, persisted in their refusal to allow us to talk. As to the incident this morning, which resulted in my arrest, I am glad of the chance to tell the facts.

"I was crossing the street to see a girl who was on the way to the factory. One of the plain clothes men stopped me with the excuse as that I was obstructing a public highway. I insisted on my rights, and told him I would continue to act as I had been acting, as I knew the law and was careful to keep within it.

"The only thing I said to the girl was 'There's a strike in the Triangle.' She became very angry and talked about my annoying her. Then she struck me. When she struck me I turned to the policeman to see if he would arrest her, as he had been doing in the case of the striking girls. The girl told him that I had been annoying and threatening her, whereupon the policeman turned to her and said, 'If you want to press the charge, come along to the station house with me.'

RELEASED AT THE STATION

"In the station the girl told the Lieutenant behind the desk that I said, 'I will split your head open if you try to go to work.' That was so palpably false that the Lieutenant refused to listen further and released me. Of course, I shall continue my work on behalf of the girls."

• • •

"Arrest Strikers for Being Assaulted," *New York Times,* November 5, 1909. Reprinted by permission.

(continued)

THUGS HIRED FOR INTIMIDATION.

The charge is made that thugs have been hired to intimidate the pickets. This has been heard in the precinct for months. At the time of the neckwear strike, ended a few weeks ago, it was asserted that bands of "strong-arm men" were imported from the Bowery and the regions east of it by certain employers to intimidate the strikers. The intimidation took the form of beatings. It is a fact that one young girl was confined to her bed for three weeks as the result of the treatment at the hands of half a dozen of these thugs.

Miss Elsie Cole, a graduate of Vassar and a member of the Woman's Trade Union League, has been helping the Triangle girl strikers. She told some of her experiences with the police yesterday. They were similar to those of Miss Dreier. She declared that one policeman, when she quoted to him the law permitting her to use moral susion in influencing strike-breakers so long as she did not try and influence them by acts expressing or implying threats, intimidations, coercion, or force, exclaimed:

"Well, you know me, young lady. None of that around here."

Miss Marot declares that when she was on picket duty a plainclothes man said to her: "You out-of-town scum, keep out of this or you'll find yourself in jail."

"THE STRIKE OF THE SHIRTWAIST MAKERS"

The World Today (March 1910)

• • •

One evening a magistrate in a night court which had become notorious for its treatment of pickets, going through his usual routine, demanded of a prisoner who had been brought in on a charge of "assault" "What is your name?"

"Mary E. Dreier," was the gentle response.

The magistrate started, and, for the first time, took the trouble to look at the prisoner.

"You any relation to that lady that has something to do with the trade union?" he asked with evident trepidation.

"I am president of the Women's Trade Union League," responded Miss Dreier.

The magistrate, forgetting his court ritual, soundly berated the officer who had brought in Miss Dreier, and making no effort to discover how her offense differed from the offenses of other young women on whom he had been imposing severe sentences, promptly dismissed the case and manifestly was anxious for her to leave the court as soon as possible.

"The Strike of the Shirtwaist Makers," *The World Today* (March 1910), 266-67.

"Girl Strikers Well Treated"
New York Times, November 6, 1909

This is the *Times's* follow-up piece to its Dreier arrest story. The headline referred to the police commissioner's denial of Dreier's charges that police were abusing strikers or that employers were bribing ("sugaring") officers. The opening paragraphs of the story, however sardonically described the police resources devoted to protecting the Triangle Shirtwaist Company from the "six slender east side girls" on picket duty. The story also includes an extended interview with Triangle Shirtwaist Company co-owner Max Blanck. Despite the *Times's* commitment to impartial reporting, the reporter's paraphrase of Blanck's remarks in the second paragraph makes subtle fun of his claim that there was no strike, a gibe picked up by the copyeditor and incorporated into the last subheadline. Only in its final paragraphs did the *Times* story detail the police commissioner's denials. It noted that he based his statements on assurances from "Inspector Daly." In its November 5 story concerning the inspector's investigation, the paper quoted WTUL activist Helen Marot's testimony: "Miss Marot declares that when she was on picket duty a plainclothes man said to her: 'You out-of-town scum, keep out of this or you'll find yourself in jail.'" Daly, the reporter noted, commented at the hearing, "Well, scum might be a nice word. How do I know what it means?"

GIRL STRIKERS WELL TREATED, SAYS BAKER

Commissioner Discredits Charge That Police Showed Sympathy with Waist Manufacturers.

No "Sugar" Going Around

Mr. Blanck Maintains There is No Strike In His Factory, but Admits There Are Strikers.

Two big policemen, whose combined weight must be about 700 pounds, were on duty in Washington Place, near Washington Square, yesterday, to see

"Girl Strikers Well Treated, Says Baker," *New York Times*, November 6, 1909. Reprinted by permission.

(continued)

that the striking girls of the Triangle Waist Company, 29 Washington Place, did not do bodily harm to the girls now at work there. Opposed to the police, so far as could be visually ascertained, were six slender east side girls, the combined weight of the sextet probably being within 50 pounds of that of the guardians of the peace, who were there to maintain order.

Miss Mary E. Dreier of 144 East Sixty-fifth Street, the wealthy champion of laboring women, who is also President of the Woman's Trade Union League, which is backing the strikers in their fight against the waist company, says that 150 girls are out as a result of a "lockout." Max Blanck, one of the two owners of the waist company, on the other hand, stoutly maintains that there is no strike. Then he says, that instead of 150 girls being out there are less than half that number. The recognition of a union, which he says does not exist, is the cause of the trouble, except that part of it is due to the efforts of Miss Dreier and others in behalf of the girls.

Mr. Blanck denied vehemently yesterday that the police were unduly sympathetic to the employers or that they were needlessly arresting the girl pickets, even going so far, according to Miss Dreier, as to arrest the pickets when they, and not the non-strikers, had been assailed. All this, Mr. Blanck said, was absolutely false. It is the girls who are still at work, he said, who are being maltreated, and to prove this he called into his office six young shirtwaist makers who corroborated him and offered to produce twice as many more.

The Triangle Waist Company employs some 400 girls. A tour through the factory yesterday proved that nearly every machine was being operated, bearing out the statement of the owners that a full force is working. Mr. Blanck said these girls had not joined the union. The lowest salary paid in the establishment, he added, was $8 a week, while at least half of the girls get as high as $16 a week.

"All of this trouble," said Mr. Blanck, "is over this union business. We did not recognize it, and we do not intend to. We told the girls that we were willing to listen to any complaints and to receive any suggestions from our employes themselves, but we had to draw the line on three or four east side gentlemen stepping in to tell us how to run our business. It is an outrage the way the girls who have remained loyal—and they are the great majority of our force—have been treated by these people and their sympathizers. I will let them tell their own stories."

Mr. Blanck then summoned the girls into his office. The ones who came represented at least three nationalities. One girl, an American, said she had been followed by strikebreakers and their sympathizers, and that a man had thrown a potato which struck her in the back, leaving a bruise that could still be seen if necessary. Another girl, an Italian, said she had been struck in the stomach by a man. The others said they had been followed and insulted frequently by the strikers and their friends.

The picket girls who were patrolling the sidewalks surrounding the building in which the factory is denied all of the stories told by the other girls. They declared that they had not been insulting and that at no time had they resorted to violence in their fight for the recognition of their union. Miss Dreier, corroborates them in this.

The police of the Mercer Street Station, the "penitentiary precinct" of the department, were not very affable when it came to talking about the strike. The Lieutenant behind the desk professed to know little or nothing of the trouble between the police and the strikers which has resulted in the arrest of so many of the girl pickets.

Police Commissioner Baker declared that the charges that the police of that station were being "sugared" was false, and the charges made by Miss Dreier that the police were taking the side of the manufacturers against the striking girls was also untrue. Inspector Daly, the Commissioner said, had assured him that all of the allegations were unfounded: in fact, that the strikers were being treated better than ever before.

Cooper Union Meeting
New York Times, November 23, 1909

This meeting, which led to tens of thousands of shirtwaist workers joining the union and going on strike, is one of the most important moments in U.S. labor history. The strike would prove to be the largest, to date, of women workers. The union would be the first successful labor organization of women workers in U.S. history. The meeting itself quickly achieved mythic status. One can trace this process by comparing the account of the meeting in the *Times,* published the morning after, with one in the "progressive" weekly, *The Survey,* published three weeks later. The *Times* carried the story of the Cooper Union meeting on page 16. It focused upon Samuel Gompers, president of the American Federation of Labor. Constance D. Leupp's account, from her "The Shirtwaist Makers' Strike," *The Survey* 23 (December 18, 1909): 384–385, focused upon Clara Lemlich's Yiddish-language "Philippic," omitted in the *Times* story, and the dramatic taking of the strike vote. It has become the standard version, cited in virtually every study of the strike. Leupp's treatment of Lemlich's speech, like several other contemporary accounts, identified her simply as a "striker" and emphasized the spontaneity of both her "Philippic" and the strike vote that ensued. Here was the stuff of romance: Veteran labor leaders waffle over the crucial question of the general strike until a "girl" galvanizes the meeting with her impromptu eloquence and her fellow workers rise as one. It was an inspiring story and did much to gain the strikers that "sympathy" that Paul Kellogg, editor of *The Survey,* pointed out was so important for their success. Yet Lemlich was not just a "striker"; she was a member of the executive committee of the local that called the strike and organized the Cooper Union meeting. Her speech, the vote, and the taking of the oath were almost certainly all planned carefully in advance by the committee.

40,000 CALLED OUT IN WOMEN'S STRIKE

Makers of Shirtwaists Vote to Quit Work After Hearing Gompers Speak.

More Pay; Shorter Hours

Cooper Union Filled with Cheering Throng—Strike Order Goes into Effect Here To-day.

After hearing Samuel Gompers, President of the American Federation of Labor, deliver an address in Cooper Union last night the audience of shirtwaist-makers which filled the hall voted to go on strike. A similar vote, also in favor of the strike, was taken in four other halls.

The auditorium was well filled, and hundreds stood outside, striving to gain admittance. B. Finegbeim of Vorwaerts presided. He spoke in Yiddish.

• • •

The conditions in the clothing trade, declared Mr. Gompers, were a blot on modern civilization as

"40,000 Called Out in Women's Strike," *New York Times,* November 23, 1909. Reprinted by permission.

he knew through investigation. The clothing trade with its tenement house work, he said, and work under unsanitary conditions breaks the spirit of men and women, and makes children prematurely old.

"Mr. Shirtwaist Maker may be inconvenienced and his profits may be diminished if you girls and boys go on strike," he went on. "And, mind you, I do not know whether a strike is necessary in this case, but there is something greater than the convenience or the profits of Mr. Shirtwaist Maker at stake—there are the lives and the future of the men and women engaged in this work. You seem to be aroused now to your interests. It is time, more than time. I am only sorry that you did not organize long ago.

"This is the time, and if you let this occasion go by it may be generations before you again get the opportunity to improve your conditions."

He told them not to enter into a strike too hastily, but when they found that the conditions were such that they could not obtain measurable relief from present conditions, better pay, better and shorter hours, he would say to them as calmly as he could "Strike!" and when they did strike to let the manufacturers know that they were on strike.

After an appeal by W. A. Coakley for organization, the Chairman read a resolution declaring that the shirtwaist makers, including the operators, finishers, buttonhold makers, and all other workers on shirtwaists except the cutters, who have their own organization, should declare a general strike. This was received with cheers, and when the Chairman asked whether all understood the conditions for which they struck, the reply was overwhelmingly in the affirmative.

The audience stood waving American flags and shouting.

"THE SHIRTWAIST MAKERS' STRIKE"
THE SURVEY, DECEMBER 18, 1909

The resolution for a general strike was taken at mass meetings held November 22. At Cooper Union Mr. Gompers spoke, and a procession of speakers, mostly Yiddish, for two hours implored their attentive audience to go about the thing soberly and with due consideration; but, if they decided to strike, to stand by their colors and be loyal to the union. The dramatic climax of the evening was reached when Clara Lemlich, a striker from Leiserson's who had been assaulted when picketing, made her way to the platform, begged a moment from the chairman, and after an impromptu Philippic in Yiddish, eloquent even to American ears, put the motion for a general strike and was unanimously endorsed. The chairman then cried, "Do you mean faith? Will you take the old Jewish oath?" And up came 2000 right hands with the prayer: "If I turn traitor to the cause I now pledge, may this hand wither and drop off at the wrist from the arm I now raise."

"The Shirtwaist Makers' Strike," *The Survey,* December 18, 1909.

First Day of General Strike
New York Times, November 24, 1909

Running the "Uprising" taxed the resources of the union to the breaking point. It had to enroll tens of thousands of members; it had to negotiate contracts with the scores, and then the hundreds, of small employers who preferred settling to losing business; it had to organize picket lines and promulgate "rules" for those on them to follow; it had to raise money to provide benefits to strikers and their families—its own treasury, built up from the dues of its hundred or so members before the strike, consisted of perhaps $100. It had to get out its version of the strike to the newspapers and magazines. And it had to do all of this virtually overnight. The following story captures something of the frenetic character of the strike's first day and of the overwhelming crush of business that inundated union officials. It also notes the key role played by Mary Dreier and the Women's Trade Union League. WTUL volunteers provided clerical services in enrolling union members; they provided publicity services, particularly with the English-language press; they served on picket lines; they raised money. They also chaired meetings of strikers because, as the small firms settled, their strikers had to ratify the new contracts. WTUL volunteers often rented the halls for these meetings as well.

WAIST STRIKE ON; 18,000 WOMEN OUT

❦

They Quit Work In Factories Here on a Signal From Their Union Leaders.

❦

Some Employers Give In

❦

East Side Halls Crowded with Strikers, and the Number is Expected to Grow to 40,000 Soon.

❦

Every available hall on the east side was filled yesterday with striking shirtwaist girls, who quit work throughout the city in obedience to the strike vote passed at the mass meeting in Cooper Union and three other halls on Monday night. There are some men among the strikers, but they were insignificant in numbers compared to the vast outpouring of women and girls from the shirtwaist factories.

In accordance with a programme arranged late on Monday night the army of waistmakers went to work as usual yesterday morning. At 10 o'clock an agent of the union in each factory gave the signal and the strike was on.

• • •

More than twenty halls were designated as meeting places, but the general tendency was to crowd into Clinton Hall, 151 Clinton Street, where the Women Waistmakers' Union has its headquarters. The office of the Shirtwaist Makers' Union is on the fifth floor. B. Weinstein, S. Goldstein, Salvatore Ninfo, Max Kasimirsky, and Solomon Schindler were looked on as a Committee of Arrangements at Clinton Hall, but the women came in such numbers that nothing could be done. The office of the union was choked up with people; so were the stairways, passages, and every assembly room in the building.

"Waist Strike On; 18,000 Women Out," *New York Times*, November 24, 1909. Reprinted by permission.

Employers began to arrive to settle with the union, but had a hard time to get near the room where the officers had agreements ready to be signed.

• • •

. . . Every time the office of the union opened the press of people behind forced men and women into it, until the man who was filling out the agreements had not room to move his elbows. The place was cleared, only to have the same thing happen every twenty minutes. It was announced that eleven employers had signed agreements with the union, and that fifty more who were ready to sign will do so to-day.

The strike leaders could make no estimate of how many workers were on strike. So far as they could guess about one-half of the shops were affected, and about 18,000 waistmakers were out. More continued to quit until the closing of the factories, and the strike is expected to be complete to-day. The leaders, who estimate liberally, cling to their original statements that 40,000 will be affected.

Miss Mary E. Dreier, President of the Women's Trades Union League, appeared at Clinton Hall in the afternoon and succeeded in persuading the striking waist girls who filled up the corridors to squeeze themselves into different assembly rooms so as to leave a passageway for employers who came to settle. There were several police around, who kept order at the doors, but were jostled around like other people if they were caught in the crowd.

Miss Dreier said that the Women's Trades Union League had formed itself into a sort of general committee of the whole to aid the strike in every possible way.

"The first day is the worst," she said. "After to-day matters will be systematized. Such a big strike as this is hard to handle at first."

Each factory has its own system of wages, which are to be filled in blanks in the agreements the employers are required to sign. There are general demands applicable to all, the principal of which are an advance of 20 per cent for piece workers and 15 per cent for week workers; a fifty-two-hour working week for the latter, pay for all legal holidays and not more than two hours in any day to be worked as overtime. The proposed agreement, of which the union is the one party and the employers the other, also provides that if either side violates its provisions the party violating it shall pay $300 for "liquidated damages."

• • •

The employers are not organized. None of them had much to say about the strike, except that it was expected.

"Waist Strike Grows"
New York Times, November 25, 1909

As the strike grew to involve approximately thirty thousand workers, the larger employers formed their own association and vowed to fight. But, even as more workers joined the strike, others were going back to work as small employers signed with the union. This meant that although up to forty thousand workers walked off the job, and although the strike dragged on for months, most were on strike for a relatively brief period. Further, because labor turnover—the incidence of workers quitting—was very high, workers on strike in one shop often took positions in others that had settled.

This decentralized nature of the garment trades posed problems for both sides. The hundreds of shops meant that the union could pursue a "divide and conquer" strategy. Each manufacturer who settled could take business away from those who held out. Hence the employers' decision to organize themselves. On the other hand, the union faced the herculean task of organizing workers in all the factories, including those in nearby Brooklyn, Newark, and even Philadelphia, because the large manufacturers could subcontract work out to nonunion shops.

Note the reference to "agents of some of the strike-breaking agencies" who hovered outside the meeting of shirtwaist manufacturers. Strikebreaking was a well-established profession, not only in New York City but also throughout the nation. The largest company engaged in it was the Pinkerton Detective Agency, which supplied armed guards for workers crossing picket lines. Its services were not engaged by the shirtwaist manufacturers. Other agencies provided workers willing to cross picket lines, and some supplied "thugs" willing to assault or otherwise intimidate strikers. The employers' use of these "thugs" and alleged "sugaring" or bribing of police to look the other way helped turn public opinion to the side of the strikers.

WAIST STRIKE GROWS.

But the Big Employers Organize to Fight—Some Giving In.

A number of the large employers in the waistmaking industry decided yesterday to get together and fight the strike of the waistmakers, which has practically tied up the trade in this city. With a view to forming a manufacturers' association in order to stop the competition likely to follow if the tendency of small firms to grant the strikers' demands is not checked, a secret meeting of the largest manufacturing firms was held yesterday afternoon at the Broadway Central Hotel. None of those who were present would talk, but it was learned that another meeting will be held to-day in the same place, at which an association will probably be formed and means taken to break the strike. Agents of some of the strike breaking agencies got wind of the meeting; and hovered around the corridors while the meeting was in progress. But they did not get an audience with the manufacturers and went away.

One of the largest of the manufacturers said yesterday: "We cannot understand how so many people can be swayed to join in a strike that has no merit. Our employes were perfectly satisfied, and they made no demands. It is a foolish, hysterical strike, and not 5 per cent of the strikers know what they are striking for."

The same scenes of confusion took place yesterday as occurred on Tuesday at Clinton Hall, 151 Clinton Street, the main headquarters of the strikers. B. Witasken of the Executive Committee of the union said that fifty employers in all had granted the demands and that there were 12,000 more strikers out than on Tuesday, making a total of about 30,000.

• • •

Policeman Lowenthal of the Elizabeth Street Station was called into a shirtwaist factory at 48 Walker Street yesterday to order out 300 striking girls who had gathered on the stairways there. He said it took him "two hours to get them down." He arrested Sophie Kleineman, 18, of 184 Forsyth Street, for slapping him in the face. In the Tombs Court later she was discharged.

"Waist Strike Grows," *New York Times*, November 25, 1909. Reprinted by permission.

"Girl Strikers Riot"
New York Times, November 27, 1909

Much of the contemporary mystique of the strike centered on the pluck of the strikers, usually described as "girls," holding their ground against burly strikebreakers and/or police. Newspaper and magazine stories often devoted much space to describing how "slender" and "tiny" the women on the picket lines were and how heavy and tall their male antagonists were. Each of these encounters gained support for the "Uprising." Yet much of the violence connected with the strike was between strikers and other women, those trying to cross the picket lines and take their jobs. The *Times* reporter referred to the latter as "non-union girls." To the strikers, they were "scabs" who were taking bread from their families' mouths. The contempt that strikers felt for scabs cannot be exaggerated, and what usually began as good-faith efforts at persuasion often turned to insult and then to violence when "non-union" girls ignored strikers' entreaties to join them. This early encounter produced exactly the sort of publicity that the union and its allies wished to avoid. Note that the "girls" became "combatants" and then "Amazons," a reference to the women warriors of classical myth. Note, too, how the focus of sympathy in the story is on Morris Parillo, the "lone man" in the fray, who expressed "relief" when he was arrested. This incident helped provide the impetus for the union's "Rules for Pickets," reprinted here, which strictly forbade the use of insult and force.

GIRL STRIKERS RIOT; QUELLED BY POLICE

Lone Man in Fight Between Pickets and Non-Union Waist Makers Glad He's Arrested.

But 600 of the Largest Manufacturers Organize to Break It—Some Others Surrender.

For about two hours yesterday there was a cyclonic time in the block in Greene Street, between Houston and Bleecker Streets, owing to a fight between pickets of the striking waistmakers and non-union girls. A crowd of onlookers, which blocked all traffic, watched the combatants while dresses were torn, faces scratched and the headgear of many girls on both sides were wrecked.

When the police came they were unable to cope with the situation and the reserves of the Mercer Street station were called out. They found a spirited running fight going on and Morris Parillo, who had undertaken to lead the pickets, was bandied hither and thither, the centre of an Amazonian attack by the non-union girls. He was literally at bay, his hair dishevelled, his collar torn loose, and in a state of utter exhaustion. It was a relief to him, he said, when he was arrested.

The fight raged near the factory of J. M. Cohen of 189 Greene Street, where the greater number of the waistmakers refused to strike. The reserves made short work of dispersing the crowd, and arrested eleven women pickets and six men, all of whom were taken before Magistrate Kernochan at Jefferson Market Court. He let the women go with a warning and fined the men $3 each.

At a meeting of the large firms in the trade in the Broadway Central Hotel permanent organization was effected under the name of the Association of Waist and Dress Manufacturers of New York, with J. B. Hyman as Chairman and Charles Weinblatt of 280 Broadway as Secretary and counsel. The new organization contains between 600 and 700 members, and will meet to-day at the Hoffman House to adopt a constitution and by laws and initiate active measures for breaking the strike.

• • •

At the request of Miss Clara Lemlich, who took the initiative in calling the strike of the waistmakers, the Central Federated Union last night appointed a committee to co-operate with the shirtwaist makers' Union in the strike.

"Girl Strikers Riot; Quelled by Police," *New York Times,* November 27, 1909. Reprinted by permission.

"Girl Strikers Go to the City Hall"
New York Times, December 4, 1909

The "girl" strikers arrested during the "riot" outside the factory of J. M. Cohen on November 26 received suspended sentences, but those strikers brought before magistrate's court in the days to follow faced stiff fines and even imprisonment for up to a month. The union and its allies, which now included prominent leaders of the suffrage movement as well as members of the Women's Trade Union League, protested that the police were arresting strikers on false pretenses. The marchers gained little satisfaction from the mayor, but they did win a good deal of favorable publicity for their cause. Crucial to their gaining the attention of the media was the participation of suffrage leaders in the march. This marks the moment of formation of that extraordinary coalition of women's organizations that fascinated and, in many cases, inspired contemporaries and has so intrigued historians. The *Times* took the occasion to provide its readers with some background information on the strike, including its first full description of the Cooper Union meeting and of Clara Lemlich's role. Of particular interest is its explanation of "why the union idea appeals" to the strikers. However condescending (sexist?) the story's tone, the *Times's* reporter early appreciated the idealism of the strikers and clearly recorded the centrality of union recognition in their list of demands.

GIRL STRIKERS GO TO THE CITY HALL

❧

Delegation from the Shirtwaist Makers' Union Protests Against Police Discrimination.

❧

"Girl Strikers Go to the City Hall," *New York Times,* December 4, 1909. Reprinted by permission.

Mayor Promises Fair Deal

❧

Strike, Following Young Girl Workers' Call, Is for Shorter Hours and Recognition of Newly Formed Union.

❧

In a gay mood despite their indignation, a thousand or more striking shirtwaist makers, supplemented by perhaps a thousand sympathizers from

(continued)

the east side, marched to the City Hall yesterday afternoon to present a written protest to the Mayor against the alleged partiality of the police in favor of the employers and against the strikers. The Mayor said he would take the matter up with Police Commissioner Baker. He wanted the young women to have a fair deal, he said. The girls are striking, primarily, for the union shop.

A mass meeting to recruit for the parade was held in Lipkin's Theatre, Bowery and Rivington Street, at 1 o'clock. The theatre could not hold all who wanted to attend. The suffragettes, who have outdistanced even the Socialists in their activity for the strikers, were in the van of the movement.

The banners in the hands of the paraders told their sentiments concisely. "Peaceful picketing is the right of every woman," said some of the banners. Others ran thus: "Fifty-two hours a week," "One hundred and fifty employers agree to union demands," "The police are for our protection, not for our abuse," "Union contracts have been signed for 13,000 workers."

POLICE HEAD THE LINE.

Headed by a squad of mounted police, in true parade style, and guarded on the side lines and in the rear by walking policemen, the paraders started for the Mayor's office. They marched down the Bowery and Park Row, where the committee that was to present their grievances to the Mayor left them, and then back up the Bowery to the theatre, where the marchers were disbanded. There was no disorder.

• • •

A committee of five took the protest to the Mayor's office. They waited patiently for him to return from lunch. Three of the committee were striking waist makers, the other two were Miss Helen Marot and Miss Mary E. Dreier, both of the Woman's Trades Union League. The three shirtwaist workers had been arrested in the strike. Mayor McClellan questioned the committee and took charge of the protest, saying he would look into the matter. Here it is:

We, the members of the Ladies' Waistmakers' Union, a body of 30,000 workers, appeal to you to put an immediate stop to the insults, intimidations, and to the abuses to which the police have subjected us while we have been peacefully picketing, which is our lawful right.

We protest to you against the flagrant discrimination of the Police Department in favor of the employers, who are using every method to incite to violence.

We appeal to you directly in this instance instead of to your Police Commissioner. We do this

because our requests during the past six months have had no effect in decreasing the outages perpetrated upon our members, nor have our requests been granted a fair hearing. Yours respectfully,

S. SHINDLER, Secretary.

After two weeks of the strike both the employes and the employers report that they are certain to win, and both sides can give many reasons why they are sure of their contention.

MANUFACTURERS TAKE BACK STRIKERS.

It was said last night at Clinton Hall, 151 Clinton Street, the headquarters of the strikers, that over 160 manufacturers have signed the union agreement, and have taken back to work on better terms some 15,000 waistmakers. That leaves about 17,000 strikers still out, it was said.

The managers and advisers of the union say they are inducing about 1,000 shirtwaist makers in non-union shops to go on strike every day now for the union agreement, and in the meanwhile they are sending back to work on the union terms almost that many every day.

On the other hand, the officials of the Associated Waist and Dress Manufacturers, the organization of employers, with headquarters at the Hoffman House, said last night they are going to hold out for the open shop; that many of the girls who struck in the beginning are going back to work; that the employers who are signing the union agreement are small manufacturers of little financial standing, who are not members of the Associated Waist and Dress Manufacturers, and that the real members of that organization of 500 men are simply holding their ground, advertising for help in their open shops, and getting it so fast that they are encouraged to let the strike run its course.

On account of its spectacular and picturesque features, this strike has attracted considerable attention, but very few know exactly what the girls are fighting for. The five floors of Clinton Hall, which swarms with the strikers day and night, all as gay and animated as if they were attending a dance or a wedding, can furnish very few girls who can tell clearly why they have left their places.

Suddenly thousands of them have come almost to worship "the union." They are not clear about what the union is, what it can do for them, and what they want it to do. They feel that they are not getting a fair deal in the work they are doing. They have noted that girls in other trades who did belong to unions seemed to be getting on better than they.

(continued)

Why the Union Idea Appeals.

The idea of union rules which provide that all workers doing the same sort of work shall get about equal pay, the idea of enforced equality in earning power, the idea of sacrificing themselves, if necessary, for the sake of a principle they believe for the good of the weaker worker as well as for the more clever worker—that appeals to them powerfully. For they are women. The idea, too, of this vague and powerful protector, "the union," as they think of it, draws them into it.

Besides, they have been on strike too short a time, and the settlements with employers have been too rapid to make them feel the touch of distress. For them the strike is a sort of gay holiday, all mixed in with a vague and pleasant new worship, with lots of speeches, lots of dancing, much running to and fro, some danger, and a very great deal of excitement.

* * *

The strike swept through the east side, through the lower west side, and up along the avenues, where the workshops are thick. The girls gained many helpers, including the Central Federated Union, the Woman's Trade Union League, and one section of the suffragettes. The strikers posted pickets outside the shops that hadn't struck. According to Mrs. Walter Weyl of the Woman's Trade Union League, who went to the aid of the strikers in the beginning . . . , all pickets were furnished with printed instructions telling them what they could do under the law, and warning them against overstepping the law.

"The laws of this State provide that pickets may walk up and down in front of a factory," said Mrs. Weyl yesterday, "and try to persuade workers from going into a non-union shop. They may argue about the good points of the union. But they cannot lay hands on a worker to prevent her going to work.

"And it is here that we have to complain about the police. We know absolutely that there are bureaus which furnish rough men for use by employ-ers in breaking up a union. These men interfere with pickets, make a disturbance, and then the police, who are, of course, on guard where there is a strike, arrest the strikers, but somehow permit the roughs and toughs to go away."

* * *

Deny Employing Toughs.

The Associated Waist and Dress Manufacturers, when Mrs. Weyl's statement was quoted to them yesterday, denied the use of bureaus of toughs, charging, on the contrary, that the pickets have attacked and intimidated their employes who wanted to work in spite of the strike.

M. E. Hyman of the firm of I. B. Hyman & Co., 126 Sixth Avenue, President of the Associated Waist and Dress Manufacturers, showed several letters yesterday, which said that the writers wanted to go to work, but that they had concluded to stay away because of the annoyance and danger of going to and from their work.

"I shouldn't blame the employers if they did use toughs," said Mr. Hyman yesterday. "These strikers do such things! Why, one of our girls was held up to-day by either a striker or a sympathizer, who cursed her and told her they'd break her back if she tried to go to work. She came in here crying."

* * *

I. B. Hyman, President of the Associated Waist and Dress Manuacturers, said of the proposed agreement of the strikers:

* * *

"It is this union thing that is in the way of settlement."

But it is that union thing which the strikers most love just now. There are dozens of meetings a day to keep blazing the union spirit. Mrs. O. H. P. Belmont, President of the Political Equality Association, and a lot of labor speakers will speak at an open-air meeting this afternoon in Rutgers Square, and to-morrow afternoon is the date for Mrs. Belmont's meeting in the Hippodrome.

The Hippodrome Meeting
New York Times, December 6, 1909

Two days after the march on City Hall (December 5, 1909) strikers and their new allies held a rally at the Hippodrome, one of the largest halls in New York. By now the strike was front-page news. Much of this was due to the involvement of Mrs. O. H. P. (Oliver Hazard Perry) Belmont and other socially prominent women. Mrs. Belmont, president of the Political Equality Association, was reputed to be the second-wealthiest woman in the country with a fortune estimated at $60 million. The *Times* quoted several of the speeches at length. Its report characterized the radical rhetoric of the speakers as an amalgam of "socialism, unionism, woman suffrage and what seemed to be something like anarchism." This last "ism" may have referred to the speech of Rose Pastor Stokes, a socialist activist and former garment worker, who spoke of the necessity of smashing the "rock" of capitalism. Implicit in the paper's coverage was a question: For how long could a coalition of women that included both Mrs. Belmont and Mrs. Stokes hold?

THRONG CHEERS ON THE GIRL STRIKERS

⌒⌒⌒⌒

8,000 Gather in the Hippodrome on Mrs. Belmont's Call to Bid Them Triumph.

⌒⌒⌒⌒

Suffrage Pleas Put In

⌒⌒⌒⌒

The Rev. Dr. Anna Shaw Declares Women Must Finally Fight for Their Rights.

⌒⌒⌒⌒

Socialism, unionism, women suffrage and what seemed to be something like anarchism were poured into the ears of fully 8,000 persons who gathered yesterday afternoon in the Hippodrome to attend the mass meeting held there by Mrs. O. H. P. Belmont, President of the Political Equality Association, in the interest of the striking shirtwaist makers of the city. But all the speakers told the girls—for 85 per cent of the audience was girls—that the strike they were engaged in was a worthy fight which they ought to win.

"Throng Cheers on the Girl Strikers," *New York Times,* December 6, 1909. Reprinted by permission.

(continued)

The chairman was the Rev. John Howard Melish, Rector of the Church of the Holy Trinity, Brooklyn.

The Hippodrome could not hold all who wanted to attend the meeting. The doors were opened at 1:30 o'clock. By 2 the Hippodrome was filled, and the police outside, of whom there were enough to suppress a riot, firmly turned back hundreds long before they approached the outside doors of the building.

• • •

The stage settings were for a woman suffrage meeting. Flags of blue on both side walls carried the words in white, "Votes for Women." Three small drops hung down from the curtain machinery, all carrying arguments in big letters which the girls in the rearmost seats could read. "We demand equal pay for equal work," the audience read; and "Give women the protection of the vote."

• • •

The Rev. Dr. Anna Shaw spoke long and passionately and these are some of the things she said:

"Our cause is your cause, and your cause is our cause. (Our cause referring to woman suffrage.)

"Personally I believe in trade unions. You can't strike a blow with one finger or two fingers, but when you want to strike you put all your fingers together, clench them hard, and then let drive. That's what the workers must do with themselves if they would be effective.

• • •

"A preacher wrote to me saying that I ought not to speak at a meeting of this kind on Sunday. He said I should not be preaching unrest on this day. My gospel is that they who resist tyranny serve God."

Dr. Shaw said there ought to be women policemen, women officials of all kinds, so that everywhere and under all conditions in this country women could be dealt with by women.

"The interests of men are not safe in the hands of women," she said, "and the interests of women are not safe in the hands of men."

• • •

Mrs. Rose Pastor Stokes defended socialism. The interests of the employer and the employe were opposed, she said, and they could not work fairly together any length of time. She painted the picture of a huge rock in the path of all the workers. They couldn't climb over it, nor get around it. The workers were now right at this rock. They had already been smashing at it with the hammer of organization, and she could see it breaking here and there. Presently, she was sure, it would go to pieces under the blows, and then the way would be clear to the co-operative commonwealth. The rock was capitalism.

She had no grudge against capitalists individually and personally. She did not hate individual mosquitoes and flies. But she refused to let them live a parasitic life on her, and so she was doing all she could to destroy the breed of parasitic capitalists.

Publio Mastello spoke in Italian, and Leonora O'Reilly delivered a labor union speech.

Colony Club Meeting
New York Times, December 16, 1909

A useful measure of the way in which sympathy for the strikers had become fashionable was the coverage given the decision of Anne Morgan, daughter of banker J. P. Morgan, to support their cause. She sponsored a meeting on December 15 at the Colony Club, perhaps the most exclusive private club in the city, at which the shirtwaist workers appealed for financial support. Among the speakers was Clara Lemlich, already celebrated for her "Philippic" at the Cooper Union meeting that led to the "Uprising." Lemlich used the Colony Club meeting to reply to a charge that she had misrepresented her own wages and those of her co-workers. The manufacturers had seized upon a story in the *New York Evening Journal* that claimed to quote Clara Lemlich as saying that she earned only $6 a week. In fact, they pointed out, she averaged $15 a week, making her one of the highest-paid shirtwaist workers in the city. Colony Club members questioned several strikers. They clearly found it unimaginable that these "girls" were supporting families on $6–$10 a week.

Meanwhile the endemic violence of the strike continued. The *Times* reported on December 16, 1910, that "it seems some of the more violent strikers have adopted aged but strong eggs as weapons against hostile men. Jacob Rosenberg, manager of a factory in Twentieth Street, was trailed to his home . . . last night by two girls and a man, who bombarded him with eggs until they were arrested . . . ." The same story recounted that when a fire broke out "in the shirtwaist factory of Max Roth on the top floor of the building at 48 and 50 Walker Street," his "non-union employes preferred risking death on the roof to running downstairs and being jeered at by the strikers who, they knew, would be on the sidewalk below." Fortunately, the fire guttered out with little damage and no loss of life.

GIRL STRIKERS TELL THE RICH THEIR WOES

$1,300 Collected at a Colony Club Meeting to Aid the Shirtwaist Workers.

"Also, it is true that I made $15 a week," said little Clara Lemlich yesterday afternoon to 150 well-to-do women gathered in the Colony Club, Madison Avenue and Thirtieth Street, at the invitation of Miss Anne Morgan, Miss Elizabeth Marbury, and Mrs. Egerton L. Winthrop, Jr., to hear representatives of the striking shirtwaist makers tell their side of the fight, now in its fourth week.

"I did not strike because I myself was not getting enough," the east side girl went on to tell her Fifth Avenue audience. "I struck because all the others should get enough. It was not for me; it was for the others."

More of the strikers spoke, as well as several women and men sympathizers, and then Mrs. Philip M. Lydig and Elsie De Wolf passed around two hats, which brought back over $1,800. It was announced, also, that the Shuberts would give 50 per cent of the receipts of one of their New York theatres all next week to the strikers, that percentage being the share of the Shuberts in the receipts.

• • •

Miss Clara Lemlich was then called to explain her part in the strike and the circumstance of her weekly wage, which has been so much discussed by the employers. She stepped quickly on to the platform. She is a small, dark, quick-eyed girl, absolutely unafraid even in the gymnasium of the Colony Club, in the presence of such an audience.

(continued)

"Girl Strikers Tell the Rich Their Woes," *New York Times*, December 16, 1909. Reprinted by permission.

"My dear ladies," she began without a smile, "I will tell you about myself. They say I caused the strike by making a motion at a meeting in Cooper Union that it should be. I did make a motion, but it is not true that I said I was making only $3 or $6 in a bad shop to work in. I said other girls were working that way.

• • •

"They say I made $15 a week in a good shop. It is true that I made it. I did not strike, dear ladies, because I myself was not getting enough. I struck because the others should get enough. It was not for me; it was for them."

WORKERS AND WAGES.

Other girls told about the places they worked in and about the pay they received. Their names were withheld, Miss Dreier said, for obvious reasons. One girl said she had made $10 a week.

"Why did you make $10 and most of the others only $6?" asked one woman in the balcony.

"Ah! I made the sample dresses," she answered.

• • •

An Italian girl said she earned $6 a week as a finisher. "Yes, I get 4 cents a dozen for waists," she declared, and the audience gasped. A priest came to our shop and told us girls that if we struck we should go—excuse me, please, ladies—to hell."

Miss Rose Schneiderman, an organizer of the Woman's Trade Union League, who is a veteran in strikes, said she had investigated many of the shops. She was sure that if some of her listeners could see where at least some of the wedding dresses are made they wouldn't want to wear them.

"In many of the places the girls are known by numbers," she went on. "Two girls will work side by side for weeks without knowing each other's names. Italians will be placed by the side of Jews, and race antagonism worked on to keep the girls at daggers' points so that there will be created a distinct feeling against any sort of organization and fellow-feeling. A good many girls in this fight have come to know each other's names and to know a sisterly feeling for the first time in their lives."

Finally Mrs. Archibald Alexander rose and asked Miss Dreier what was most needed.

"Money to fight with," answered Miss Dreier.

"I hope I may have the honor of beginning the collection," said Mrs. Alexander. And then Mrs. Lydig and Miss De Wolf made their rounds.

The east side girls went to tea with some of the members of the club.

Violet Pike Arrest

Women's Trade Union League volunteers continued their publicity campaign on behalf of the strikers because they believed that "sympathy" of the sort that Paul Kellogg described was the key to winning. Violet Pike, identified in this story simply as a school teacher and suffragist, was a WTUL member who had been active on the picket lines from the earliest days of the strike. The *Times* implied she deliberately sought to be arrested by refusing to seek a permit to speak and then by refusing to move along when ordered to do so by a police officer. Whether this was the case or not, much of the "sympathy" the strike generated arose from the arrests of affluent and professional women like Pike and Mary Dreier. The arrests helped persuade other middle- and upper-class women that, in the words of Dr. Anna Shaw at the Hippodrome rally, "our cause is your cause, and your cause is our cause." The arrests also helped persuade strikers, who doubted that "rich women" could sincerely take an interest in their plight, that the WTUL women were willing to make the same sacrifices as they were.

ARREST SUFFRAGIST TALKER

Miss Pike, School Teacher, Wanted No Permit for Street Speaking—Failed Employer Denounces the Union.

New York Times, December 19, 1909

• • •

Miss Violet L. Pike, who said she was a teacher in a private school and a suffragist also, was arrested in front of 48 West Thirty-fifth Street about 5:30 last evening, where she was making an appeal for aid for the girl strikers to a crowd of about 200 men and women. Miss Pike was arrested by Policeman Ahrens of the West Thirtieth Street Station for causing a crowd to collect and speaking in the street without a permit.

"Arrest Suffragist Talker," *New York Times*, December 19, 1909. Reprinted by permission.

MORE PLACARDS.

Miss Pike was sandwiched between two big cardboard signs, on which were legends declaring that 30,000 girl shirtwaist operators on strike needed help badly. She removed these on the way to the station house, and refused to show them to reporters.

Miss Pike protested against her arrest, telling the policeman that she was a citizen and had a right to speak where she pleased.

"All right," said Ahrens, "you can speak if you have a permit. If you haven't you will have to get one, move on, or be arrested."

"I haven't a permit," the policeman says Miss Pike replied, "I don't intend to get one, and I don't intend to stop speaking. Go ahead and arrest me if you dare."

She made no resistance when the policeman told her she would have to go with him. About a hundred of her audience followed her to the station house, some jeering her and some with cries of "Shame!" for the policeman.

At the station house Miss Pike said she was 24 years of age and lived at 43 East Twenty-second Street. She did not seem to be at all dismayed by her arrest. The signs that had decorated her when she was speaking she held together tightly with the reading matter inside to hide it from view. She took the placards to her cell with her.

POLICE BREAK UP STRIKERS' MEETING

Raid Union Members to Arrest Eight Accused of Attacking Shirtwaist Workers.

"Police Break Up Strikers' Meeting," *New York Times*, December 22, 1909. Reprinted by permission.

Pickets Parade in Autos

Miss Morgan and Mrs. Belmont Lend Their Machines— Miss Mulholland Drives Her Own.

New York Times, December 22, 1909

Reception for Strikers Released from Workhouse
New York Times, December 23, 1909

Sorority remained a key theme of the strike as members of the Women's Trade Union League, Local 25 of the International Ladies Garment Workers Union, and socialites like Inez Mulholland, whose ability to drive her own auto in the Fifth Avenue parade had occasioned much comment in the press, jointly hosted a dance for the strikers just released from the workhouse where they had served five-day sentences for allegedly assaulting nonstrikers. Magistrates had turned to jail sentences because affluent supporters, such as Mrs. O. H. P. Belmont, raised so much money to pay fines and bail charges that the strikers could simply ignore them. Mrs. Belmont's role became notorious, as Minnie Cohen's purported remark at the end of this excerpt from the *New York Times* of December 23 makes plain. This notoriety derived largely from an incident of December 19, as reported in the *Times* and other papers the following day. Mrs. Belmont often attended night court in order to post bail for arrested strikers. Magistrate Butts "remarked that he would require $800 surety" for the four "girls" under arrest. Mrs. Belmont offered to put up her town house:

> Not recognizing the volunteer bailer, Magistrate Butts asked her if she was sure the house was worth $800.
>
> "I think it is," replied Mrs. Belmont. "It is valued at $400,000. There may be a mortgage on it for $100,000."
>
> The girls were then freed on this bail.

Meanwhile the arrests continued.

PICKETS FROM PRISON ARE GUESTS OF HONOR

❦

Floral Tributes at Reception and Dance for Shirtwaist Girls Released from Workhouse.

❦

Strikers Accused in Court

❦

Girl shirtwaist strikers who have been arrested and sent to the workhouse for doing picket duty were the guests of honor last night at a reception and dance held in Arlington Hall, 12 St. Mark's Place. Their hostesses were other girl strikers who have avoided arrest, assisted by many women from the Women's Trade Union League and other organizations of women.

• • •

The girls from the Workhouse were Jessie Alter, Mary Abelson, Ida Brodin, Lena Lapido, Annie Rosen, Sarah Morgen, and Edith Perr, the latter being only 16 years of age. Each was presented with a big bouquet of American Beauty roses. These came from the strikers who had obtained their demands. In presenting the floral tributes Miss Leonora O'Reilly said:

"Usually a term in prison is looked on as a sign of degradation. There are cases in history where it has been a mark of honor. These girls did no wrong, they violated no law. They were on duty

---

"Pickets from Prison Are Guests of Honor," *New York Times*, December 23, 1909. Reprinted by permission.

for a cause, and bore their unjust imprisonment with fortitude. In their case imprisonment was an honor and not a degradation."

• • •

MANY STRIKERS UNDER ARREST.

While preparations for the reception and dance were under way in the afternoon many luckless strikers were being arraigned in the several police courts of the city.

In the Essex Market Court Morris Wohl, accused of assaulting Morris Polowitz in a riot at a strikers' meeting in Second Street last night, was admitted to $1,000 bail to await trial. Mrs. Lena Breit of 63 East Ninety-Ninth Street, who says she supports herself and two children, charged with assaulting Mary Abramowitz of 153 Ludlow Street, was held in $500 bail.

Two strikers, who were fined $3 each, were charged by Policeman Scott of the Union Market Station with interfering with him when he made seven arrests last night at the strikers' meeting in Second Street. Mrs. Fannie Harawitz, counsel for the strikers, said that the police raided the meeting for the purpose of breaking it up. She said two men started a fight and then called in the police. Harry Schorr, one of the prisoners, had his head bandaged. He had been struck with a club. Policeman Scott's seven prisoners were fined.

• • •

BAIL EASY TO GET, SAYS MAGISTRATE.

Morris Gerstein of 78 Avenue B had a lump on his head. He said Minie Cohen of 66 Stanton Street struck him with a blunt weapon. Morris told the court that the young girl told him she was not afraid of him, adding:

"Mrs. Belmont has enough money."

A lawyer representing the girls said that they would not be able to get bail.

"Tut! Tut!" exclaimed Magistrate Cornell. "Why the women of this town are all frantic to go bail."

Strikers Reject Arbitration Agreement
New York Times, December 28, 1909

From the first, as the *Times* story of December 4 (reprinted here) made clear, the strike had been about union recognition. When the executive committee of Local 25 called the Cooper Union meeting, the goal was to use an industry-wide strike to recruit enough members to force the employers to accept the union as their official bargaining agent. Wage increases, shorter hours, elimination of the subcontracting system (i.e., the system of farming out portions of orders to other shops) all were important demands, but recognition came first. It is worth recalling that the only members voting were those who were still out on strike. As individual employers had settled with the union, their workers had voted on those agreements. Arbitration would have applied only to the employees of the firms belonging to the Associated Waist and Dress Manufacturers. These were the largest employers, and it was their workers who rejected this settlement. It would have granted them a shorter workweek (fifty-two hours with mandatory overtime limited to two hours in any one day) and four paid holidays a year. It would also have required employers to provide such necessary supplies as needles, thread, and "all other appliances." The agreement further stipulated that employers would not discriminate against strikers and would, "so far as is practicable" reinstate them in their jobs. The sticking point was article eight. It read:

> The Associated Waist and Dress Manufacturers will welcome communications at any time, from any source, as to alleged violations by any of its members of any of the foregoing provisions, and will take necessary steps to correct such grievances as upon investigation are found to exist, and will welcome conferences as to any differences which may hereafter arise and which may not be settled between the individual shop and its employes.

To this the union offered the following substitute:

> The Associated Waist and Dress Manufacturers will confer with employes and the representatives of the Lady Waistmakers' Union as to any differences which may arise hereafter, and which may not be settled between the individual shop and its employes.

When the manufacturers' association rejected this, the union officials recommended that their members reject the entire agreement. It was a controversial decision and cost the union much public support.

SHIRTWAIST STRIKE PEACE PLAN FAILS

Negotiations for a Settlement End, the Strikers Refusing to Accept the Terms.

Employers Stand Firm

Say They Will Never Agree to a Definite Recognition of the Union.

Crowded meetings of striking shirtwaist makers in several halls in different parts of the city voted down yesterday the agreement entered into last Wednesday and Thursday by representatives of the strikers and of the Associated Waist and Dress Makers, and so put an end to all hope of an immediate settlement of the strike.

The rock upon which the peace plan was shattered and which caused the strikers to repudiate their own representatives was the eighth and last article in the tentative agreement drawn up by the conference. It referred to the settlement of future differences, and the strikers felt that while inferentially recognizing the existence of a union, the clause was not sufficiently explicit in this avowal. For this reason the members of the Executive Committee of the strikers declined to recommend its acceptance, and the articles were rejected as a whole.

• • •

President I. D. Hyman of the manufacturers said that the action of the strikers was a surprise to the members of his organization, who had felt certain that the strike would be settled by to-day.

"Will the manufacturers consider a proposal involving a more explicit recognition of the union?" Mr. Hyman was asked.

"Not under any circumstances," he replied. "We insist upon an open shop, the right to employ union and non-union employes without discrimination, and from that stand we will not budge."

"Shirtwaist Strike Peace Plan Fails," *New York Times,* December 28, 1909. Reprinted by permission.

Carnegie Hall Meeting
New York Times, January 3, 1910

The Carnegie Hall meeting of January 2, 1910, was the last great public gathering of the various groups who supported the strikers' cause. Leonora O'Reilly, a former garment worker and Women's Trade Union League activist, hailed the display of sisterhood across class, ethnic, and religious lines. The strike, she said, had done more to make women recognize their common interests than all the preaching in all the churches. Yet the spirit of sorority was not to last. Within days Anne Morgan would criticize the socialists as having contributed nothing beyond "rhetoric"; socialists like Theresa Malkiel, another former garment worker, who covered the strike for the *New York Call*, would reply in kind about rich women pretending to sympathize with the plight of the working girl while really trying to advance their own suffragist agenda, and the dream of sorority across class and ethnic lines would begin to vanish. But it was still very much alive in early January.

THE RICH OUT TO AID GIRL WAISTMAKERS

Carnegie Hall Packed at Protest Meeting Against the Arrest of Their Pickets.

Magistrates Denounced

Fifth Avenue and the lower east side, both represented chiefly by women and girls, joined last night in filling Carnegie Hall to protest against what was called the "continued encroachment of the police and the Police Magistrates" upon the rights of the striking shirtwaist makers and their sympathizers.

• • •

In addition to the emphatic protest against the police and Magistrates which the meeting served to register, it gave heart to the strikers to continue their fight for the principles for which they began to fight some weeks before Christmas.

"The Rich Go Out to Aid Girl Waistmakers," *New York Times*, January 3, 1910. Reprinted by permission.

There are still 6,000 of the 30,000 shirtwaist makers out of work, and the organization of employers has not, as a body, agreed to recognize the union, though 251 individual employers have come to terms with the strikers.

It was an uprising of women last night. Leonora O'Reilly, one of the speakers, boasted that this strike of six weeks had done more to make people of all classes in this city recognize their common bond of kinship than the preaching of all the churches and all the ethical schools had done in years.

• • •

The stage platform was crowded to its utmost limit by some 350 girls wearing wide strips of paper, upon which were printed in huge black letters, "Arrested." Down among the audience were other girls so labeled. In the very front rank of the stage were twenty girls whose placards read, "Workhouse," indicating that these were they who had actually served time for "the cause."

Everywhere to be seen were the active college girls, who have thrown themselves into this fight. Elizabeth Dutcher, Mary Dreier, Ida Rauh and Miss Elsie Cole are graduates and students who have been in the thickest of the warfare for six weeks.

• • •

Rose Perr, 16 years old, told how she had been sent to the workhouse for five days, because, as she said, she had asked non-union workers not to take the bread out of their sisters' mouths, and had then protested to a Police Captain against a policeman hitting a fellow-striker on the breast.

Postscript to News Accounts

February 15, 1910, marked the official end of the strike. The *Times* did not even bother to report the International Ladies Garment Workers Union proclamation that all of its members would be returning to work. Nor did it attempt to cast a final balance of which side gained, or lost, what. In fact, the great majority of the members of the manufacturers' association ultimately accepted the union's demand for recognition. A handful of the very largest manufacturers, led by the Triangle Shirtwaist Company, however, did not. Triangle's owners kept their factory open using "non-union girls," a fact that the union belatedly accepted in mid-February. Its treasury was empty. The remaining strikers were desperate. So, although the strike produced union agreements with most of the employers, and higher wages and better working conditions for most of the workers, it failed against those employers large enough to hold out.

There was a certain symmetry to the newspapers' lack of interest in the final days of the struggle. Most of the city's newspapers ignored the strike's beginnings when workers at Leiserson's and Triangle first walked out. It had taken the participation first of Mary Dreier and then Mrs. O. H. P. Belmont and Anne Morgan for the strike to become "news." The press continued to focus upon these "society ladies." The strikers' own stories reached the general public, with the exception of the special edition of the *Evening Journal* devoted to the strike, mainly through the almost daily accounts of their appearances in the magistrates courts and through accounts in magazines written by sympathetic journalists, most of whom were women.

MRS. BELMONT HOLDS STOCK IN UNION SHOP

Subscribes to Preferred Shares of Co-operative Factory to Aid Striking Waistmakers.

Common Stock $1 a Share

Will Be Sold Only to Those Holding a Card in the Waistmakers' Union— Many Strikers Arrested.

New York Times, January 15, 1910

"Mrs. Belmont Holds Stock in Union Shop," *New York Times,* January 15, 1910. Reprinted by permission.

STRIKE PARTICIPANTS' ACCOUNTS

"The Spirit of the Girl Strikers"

A large majority of the scores of magazine articles dealing with the strike sympathized with the shirtwaist makers' cause. Miriam Finn Scott's "The Spirit of the Girl Strikers" is unusual in its attempt to report the strike in the "girls'" own words. How should one read this "first-hand" account? *The Outlook* was a generally "progressive" magazine and favored the strikers' cause, but it editorialized that arbitration rather than strikes was the best means of settling disputes.[1] One of the stories that Finn Scott recorded, that of Rose Perr, is told at much greater length, but with the use of a pseudonym, in the next selection. Perr was one of the most celebrated of the strikers; she spoke of her ordeal in prison before the packed Carnegie Hall meeting on

[1] See, for example, the editorial, "The Garment Workers' Strike," *The Outlook* 103 (January 11, 1913): 55: ". . . The only real hope of settling industrial disputes is in compromise, conciliation, and arbitration, not in fighting to the bitter end."

January 2, for example. And she accompanied Rose Schneiderman for a portion of her speaking tour to raise money for the strike (see Schneiderman's account, reprinted here). Finn Scott did not mention Perr's experience on the platform in her article. Instead she described her as "a little fifteen-year-old girl" with a look of "wonderment and pain in her face" as she pondered why she had been arrested. Perr was, in fact, only fifteen when the events in question occurred. But her account was not the disingenuous outpouring that Finn Scott and then others would make it out to be. She had told her story before numerous audiences, knew from experience what portions of it had the greatest impact upon middle- and upper-class audiences, knew, too, what details those audiences wished to hear. This does not mean that her story is less than accurate. But it does mean that the journalists supporting the strike who insisted upon the naiveté and youth of the strikers misled their readers and not a few historians. The strikers were young; they were inexperienced. They were also exceedingly tough-minded and resourceful, as their employers came to know only too well.

THE SPIRIT OF THE GIRL STRIKERS

BY MIRIAM FINN SCOTT

The "Grand American Palace" was packed with a strangely unaccustomed crowd. Every night "Professor" Somebody's orchestra (the "professor" and two pasty-faced helpers) dispensed music from the little platform in the corner, and some scores of work-worn immigrant boys and girls, at so much per head, struggled and giggled through the waltz and the two-step. But now, instead of these weary revelers, from gaudy wall to gaudy wall were jammed girls with determined, workaday faces. Strikers they were—a group of shirtwaist makers, whose strike in New York has been the biggest and most bitter strike of women in the history of American labor troubles.

And the faces of this group were fixed on the "Professor's" stage, and on that stage stood a slight, pale girl of perhaps nineteen, her dark eyes flashing. "Girls, from the bottom of my heart," she cried, "I beg you not to go back to work. We are all poor, many of us are suffering hunger, none of us can afford to lose a day's wages. But only by fighting for our rights, and fighting all together, can we better our miseries; and so let us fight for them to the end!"

The strikers applauded long, and in scores of other East Side dance-halls at the time when the strike was at its height and forty thousand girls were out, just so at this same hour were other speakers applauded by other groups; and by meetings such as this was the spirit kept in the girls for their remarkable fight. When the girl left the platform, I edged my way to her and asked her for her story. She had come from Russia, she told me—come with her parents, who had found life in the land of the Czar no longer endurable.

Miriam Finn Scott, "The Spirit of the Girl Strikers," *The Outlook* 94 (February 19, 1910), 392–97.

(continued)

"Close your eyes and point to any girl in this hall," said the little shirt-waist maker, "and my story will be her story. We are all the same. Why do we strike? I will tell you where we work, how we work; from that perhaps you will understand. My shop is a long and narrow loft on the fifth floor of the building, with the ceiling almost on our heads. In it one hundred electric-power machines are so closely packed together that, unless I am always on the lookout, my clothes or hair or hand is likely to catch in one of the whizzing machines. In the shop it is always night. The windows are only on the narrow ends of the room, so even the few girls who sit near them sew by gaslight most of the time, for the panes are so dirty the weak daylight hardly goes through them. The shop is swept only once a week; the air is so close that sometimes you can hardly breathe. In this place I work from eight to six o'clock six days a week in the ordinary season; and in the busy season, when we are compelled to work nights and Sundays, I put in what equals eight work-days in the week. Thirty minutes is allowed for lunch, which I must eat in the dressing-room four flights above the shop, on the ninth floor. These stairs I must always climb; the elevator, the boss says, is not for the shopgirls.

"I began as a shirt-waist maker in this shop five years ago. For the first three weeks I got nothing, though I had already worked on a machine in Russia. Then the boss paid me three dollars a week. Now, after five years' experience, and I am considered a good worker, I am paid nine. But I never get the nine dollars. There are always 'charges' against me. If I laugh, or cry, or speak to a girl during work hours, I am fined ten cents for each 'crime.' Five cents is taken from my pay every week to pay for benzine which is used to clean waists that have been soiled in the making; and even if I have not soiled a waist in a year, I must pay the five cents just the same. If I lose a little piece of lining, that possibly is worth two cents, I am charged ten cents for the goods and five cents for losing it. If I am one minute late, I am fined one cent, though I get only fifteen cents an hour; and if I am five minutes late, I lose half a day's pay. Each of these things seems small, I know, but when you only earn ninety dimes a week, and are fined for this and fined for that, why, a lot of them are missing when pay day comes, and you know what it means when your money is the only regular money that comes in a family of eight."

• • •

The "fining" system just referred to is not the only method by which, the girls claim, their meager wages are subtracted from. "There ain't

nothing too low for my boss to do to make a few cents' extra profit," said another girl. "He ain't ashamed to do plain stealing from us girls. In our shop we have no books to mark down our work—just little slips of paper, checks, are given us when we turn in a bundle of work. For these slips we are given money at the end of the week. The boss has these slips made small purposely, so they'll be easier to lose. One week I lost two of these tiny pieces of paper, and I could not get one cent for the work I had done. It was half my week's wages. Every day some of us lose these tickets. But our loss is the boss's gain, so he won't change the system."

There is one very simple explanation for the wretched conditions under which the girls have worked—they have been very easy to exploit. Ninety per cent of the workers are Russian and Italian girls between eighteen and twenty-five. These girls enter the shop almost immediately after landing in America. They come from great poverty and oppression, where they were compelled to accept conditions without complaint. And so, accustomed to fear and obey, these girls have for years suffered their grievances here, and kept silent.

• • •

Everywhere was ferment. The girls were ripe for the strike, as was shown by the quickness and unanimity with which the girls responded to the call for the strike. But, even so, among the girls were leaders each of whom roused and led her own group of less militant comrades. Among these was Eva Goldstein, and this is her story of how she "called down" her shop:

"I knew our girls were dissatisfied, I knew other shops were already on strike, I knew it only needed some one to talk to the girls a little and they would join the strikers. So I began to talk to the girls whenever I got the chance. I went to their houses in the evening; I met them early in the morning. At first some girls would not listen to me; they were afraid to lose their 'grand job.' But at last we all agreed. Tuesday morning we came to work as usual, but after we were thirty minutes at our machines I got up and called to them:

"'Girls, other waist-makers are on strike! Will you join them?'

"Every girl got up from her machine. As we were all starting for the door the boss rushed in and began to shout, 'Sit down; sit down, girls.' But not one of us took her seat. The boss came over to me; he was very mad. 'I know you are the trouble-maker,' he said. 'Tell the girls to sit down; tell me what you want. Here is an agreement,' and he drew out a sheet of paper and a pencil from his pocket.

(continued)

'I will sign this agreement. I'll give you a raise. If you sign that, too, you and the girls won't have to strike in this shop.'

"I just smiled at him, for I knew it wasn't a real agreement, but just a trick, a fake, and I said, 'Mr. ——, if you are willing to settle, you must go to the union headquarters to sign the agreement. I have no right to sign.' Then I just said, 'Girls, are you coming?' and we all walked out and left him there alone."

• • •

Annie is the swiftest sample-trimmer of the Blank Waist Company. She works at a fixed salary of $15 a week. In three years Annie missed only one day's work, and there were three good reasons for such faithfulness to her job—a blind mother and two little sisters. After the first week on strike Annie went back to the shop to get wages still due her. The boss, knowing her circumstances, tempted her to return to work by offering her a raise of $5 a week, but to that Annie promptly replied: "Mr. Baum, you cannot buy my conscience for money!"

It is ten long, bitter weeks since Annie went out; she has been picketing, speaking, organizing every day since. During all these weeks she never had more than two meals a day, often only one; lately, days pass practically without her tasting food. But the blind mother and the two little ones still have their food and roof, and do not know of Annie's sacrifices.

But to appreciate what sufferings these girls are undergoing for the sake of better conditions in the future, one must know a little of how they live in times when there is no strike. Some of the girls earn but $3 or $4 a week: a few exceptionally clever girls, working in exceptionally well run shops, earn as high as $20 and $25. The story circulated by the bosses that some of the girls get $35 and $40 a week is false, and the evidence by which they seek to substantiate the story amounts to a mere trick of bookkeeping. The average wages for the forty thousand workers is $9, and this is not for fifty-two weeks in the year, but only for the busy season, a period of about three months.

• • •

Almost every shirt-waist maker who has taken an active part in the strike—and few indeed there are who have not—has some terrible experience to tell of her contact with the representatives of the law. Fannie Goldmark has deep-set, sorrowful eyes, yet she was calm and often smiled as she told me her story. She was born at Kishineff, and lost every member of her immediate family in the great massacre. She had heard of America as the land of liberty and justice, and in

fear and hope she fled from Kishineff. Arrived in New York, she at once entered a shop and learned shirt-waist making. In Russia she had been a student, and had gone about among the Russian workmen trying to spread the lesson of organization. So, when the strike broke out, she was among the first to enlist. She was very successful as a speaker, as an organizer, and particularly as a picket. While picketing she was arrested three times. The first two charges against her were for "disturbing the peace," when in fact she was quietly, and legally, walking up and down in front of her shop. Each of these two times she was fined five dollars. The third time she was arrested she was dragged to the station-house like a disorderly woman, on the charge of assaulting a six-foot policeman. As a matter of fact, the policeman tripped her, and she fell off the sidewalk near the place where the policeman stood. She was thrown into a cell and for ten hours she was absolutely refused permission to communicate with the union about her arrest unless she paid fifty cents for the telephone message, which amount she did not possess. At the trial she was severely reprimanded by the magistrate and warned that the next time "her foot entered the court-room she would land in the workhouse."

It was nearly midnight when Fannie, dizzy with weariness, hunger, and cold, reached the flat of her "missus." But her key no longer fitted the door. In the very dim light she saw her few belongings stacked up in the hallway. She had been dispossessed and had a home no more.

She went back into the night. Finally she found a sleeping-place with a friend who lives with her parents. An now, despite it all, she is still picketing, morning, noon, and night.

An example of what may be the dangers of picketing, and an example also of the relations that have existed in many cases between employer and police, is in the story of Minnie Sussman. When Minnie's shop went on strike, Minnie informed the girls that she had worked for the same firm in their Newark shop, which is twice as big as the shop in New York, and where conditions are the worst. She declared that unless the Newark shop was "taken down" the work of the New York shop would be done in Newark and they would never win. Minnie was therefore appointed with a few other girls to picket the Newark shop. This news reached the employer, who at once went to Newark. While Minnie was talking to one of the non-union girls, who was perfectly willing to listen to her, her employer jumped out of an automobile, sprang on her like a cat, grabbed her by the throat and nearly choked her. She was helpless, *(continued)* but the girl she was talking to screamed, which caused a policeman to appear from around the corner. The employer then came to his senses, and immediately saw his danger. Slipping a handful of silver to the policeman, he ordered that Minnie be arrested on the charge of assaulting the non-union girl. The policeman was about to obey when the employer noticed that Minnie was unconscious, and that the other pickets were eager to be taken to court with her to testify as to what had really happened. He quickly changed his mind. Slipping the policeman a further fee, he ordered the officer to call an ambulance, which the policeman did. Minnie was taken to the hospital, where she remained for two weeks—and there was the end of the story.

Of all the wearying duties that have devolved upon the girls, none has been so trying and dangerous as this duty of picketing. It means long and weary hours of walking and waiting, often in bitter cold and rain, often with little food to keep you warm within and too little clothing to protect you from without. It means exposure to the street loafer; it often means abuse and insult from the boss; it has meant, as has been shown, suffering from the lawlessness of police and magistrates, for merely performing an act which is a legal right according to the statutes of the State of New York; it has meant being thrown into cells with the most degraded women of the street, and finally, for many, a sentence to five days in the workhouse.

"Why was I sent to the workhouse?" repeated Rose Perr, a little fifteen-year-old girl, with wonderment and pain in her face. "It happened so: Before I go to picket I always read my little piece of paper with the picketing rules printed on it, so as not to get arrested. '1. Don't call *Scab.* 2. Don't touch *Scab* while you speak to her. 3. Don't speak to *Scab* when she says "stop." 4. Don't stand with *Scab* on sidewalk; keep on walking.'

"One evening a friend and I were picketing a shop when a great big fat policeman came over to us. Holding out his club as a threat, he told us in a rough way, 'You girls go home and mind your own business!'

"We did not answer, but walked on. Just then a scab came down from the shop, and we quietly told her the usual thing: 'This shop is on strike; won't you please join the union?' While we were speaking a thug came suddenly over and hit my friend right in the chest. She fell down crying. I turned to the policeman, who saw the whole thing, and asked him to arrest the thug. 'All right.' he said. 'but you must come along as a witness.'

"I went with him. But at the stationhouse we were treated as the criminals. We were insulted by everybody; men pulled at our hats and coats, talked to us in a way that is impossible for a decent person to repeat. We were thrown into a cell and kept there six hours with drunken women— oh, the worst kind of women! When our case came up we had no chance to say a word. In the courtroom was the employer with the scab. She was Italian and could not speak English, so the boss spoke for her. He made a complaint against my friend and myself; he said that we hit her; and the judge sent my friend and myself for five days to the workhouse."

Some of the actions of the magistrates seem almost unbelievable, but are only too sadly, too frequently, true. There is one little girl who is always doing something at the union's headquarters— you can distinguish her from the rest because she wears her coat like a cape. There is a reason for that, for her right arm is in a sling. When she arose in her shop to announce to the workers that a strike had been called and asked them to join the union, the boss in his fury threw a pair of scissors at her, which inflicted a deep wound in her forearm. When she applied at court for a warrant for the arrest of her assailant, the magistrate expressed himself as follows:

"You cannot have a warrant. You are a criminal, and you have got no more than your just deserts. God says in the Bible that by the sweat of his brow every man must earn his bread. You are keeping the girls from earning their bread. Your strike is a strike against God!"

But despite it all—despite cold, hunger, police brutality, magisterial insult and injustice, the shame and degraded companionship of the workhouse—these girls have kept up their spirit, a spirit that has brought them much sympathetic outside aid, a spirit that is, as I write, bringing toward a successful close the longest, biggest, bitterest struggle for better living conditions ever waged by women in America.

Natalya Perovskaya's "Tale of Adventure"

According to Edith Wyatt, who wrote the following account of a single shirtwaist striker's experiences with Sue Ainsley Clark, it is "the word-of-mouth tale of Natalya Perovskaya, a household tale of adventure, repeated just as it was told to the present writer and to her hostess' family and other visitors during a call on the East Side on a warm summer evening [in 1910]." Wyatt and Clark wrote that their informant was "a young Russian Jewess of sixteen, who may be called Natalya Urusova." Her "tale" is actually that of Rose Perr, whose story is recounted in Miriam Finn Scott's "The Spirit of the Girl Strikers," reprinted earlier. Why would Clark and Wyatt use a fictitious name? The most obvious answer is to protect their source. Employers, strikers often feared, maintained a list of activists and would refuse to hire them. As a result, some strikers asked reporters not to use their real names. This, however, would not apply in Rose Perr's case. As noted earlier, she had achieved a good deal of notoriety during the strike. Her name appeared in newspaper accounts. She spoke publicly of her experiences on several occasions and even accompanied Rose Schneiderman of the Women's Trade Union League on a fund-raising tour of New England. Further, the authors inadvertently identified her themselves in a footnote in which they cite "the court stenographer's minutes of the proceedings in the Per [sic] trial." If the shirtwaist manufacturers had a blacklist, Rose Perr's name was already on it. On the other hand, calling their informant Natalya Perovskaya (and/or Urusova) advanced the authors' evident intention of presenting their account as the ingenuous and unrehearsed outpouring of a young girl. Their concluding paragraph makes especially interesting reading in this light. The concern they express there about "Natalya's" innocence being jeopardized by contact with "women of the street" and their "cadets," that is, pimps or procurers, was both heartfelt and widespread. Many of the "new women," including the Dreier sisters, who became interested in the plight of the working "girl" did so because of their concern over ending the "social evil," namely prostitution. As Rose Schneiderman told a meeting of the Women's Education Society (see the excerpt from her autobiography reprinted here) "the women on strike were fighting for conditions that would make it possible for working women to live decently and not be prey to procurers."

The National Consumers League[1] commissioned *Making Both Ends Meet,* a study of "the income and outlay of New York working girls", before the shirtwaist strike began, and authors Sue Ainsley Clark, who collected the data, and Edith Wyatt, who wrote up the results, quickly expanded its scope to include an account of the "Uprising," which they first published in *McClures's Magazine,* the leading "muckraking" publication of the day.

---

[1] The league, founded in the late nineteenth century by philanthropist and reformer Josephine Lowell Shaw, campaigned to improve the working conditions of women and children through the creation of a "white list" of manufacturers whose factories met league standards. Members, who numbered in the hundreds of thousands by 1910, promised not to buy products made by firms not on the list. Interest in working-class budgets in the United States goes back to the pioneering studies of Carroll Wright, commissioner of the Bureau of the Statistics of Labor for Massachusetts, published in his *Sixth Annual Report* (1875). *Making Both Ends Meet* is dedicated to Consumers League president Florence Kelley.

"THE SHIRT-WAIST MAKERS' STRIKE"

By Sue Ainsley Clark and Edith Wyatt

Among the active members of the Ladies Waist Makers' Union in New York, there is a young Russian Jewess of sixteen, who may be called Natalya Urusova. She is little, looking hardly more than twelve years old, with a pale, sensitive face, clear dark eyes, very soft, smooth black hair, parted and twisted in braids at the nape of her neck, and the gentlest voice in the world, a voice still thrilled with the light inflections of a child.

She is the daughter of a Russian teacher of Hebrew, who lived about three years ago in a beech-wooded village on the steppes of Central Russia. Here a neighbor of Natalya's family, a Jewish farmer, misunderstanding that manifesto of the Czar which proclaimed free speech, and misunderstanding socialism, had printed and scattered through the neighborhood an edition of hand-bills stating that the

---

Sue Ainsley Clark and Edith Wyatt, "The Shirt-Waist Makers' Strike," from *Making Both Ends Meet: The Income and Outlay of New York Working Girls* (New York: Macmillan, 1911), 44–46, 47–48, 61–63, 64–76, 77–78.

Czar had proclaimed socialism, and that the populace must rise and divide among themselves a rich farm two miles away.

Almost instantly on the appearance of these bills, this unhappy man and a young Jewish friend who chanced to be with him at the time of his arrest were seized and murdered by the government officers— the friend drowned, the farmer struck dead with the blow of a cudgel. A Christian mob formed, and the officers and the mob ravaged every Jewish house in the little town. Thirty innocent Jews were clubbed to death, and then literally cut to pieces. Natalya and her family, who occupied the last house on the street, crept unnoticed to the shack of a Roman Catholic friend, a woman who hid sixteen Jewish people under the straw of the hut in the fields where she lived, in one room, with eight children and some pigs and chickens. Hastily taking from a drawer a little bright-painted plaster image of a wounded saint, this woman placed it over the door as a means of averting suspicion. Her ruse was successful. "Are there Jews here?" the officer called to her, half an hour afterward, as the mob came over the fields to her house.

"No," said the woman.

"Open the door and let me see."

The woman flung open the door. But, as he was quite unsuspecting, the officer glanced in only very casually; and it was in utter ignorance that the rage of the mob went on over the fields, past the jammed little room of breathless Jews.

As soon as the army withdrew from the town, Natalya and her family made their way to America, where, they had been told, one had the right of free belief and of free speech. Here they settled on the sixth floor of a tenement on Monroe Street, on the East Side of New York. Nothing more different from the open, silent country of the steppes could be conceived than the place around them.

● ● ●

As soon after her arrival as her age permitted, Natalya entered the employment of a shirt-waist factory as an unskilled worker, at a salary of $6 a week. Mounting the stairs of the waist factory, one is aware of heavy vibrations. The roar and whir of the machines increase as the door opens, and one sees in a long loft, which is usually fairly light and clean, though sometimes neither, rows and rows of girls with heads bent and eyes intent upon the flashing needles. They are all intensely absorbed; for if they be paid by the piece, they hurry from ambition, and if they be paid by the week, they are "speeded up" by the foreman to a pace set by the swiftest workers.

In the Broadway establishment, which may be called the Bruch Shirt-waist Factory, where Natalya worked, there were four hundred girls—six hundred in the busy season. The hours were long—from eight till half past twelve, a half hour for lunch, and then from one till half past six.

Sometimes the girls worked until half past eight, until nine. There were only two elevators in the building, which contained other factories. There were two thousand working people to be accommodated by these elevators, all of whom began work at eight o'clock in the morning; so that, even if Natalya reached the foot of the shaft at half past seven, it was sometimes half past eight before she reached the shirt-waist factory on the twelfth floor. She was docked for this inevitable tardiness so often that frequently she had only five dollars a week instead of six. This injustice, and the fact that sometimes the foreman kept them waiting needlessly for several hours before telling them that he had no work for them, was particularly wearing to the girls.

• • •

One day she saw a girl, a piece-worker, shaking her head and objecting sadly to the low price the foreman was offering her for making a waist. "If you don't like it," said the foreman, with a laugh, "why don't you join your old 'sisters' out on the street, then?"

Natalya wondered with interest who these "sisters" were. On making inquiry, she found that the workers in other shirt-waist factories had struck, for various reasons of dissatisfaction with the terms of their trade.

The factories had continued work with strike breakers. Some of the companies had stationed women of the street and their cadets in front of the shops to insult and attack the Union members whenever they came to speak to their fellow-workers and to try to dissuade them from selling their work on unfair terms. Some had employed special police protection and thugs against the pickets.

There is, of course, no law against picketing. Every one in the United States has as clear a legal right to address another person peaceably on the subject of his belief in selling his work as on the subject of his belief in the tariff. But on the 19th of October ten girls belonging to the Union, who had been talking peaceably on the day before with some of the strike breakers, were suddenly arrested as they were walking quietly along the street, were charged with disorderly conduct, arraigned in the Jefferson Market Court, and fined $1 each. The chairman of the strikers from one shop was set upon by a gang of thugs while he was collecting funds, and beaten and maimed so that he was confined to his bed for weeks.

A girl of nineteen, one of the strikers, as she was walking home one afternoon was attacked in the open daylight by a thug, who struck her in the side and broke one of her ribs. She was in bed for four weeks, and will always be somewhat disabled by her injury. These and other illegal oppressions visited on the strikers roused a number of members of the Woman's Trade-Union League to assist the girls in peaceful picketing.

● ● ●

It was to these events, as Natalya Urusova found, that the foreman of the Bruch factory had referred when he asked the girls, with a sneer, why they didn't join their "sisters." Going to the Union headquarters on Clinton Street, she learned all she could about the Union. Afterward, in the Bruch factory, whenever any complaints arose, she would say casually, in pretended helplessness, "But what can we do? Is there any way to change this?" Vague suggestions of the Union headquarters would arise, and she would inquire into this eagerly and would pretend to allow herself to be led to Clinton Street. So, little by little, as the long hours and low wages and impudence from the foreman continued, she induced about sixty girls to understand about organization and to consider it favorably.

On the evening of the 22nd of November, Natalya, and how many others from the factory she could not tell, attended a mass meeting at Cooper Union, of which they had been informed by hand-bills. It was called for the purpose of discussing a general strike of shirt-waist workers in New York City. The hall was packed. Overflow meetings were held at Beethovan Hall, Manhattan Lyceum, and Astoria Hall. In the Cooper Union addresses were delivered by Samuel Gompers, by Miss Dreier, and by many others. Finally, a girl of eighteen asked the chairman for the privilege of the floor. She said: "I have listened to all the speeches. I am one who thinks and feels from the things they describe. I, too, have worked and suffered. I am tired of the talking. I move that we go on a general strike."

The meeting broke into wild applause. The motion was unanimously indorsed. The chairman, Mr. Feigenbaum, a Union officer, rapped on the table. "Do you mean faith?" he called to the workers. "Will you take the old Jewish oath?" Thousands of right hands were held up and the whole audience repeated in Yiddish: "If I turn traitor to the cause I now pledge, may this hand wither from the arm I now raise."

This was the beginning of the general shirt-waist strike. A committee of fifteen girls and one boy was appointed at the Cooper Union meeting, and went from one to the other of the overflow meetings, where the same motion was offered and unanimously indorsed.

"But I did not know how many workers in my shop had taken that oath at that meeting. I could not tell how many would go on strike in our factory the next day," said Natalya, afterward. "When we came back the next morning to the factory, though, no one went to the dressing-room. We all sat at the machines with our hats and coats beside us, ready to leave. The foreman had no work for us when we got there. But, just as always, he did not tell when there would be any, or if there would be any at all that day. And there was whispering and talking softly all around the room among the machines: 'Shall we wait like this?' 'There is a general strike.' 'Who will get up first?' 'It would be better to be the last to get up, and then the company might remember it of you afterward, and do well for you.' But I told them," observed Natalya, with a little shrug, "'What difference does it make which one is first and which one is last?' Well, so we stayed whispering, and no one knowing what the other would do, not making up our minds, for two hours. Then I started to get up." Her lips trembled. "And at just the same minute all—we all got up together, in one second. No one after the other; no one before. And when I saw it—that time—oh, it excites me so yet, I can hardly talk about it. So we all stood up, and all walked out together. And already out on the sidewalk in front the policemen stood with the clubs. One of them said, 'If you don't behave, you'll get this on your head.' And he shook his club at me.

"We hardly knew where to go—what to do next. But one of the American girls, who knew how to telephone, called up the Woman's Trade-Union League, and they told us all to come to a big hall a few blocks away. After we were there, we wrote out on paper what terms we wanted: not any night work, except as it would be arranged for in some special need for it for the trade; and shorter hours; and to have wages arranged by a committee to arbitrate the price for every one fairly; and to have better treatment from the bosses.

"Then a leader spoke to us and told us about picketing quietly, and the law.

"Our factory had begun to work with a few Italian strike breakers.[1] The next day we went back to the factory, and saw five Italian girls taken in to work, and then taken away afterward in an automobile. I was with an older girl from our shop, Anna Lunska. The next morning in front of the factory, Anna Lunska and I met a tall Italian man going into the factory with some girls. So I said to her: 'These girls fear us in some way. They do not understand, and I will speak to them, and ask them why they work, and tell them we are not going to harm them at all—only to speak about our work.'

"I moved toward them to say this to them. Then the tall man struck Anna Lunska in the breast so hard, he nearly knocked her down. She couldn't get her breath. And I went to a policeman standing right there and said, 'Why do you not arrest this man for striking my friend? Why do you let him do it? Look at her. She cannot speak; she is crying. She did nothing at all.' Then he arrested the man; and he said, 'But you must come, too, to make a charge against him.' The tall Italian called a man out of the factory, and went with me and Anna Lunska and the three girls to the court."

But when Natalya and Anna reached the court, and had made their charge against the tall Italian, to their bewilderment not only he, but they, too, were conducted downstairs to the cells. He had charged them with attacking the girls he was escorting into the factory.

"They made me go into a cell," said Natalya, "and suddenly they locked us in. Then I was frightened, and I said to the policeman there, 'Why do you do this? I have done nothing at all. The man struck my friend. I must send for somebody.'

"He said, 'You cannot send for any one at all. You are a prisoner.'

"We cried then. We were frightened. We did not know what to do.

"After about an hour and a half he came and said some one was asking for us. We looked out. It was Miss Violet Pike. A boy I knew had seen us go into the prison with the Italian, and not come out, and so he thought something was wrong and he had gone to the League and told them.

---

[1] In the factories where the Russian and Italian girls worked side by side, their feeling for each other seems generally to have been friendly. After the beginning of the strike an attempt was made to antagonize them against each other by religious and nationalistic appeals. It met with little success. Italian headquarters for Italian workers wishing organizations were soon established. Little by little the Italian garment workers are entering the Union.

"So Miss Pike had come from the League; and she bailed us out; and she came back with us on the next day for our trial."

On the next morning the case against the tall Italian was rapidly examined, and the Italian discharged. He was then summoned back in rebuttal, and Natalya and Anna's case was called. Four witnesses, one of them being the proprietor of the factory, were produced against them, and stated that Natalya and Anna had struck one of the girls the Italian was escorting. At the close of the case against Natalya and Anna, Judge Cornell said:[2] "I find the girls guilty. It would be perfectly futile for me to fine them. Some charitable women would pay their fines or they could get a bond. I am going to commit them to the workhouse under the Cumulative Sentence Act, and there they will have an opportunity of thinking over what they have done."

"Miss Violet Pike came forward then," said Natalya, "and said, 'Cannot his sentence be mollified?'

"And he said it could not be mollified.

"They took us away in a patrol to the Tombs.

"We waited in the waiting-room there. The matron looked at us and said, 'You are not bad girls. I will not send you down to the cells. You can do some sewing for me here.' But I could not sew. I felt so bad, because I could not eat the food they gave us at noon for dinner in the long hall with all the other prisoners. It was coffee with molasses in it, and oatmeal and bread so bad that after one taste we could not swallow it down. Then, for supper, we had the same, but soup, too, with some meat bones in it. And even before you sat down at the table these bones smelled so it made you very sick. But they forced you to sit down at the table before it, whether you ate or drank anything or not. And the prisoners walked by in a long line afterward and put their spoons in a pail of hot water, just the same whether they had eaten anything with the spoons or not.

"Then we walked to our cells. It was night, and it was dark—oh, so dark in there it was dreadful! There were three other women in the cell—some of them were horrid women that came off the street. The beds were one over the other, like on the boats—iron beds, with a quilt and a blanket. But it was so cold you had to put both over you; and the iron springs underneath were bare, and they were dreadful to

---

[2] Extract from the court stenographer's minutes of the proceedings in the Per trial.

lie on. There was no air; you could hardly breathe. The horrid women laughed and screamed and said terrible words.

"Anna Lunska felt so sick and was so very faint, I thought what should we do if she was so much worse in the night in this terrible darkness, where you could see nothing at all. Then I called through the little grating to a woman who was a sentinel that went by in the hall all through the night, 'My friend is sick. Can you get me something if I call you in the night?'

"The woman just laughed and said, 'Where do you think you are? But if you pay me, I will come and see what I can do.'

"In a few minutes she came back with a candle, and shuffled some cards under the candlelight, and called to us, 'Here, put your hand through the grate and give me a quarter and I'll tell you who your fellows are by the cards.' Then Anna Lunska said, 'We do not care to hear talk like that,' and the woman went away.

"All that night it was dreadful. In the morning we could not eat any of the breakfast. They took us in a wagon like a prison with a little grating, and then in a boat like a prison with a little grating. As we got on to it, there was another girl, not like the rest of the women prisoners. She cried and cried. And I saw she was a working girl. I managed to speak to her and say, 'Who are you?' She said, 'I am a striker. I cannot speak any English.' That was all. They did not wish me to speak to her, and I had to go on.

"From the boat they made us go into the prison they call Blackwell's Island. Here they made us put on other clothes. All the clothes they had were much, much too large for me, and they were dirty. They had dresses in one piece of very heavy, coarse material, with stripes all around, and the skirts are gathered, and so heavy for the women. They almost drag you down to the ground. Everything was so very much too big for me, the sleeves trailed over my hands so far and the skirts on the ground so far, they had to pin and pin them up with safety-pins.

"Then we had the same kind of food I could not eat; and they put us to work sewing gloves. But I could not sew, I was so faint and sick. At night there was the same kind of food I could not eat, and all the time I wondered about that shirt-waist striker that could not speak one word of English, and she was all alone and had the same we had in other ways. When we walked by the matron to go to our cells at night, at first she started to send Anna Lunska and me to different cells. She would have made me go alone with one of the terrible women from the street. But I was so dreadfully frightened, and cried so, and begged her so to let Anna Lunska and me stay together, that at last she said we could.

"Just after that I saw that other girl, away down the line, so white, she must have cried and cried, and looking so frightened. I thought, 'Oh, I ought to ask for her to come with us, too.' But I did not dare. I thought, 'I will make that matron so mad that she will not even let Anna Lunska and me stay together.' So I got almost to our cell before I went out of the line and across the hall and went back to the matron and said: 'Oh, there is another Russian girl here. She is all alone. She cannot speak one word of English. Please, please couldn't that girl come with my friend and me?'

"She said, 'Well, for goodness' sake! So you want to band all the strikers together here, do you? How long have you known her?'

"I said, 'I never saw her until to-day.'

"The matron said, 'For the land's sake, what do you expect here?' but she did not say anything else. So I went off, just as though she wasn't going to let that girl come with us; for I knew she would not want to seem as though she would do it, at any rate.

"But, after we were in the cell with an Irish woman and another woman, the door opened, and that Russian girl came in with us. Oh, she was so glad!

"After that it was the same as the night before, except that we could see the light of the boats passing. But it was dark and cold, and we had to put both the quilt and the blanket over us and lie on the springs, and you must keep all of your clothes on to try to be warm. But the air and the smells are so bad. I think if it were any warmer, you would almost faint there. I could not sleep.

"The next day they made me scrub. But I did not know how to scrub. And, for Anna Lunska, she wet herself all over from head to foot. So they said, very cross, 'It seems to us you do not know how to scrub a bit. You can go back to the sewing department.' On the way I went through a room filled with negresses, and they called out, 'Look, look at the little kid.' And they took hold of me, and turned me around, and all laughed and sang and danced all around me. These women, they do not seem to mind at all that they are in prison.

"In the sewing room the next two days I was so sick I could hardly sew. The women often said horrid things to each other, and I sat on the bench with them. There was one woman over us at sewing that argued with me so much, and told me how much better it was for me here than in Russian prisons, and how grateful I should be.

"I said, 'How is that, then? Isn't there the same kind of food in those prisons and in these prisons? And I think there is just as much liberty.'"

On the last day of Natalya's sentence, after she was dressed in her own little jacket and hat again and just ready to go, one of the most repellent women of the street said to her, "I am staying in here and you're going out. Give me a kiss for good-by." Natalya said that this woman was a horror to her. "But I thought it was not very nice to refuse this; so I kissed her a good-by kiss and came away."

The officers guarded the girls to the prison boat for their return to New York. There, at the ferry, stood a delegation of the members of the Woman's Trade-Union and the Union waiting to receive them.

● ● ●

. . . it would convey a false impression to imply that every striker arrested had as much sense and force of character as Natalya Urusova. Natalya was especially protected in her ordeal by a vital love of observation and a sense of humor, charmingly frequent in the present writer's experience of young Russian girls and women. With these qualities she could spend night after night locked up with the women of the street, in her funny, enormous prison clothes, and remain as uninfluenced by her companions as if she had been some blossoming geranium or mignonette set inside a filthy cellar as a convenience for a few minutes, and then carried out again to her native fresh air. But such qualities as hers cannot be demanded of all very young and unprotected girls, and to place them wantonly with women of the streets has in general an outrageous irresponsibility and folly quite insufficiently implied by the experience of a girl of Natalya's individual penetration and self-reliance.

"The Spirit of the Strikers"

Mary Brown Sumner's "The Spirit of the Strikers" did much to promulgate the notion that the strike's leadership arose spontaneously out of the needs of the moment. "Into the foreground of this picture comes the figure of one girl after another as her services are needed." Brown Sumner also promoted the contradictory notion that "the soul of this young women's revolution is Clara Lemlich," who offered the general strike motion at the Cooper Union meeting. Indeed "The Spirit of the Strikers" contains perhaps the most detailed contemporary biographical sketch of Clara Lemlich. Brown Sumner's Lemlich was "a spirit of fire and tears, devoid of egotism, unable to tolerate the thought of human suffering." She was also a socialist who quoted Karl Marx's call to revolution in the *Communist Manifesto* in her report to the union the day after her resolution was adopted. Lemlich's radical politics did not trouble Brown Sumner or her editor, Paul U. Kellogg, who quoted Lemlich's brother in his introduction to the special issue that *The Survey* magazine devoted to the strike:

> If she is to make anything she must make it, that is all. She was always that way in Russia and here. If she had to finish a book of three hundred pages or three thousand, she does not do anything else until she finishes that—eating, sleeping, nothing else matters. And when she works she works, and when she strikes she strikes. That is Clara.[1]

Progressives like Kellogg were willing to indulge the radical impulses of Lemlich and many other strikers because they assumed that these young women would grow more moderate if their strike succeeded and their circumstances improved. Further, because they associated the strikers' socialist and anarchist politics with their Russian background, they further assumed that the strikers would gradually abandon their politics as they became more assimilated.

---

[1] Paul U. Kellogg, "The Common Welfare: The Survey This Week," *The Survey* 23 (January 22, 1910): 538.

THE SPIRIT OF THE STRIKERS

BY MARY BROWN SUMNER

"I hear them say this strike is historical," said a young working girl who stood watching a group of shirtwaist pickets. She did not follow her words up; probably she did not know exactly what she meant to express, but between the lines of slighting jocularity in the newspaper accounts of the strike and the strikers, she had somehow caught an idea that made a strong appeal to her imagination.

And well it might, for this spontaneous strike of the 20,000 is the greatest single event in the history of woman's work. Most remarkable of all, these girls—few of them are over twenty years old—are under the domination of no strong individuals. Secretary Schindler handles the enormously increased volume of executive work quietly and unobtrusively, aided by the volunteer services of Secretary Goldstein of the Bakers' Union. Committees

Mary Brown Sumner, "The Spirit of the Strikers," *The Survey* 23 (January 22, 1910), 550-51, 554-55.

(continued)

of the various shops meet nightly, then between midnight and three in the morning report in Clinton Hall to the general executive committee which arranges the next day's campaign. Beside them as an efficient advertising medium stands the Woman's Trade Union League which co-operates with the union in committee work, shop meetings and picket duty. Behind them is the Central Federated Union and their faithful reporter, the New York *Call,* whose employes even gave extra service to get out the strike edition. But where are the agitators, where are the labor leaders who, the girls in the settled shops say their employers tell them, must be plotting for power and pelf somewhere in the background?

There are none—or rather, "their name is legion." Into the foreground of this great moving picture comes the figure of one girl after another as her services are needed. For the time being she is perfectly regardless of self. With extraordinary simplicity and eloquence she will tell before any kind of audience, without false shame and without self-glorification, the conditions of her work, her wages, and the pinching poverty of her home and the homes of her comrades. Then she withdraws into the background to undertake quietly the danger and humiliation of picket duty or to become a nameless sandwich-girl selling papers on the street; no longer the center of interested attention, but the butt of the most unspeakable abuse. "Streetwalker" is one of the terms that the police and the thugs apply daily to the strikers, in fact it has become in their vocabulary almost synonymous with striker.

•   •   •

. . . the soul of this young women's revolution is Clara Lemlich, a spirit of fire and tears, devoid of egotism, unable to tolerate the thought of human suffering. The dramatic climax of the strike came when this girl was raised to the platform at Cooper Union and "with the simplicity of genius," as one reporter says, put the motion for the general strike. "I have listened to all the speakers and I have no patience for talk. I am one who feels and suffers for the things pictured. I move that we go on a general strike," she said. Dramatic, too, was the moment two years before when she stood, a solitary little figure, distributing circulars of her union to the girls employed in "the worst shop in New York." For this "disorderly conduct" she was arrested and had her first experience of a prison cell.

Under pressure she will tell her story simply and straightforwardly, but with a proud shyness about taking the public into her private life. Her attitude toward herself is well expressed in her words to the Colony Club: "I could tell you, ladies, how I spend my life and live on fifteen dollars, but I have no right to speak when there are others who make three dollars a week." Her old father

and mother brought their half-grown children to America, hoping to give them opportunities in life that they could not get at home. The opportunities did not prove so plentiful as they expected. Nothing but the garment trades was open for a girl who spoke no English. From a Russian high-school girl, knowing nothing of the double struggle with want and overwork, she became a wage earner in a factory. "I know now," she says, "that my father must have had a battle to keep us going at home, but I did not know it then. I was buried in my books."

At sixteen her real education began—in the shop. . . . What outraged her most from the beginning were the petty persecutions, the meannesses, and the failure to recognize the girls as human beings. She tells of the forewoman following a girl if she left the room and hurrying her back again, of the pay of the new girls kept down because they did not know what the market rate was, of excessive fines, of frequent "mistakes" in pay envelopes hard and embarrassing to rectify; of a system of registering on the time clock that stole more than twenty minutes from the lunch hour, of the office clock covered so that the girls could not waste time looking at it, or put back an hour so that they should not know that they were working overtime. She sat and worked and observed, and her greatest wonder was that the workers endured this constant dragging down of their self-respect.

Very soon she began to say things that made her parents call her a "socialist." She thought more deeply about her industrial experiences in America, and became one. At the same time she joined the International Union of Shirtwaist Makers—one of the handful who fought for years to keep that infant union alive. From that time she became an agitator in a small way. She had no personal grievance. She was a draper, always well paid and in demand. She needed money, furthermore, because she wished to take a course in medicine, but this did not prevent her from trying persistently to organize every shop she worked in. She tells of one time when she felt that she must keep her place and determined to be "a good girl"—from the boss's point of view—but in two days found herself talking unionism again.

•   •   •

In this present strike the girls "walked out to prevent themselves from being starved out," she says. Their employer who is reckoned worth $100,000— the whole of it made in the garment trade in the last three years—decided that his employes were too expensive and . . . tried to get rid of them gradually on the ground of slack work. Soon the girls found that he was sending his work to a cheap shop he had started downtown, or giving it to the low paid girls in their own shop. Then the battle was joined in good earnest. Clara went on picket

(continued)

duty, was attacked and so badly hurt that she was laid up for several days. This did not deter her; she went back to her post and, being a logical talker, straightforward and well fitted to gain the confidence of her comrades, she was able to add to the number of strikers. She even gathered a crowd around her on the street corner and enlisted their sympathies in the strikers.

Through the monotonous years when nobody took an interest in the union, when even those who were nominally members would not attend or properly support it, Clara Lemlich's hope lived in the vivid appeal to the imagination of the idea of the brotherhood of labor, and the pitiful plight of the young and lightheaded and helpless in her trade kept her fighting spirit up. And now with the general strike her faith had justified itself far beyond her expectation. "We never really expected," she said after the Cooper Union meeting, "that the mass of the workers would be inspired and come out." But they did, and so strongly was she moved by their action that, she tells you with a faint flush, she ended her report on the floor of the Central Federated Union the next day with the words, "I seem to see the realization of the words of Karl Marx: 'Workers of the world, unite. You have nothing to lose but your chains; you have the world to gain.'"

But all is not exhilaration in this struggle. There is much hard work and much discouragement. The hard work she has done bravely. She has refused a paid position in the union but speaks continually in public in its behalf, serves on shop committees and on the general executive committee. She faces with a full realization the long, discouraging task of keeping alive the union spirit and putting it on the basis of a permanent intellectual and moral appeal. She faces the laborious task of adjusting the details of agreements with employers in the various shops and is already looking forward to the next steps, when they shall demand the union label on shirtwaists and set on foot a broad system of training for learners in the shops. She does not believe that the strike can fail for it has a spirit that will carry it through, and she feels that even after "the tumult and the shouting dies," a new understanding of their relation to each other will have dawned on the girls, and from this time on the workers in the garment trades will stand together.

All for One

Shortly after publishing her "lifelet" in *The Independent* in 1905, Rose Schneiderman joined the New York branch of the Women's Trade Union League. She was, she explained in her autobiography, initially suspicious of the well-meaning, affluent, American-born women who made up most of its membership. Why were they so eager to help working-class immigrant workers like herself? It is a question that historians still ask. One part of the answer seems to be that WTUL activists, like Schneiderman herself, saw a clear connection between the low wages, bad working conditions, and sexual harassment that women encountered in the labor market and prostitution. Both believed that trade unions were the most effective way to combat the social conditions that fostered the "social evil" as their generation referred to prostitution. Another part of the answer, some historians argue, is that, again like Schneiderman, WTUL volunteers were looking for ways to make something of their own lives and, again like her, found they could build careers for themselves on service to others.

Schneiderman had a second question about her new allies: Could they be counted on when the going got rough? Schneiderman decided to take a chance on the league, at least in part because it was willing to pay her to work as a full-time union organizer. In the years following the Triangle fire (and the WTUL's feud with the leaders of the International Ladies Garment Workers Union), she was on the losing side of a struggle over whether the league should continue its organizational work among immigrant workers or concentrate upon the American-born and upon "protective" legislation. Later, in the 1920s, Schneiderman became president of the New York branch of the league, an office she held until the organization dissolved after World War II. In the excerpts that follow she described her own role and that of the WTUL in the strike. It is worth noting that Schneiderman wrote her autobiography almost sixty years after the events recounted here. Unsurprisingly, she got several details wrong. It was the New York *Evening Journal*, for example, and not the *American*, that published a special strike edition.

EXCERPTS FROM *ALL FOR ONE*

By Rose Schneiderman (with Lucy Goldthwaite)

The League entered this new fight with fervor and dedication. Our headquarters housed a number of the striking women and we became responsible for their administration and welfare. A volunteer picket line of seventy-five prominent League members and their friends was organized. This was the first picket corps recruited outside labor's own ranks. The women in it endured the rough treatment meted out to strikers in those days. They ran the risk of being assaulted by the police as well as by the goons hired by the employers to protect the scabs. When they were arrested, they asked no favors.

• • •

One of the volunteers, Carola Woerishoffer, a young Bryn Mawr graduate, divided her time, day after day, between the Jefferson Market

Rose Schneiderman (with Lucy Goldthwaite), *All for One* (New York: Paul S. Eriksson, 1967), 91–95. Reprinted by permission of the publisher.

and Essex Street courts, supplying bail for the arrested workers. As guarantee she put up her own property, a house her mother deeded to her for this purpose. When necessary, Carola rebonded the workers for Special and General Sessions. During the strike she furnished bail to the extent of $29,000. . . .

There were other members who furnished bail and money guarantees. Mrs. Henry Morgenthau, Sr. deeded property to the Henry Street Settlement so that it could furnish bail also for the hundreds of women who were arrested on flimsy charges and herded into police cells with prostitutes, drunks, and hardened criminals. Judges were unsympathetic because they did not understand the industrial situation which led to the strike, and they meted out workhouse sentences at the least provocation.

The League's publicity committee, made up of three young Vassar women, Elizabeth Dutcher, Violet Pike and Elsie Cole, kept the strike on the front page of every New York newspaper. The New York *American* donated one of its editions to the cause. The strikers sold it on street corners and added five thousand dollars to the strike fund. Mary Dreier, Helen Marot, Leonora O'Reilly, who was a particularly gifted speaker, and I spoke at all kinds of meetings.

At a meeting of the Women's Education Society, the program was devoted to the Cable Bill which proposed to curb prostitution by arresting the women involved but letting the men go free. The women speakers were opposed to it and when my turn came I linked prostitution with poverty, pointing out that the women on strike were fighting for conditions that would make it possible for working women to live decently and not be prey to procurers.

After my speech, I received a note from Anne Morgan asking me to come to see her in connection with the strike. On Monday I showed the card to my co-workers at the League and asked them what they thought of it. They said, "For Heaven's sake, call her up and make an appointment. You know she is the daughter of J. P. Morgan, don't you?" "Yes, I know," I answered cynically, "but what does the daughter of that capitalist want from us?"

I did go to see Miss Morgan that week and she was a very nice and intelligent person. I don't remember whether she gave any money toward the strike but I do know she helped swell the picket line, which made quite a publicity scoop.

At a meeting at the Colony Club, a collection was taken up after we got through speaking. We were disappointed because it was only a thousand dollars, and we had expected more from ladies of means.

In January I was sent by the League to Massachusetts to raise money for the strikers. I took with me one of the strikers, Rose Perr, who was only sixteen years old, but who, like hundreds of others, had been arrested while on the picket line and had served thirty days in the penitentiary. Mary Dreier and I had gone to see Judge Barlow who had sentenced Rose and had tried to make him understand that she had done nothing wrong. We asked if he realized what it would mean to a girl her age to be locked up with prostitutes, thieves, and narcotic addicts. "Oh," he said, "it will be good for her. It will be a vacation."

My first speech was in Boston in Faneuil Hall. To me, it was most exciting and thrilling to speak from the platform of so historic a place. Rose, who was as tiny as I, looked completely beaten as she told of her experience. The audience was aghast at her life in the penitentiary and applauded vigorously after she sat down. Rose went back to New York but I continued the work of raising money.

In the evenings I went to union meetings . . . . I was also invited to speak at parlor meetings and let it be known that I would expect at least one hundred dollars a meeting for the strikers. . . .

I spoke at Radcliffe College and some of the Harvard boys came over to listen. Then I went to Wellesley where two of the co-founders of the National League, Ellen Hayes and Vida Scudder, arranged a meeting of students, who were intensely interested in the struggle the women in New York were making. They were very impressed that we had opened a Union Label shirtwaist shop in New York to help employers who had signed up with the union. One of the girls wanted to buy a thousand dollars' worth of shirtwaists and sell them to her classmates. I was stunned, of course, by the offer but talked her out of it because I was afraid she would lose a lot of money on the enterprise. Also, it would have been a complicated proposition because of sizes and styles.

From Wellesley I went to Mount Holyoke College. On the way from Boston I had stopped at every industrial center to cover the union meetings. I had slept in a different bed in a different hotel every night for four weeks. When I got to Holyoke I was really tired and it was a godsend to be given a luxurious guestroom in the college. The next evening there was a meeting of students, augmented by some Smith college girls.

Back in New York I was very happy to learn that the amount of money raised on the trip was ten thousand dollars, a small fortune in those days. Never had a strike aroused so much public sympathy, not only in New England but all over the country.

• • •

I got home in time for a mass meeting that the League had organized at Grand Central Palace to honor all the strikers who had served time in prison. Wearing sashes on which were printed the dates of their sentences, they were cited that night for bravery and outstanding service to their fellow strikers.

CONTEMPORARY ASSESSMENTS

"The Hygienic Aspects of the Shirtwaist Strike"

The "Uprising of the Twenty Thousand" provoked an immense outpouring of reportage, analysis, commentary, and editorial judgment. One of the most systematic assessments was undertaken at the behest of *The Survey* magazine by a volunteer committee chaired by Dr. Woods Hutchinson, a well-known expert on public health. Hutchinson's group visited a representative sample of shops, examined sanitary and other working conditions, sought to determine hours of work and wages, carefully described the subcontracting system used in many shops, and explored the wage differentials between male and female workers. In the following excerpt Hutchinson reported how his committee determined which shops to investigate and summarized its findings about the causes, possible outcome, and significance of the strike. As a physician, he stressed his own "scientific" credentials in approaching these highly controversial issues. He was, he claimed, "an unprejudiced observer." And he did not claim to know the full truth about the competing claims of workers and employers. Yet, he also drew upon his scientific credentials to buttress his claim that his committee's report represented "civilized" and "progressive" opinion. Hutchinson further pointed out that he was a native-born citizen and implied that this gave him, and people like him, a greater right to determine what was or was not "un-American" than the immigrant employers and strikers. His concluding paragraph makes his committee's overall sympathies clear. Of the key issue of the strike, that of union recognition, he wrote "any manufacturer who absolutely declines to deal on any terms with an organization of his employes, large or small, is out of place and out of date here in this twentieth century."

THE HYGIENIC ASPECTS OF THE SHIRTWAIST STRIKE

BY WOODS HUTCHINSON, M. D.

Some two weeks ago I was asked by the editor of **The Survey** whether I would be willing to undertake a brief, bird's-eye, first-hand investigation of the sanitary conditions and aspects of the strike. With grave misgivings as to whether it would be regarded as any of my business, but because of a long cherished belief that strikes and many other economic disturbances are really at bottom matters of sanitary and hygienic consideration, problems of public medicine and social engineering, I undertook the task. The plan was simply to visit and carefully inspect a moderate number of sample or typical shops, to gather all the information possible from the employers, the workers, the pickets and our own eyes and ears and noses; then to present these results to the public for whatever they might be worth.

It is believed that the community is not merely interested in knowing, but has the right to know, what are the wages received, the hours worked, the sanitary conditions under which the work is done, in this or any other industry, for the simple reason that if these wages and these hours and conditions impair the health or stunt the development of the workers, these ultimately become, sooner or later, from sickness, premature age or accident, dependents upon the private or public charity of the community. In other words, if wages are below or hours of work above that standard which will render possible the maintenance of good health and vitality by the worker, the community sooner or late pays the deficit; and the employer as well as the employe becomes an object of charity and should be treated as such.

The interest of the community becomes all the keener and its right to know and interfere the stronger, when these workers happen to be young and particularly when they are of the sex who will become the mothers of the future generation. The right therefore of the employer, to declare that "it's nobody's damn business what I pay my employes" or that of the employe that it is none of the public's affair for what wages or under what conditions he is willing to work, both belong to the dark ages, and no longer exist in communities calling themselves civilized and progressive.

Indeed the keenness of the interest taken by the public in this problem is fairly shown by the columns after columns devoted to it every day in the daily press. But these were so widely divergent in their statements, so contradictory and confusing that it was hoped that a firsthand investigation by a committee which was as nearly as possible disinterested and not connected in any way with either side, might be of some interest. Whether we have done more than add to this confusion is for the reader to judge. We have no conclusions to suggest for the simple reason that we couldn't come to any. If anyone else can from the data we present, that is his privilege. For the same reason we have no solution of the problem to suggest, or responsibility to apportion, or motives to attribute—all are beyond our powers; simply to report the facts as they presented themselves to us, with such explanations of the methods of their securing as will enable you to judge of their value.

The investigation was carried out by a volunteer committee of four persons consisting of Mary Van Kleeck, and Alice P. Barrows of the Committee

Woods Hutchinson, M.D., "The Hygienic Aspects of the Shirtwaist Strike," *The Survey* 23 (January 22, 1910), 541–42, 547–50.

(continued)

on Women's Work, who were already trained investigators of women's trades and rendered invaluable service, Arthur P. Kellogg of **The Survey** and the writer. After several conferences the plan adopted was to secure from both employers and employes a list of shops in which strikes either had occurred or were still in progress. From these were selected as nearly as might be upon the principle of accidental average, that is to say taking each fifth or sixth shop upon the list, a number of shops and from this chance list were again picked out such a list of twenty as would include three or more of each kind of shops involved in the dispute; three or four "good" shops, which were described by both parties as having good sanitary conditions, good wages, and for the most part friendly relations between the employers and employes. An equal number of "bad" shops were selected, judged by the same standards, the two shops where the strike began, three or four small or so-called "contractor" shops, while the remainder of the list consisted of average or unselected shops. In all, some seventeen shops were visited, which included two of the largest in the trade, employing 350 and 650 operators, respectively; three of the smaller shops employing fifty, thirty-five and twenty-five; while the remaining shops averaged about 150. Five of these had recognized the union, four had settled directly with their employes and the remainder were still on strike, so far as their old employes were concerned. The committee will not guarantee that this group of shops forms a typical or reliable sample of the entire 350 or 400, only that it exerted its best efforts to make it so.

It was anticipated in advance that there would be great difficulty in getting accurate, reliable "documented" evidence and data covering a sufficient number of cases to be of value for drawing averages. But the reality was worse and beyond the wildest expectations. The employers of a particular shop would give us one set of facts about the situation and points of dispute in their case; the employes of the same shop would give another in many important details radically different and even contradictory statement. As no official authority or indeed any other third party, had records or first-hand information by which these statements could be checked up, it was obviously difficult to determine where the truth lay between the two extremes. It was most difficult to get either side to come down to detailed, circumstantial figures or statements, whether as to wages, hours, points in dispute, number of days worked in the years, or what not. Each preferred to dwell eloquently upon its own grievances, and to mention such individual instances of long or short hours, high or low wages, good or bad treatment, as

happened to support its particular point of view,—which of course is but natural and to be expected.

• • •

According to employers and employeresses, the girls had always been treated "chust as if they vere my own *cheeldrun.*" All the comforts of a home, including dance music on a graphophone, and fifteen cents for supper when kept to work overtime at night. "Chust, look at that girl," said one employer, "vashing her hands, and viping them on the towel, eggsackly as if she vas at home, and better too. She vouldn't have no such sink to vash in all by herseluf if she was home."

On the other hand, the girls declare that they were bossed about and picked at and tyrannized over, docked half a day if they came five minutes late, locked into the shop when they objected to staying late at night and working overtime, watched and driven incessantly by the forewoman, scolded for wasting their employer's time and machine power if they so much as lifted their hands to adjust a pin in their collar or straighten their hair, compelled to eat the suppers furnished them with one hand, while running the machine with the other, refused permission to go home when feeling unwell, or even when there was serious illness in their family, until their lives became a burden and the question of wages of minor importance. It is inconsistent and even unreasonable, but it is, alas, human nature, that while in the main and in essentials and most important respects, so far as we could come to any opinion, it appeared that eighty per cent of the girls have been fairly, moderately, justly, and even kindly treated, yet there had been allowed to grow up a system of nagging and espionage, and petty tyrannies, favoritisms and little annoyances—in some cases little more than rudenesses and discourtesies, which, though trifling in themselves, by constant dropping produced such a state of chronic irritation in the minds of the girls that as soon as the spark of a definite, substantial, public grievance was applied the flame of the strike broke out at once. It is probably not too much to say, though here I would not involve any other members of the committee, that at least one-third of the strike and the feeling that led to it, was due to an overwhelming desire on the part of girls who had little to complain of personally in point of wages and hours, to put a stop to the serious injustices practiced upon their less fortunate sisters, and the incessant annoyances, tyrannies, favoritism and drivings to which they themselves were subjected. Politeness costs little, but it saves a great deal of expense and trouble in the long run, especially when dealing with the gentler sex.

(continued)

The most serious drawback of the entire trade, next to the contractor system and the utter absence of a uniform standard of wages, is the casual or seasonal character of the work. Physiologically speaking it results in the employes being overworked and overpaid, by overtime, four months out of the year; moderately worked and moderately paid for six months, and little work and less pay for two months. With all due deference as a mere scientist and one entirely unversed in practical affairs, this would appear to be due to the newness of the trade, the lack of concerted action or agreement among the manufacturers and the absence of reasonable foresight and planning in advance on the part of those engaged in it. In other words, the trade and the workers both are, as one of the employeresses repeatedly told us of her girls, as yet "onceevilized," in more senses than that all concerned have come over from the Russian Ghettos within the last five months to fifteen years. If the workers would organize themselves and standardize wages even approximately, they would confer a lasting benefit upon the fair and honorable employers, who would thereby be protected from cut-throat competition and under-bidding in the labor cost of their product by unscrupulous rivals. If, on the other hand, the employers were organized so that they could deal with the buyers and the trade, demanding the placing of orders a reasonable time in advance of delivery of the goods, they would be able to spread their productive season over two-thirds of the year instead of one-third as now, give reasonable hours of work and steady and adequate wages to all of their employes, instead of taking on a number of comparatively unskilled transient workers in the busy season and then discharging them for the remainder of the year.

The most potent single influence in spreading the strike after it had once been started, was the conduct and attitude of the police. We were informed that shop after shop struck solely on account of the manner in which they had either seen or heard the police treat strikers and pickets. Of this phase of the strike our committee only saw a small "cross section," which did not happen to include any rioting, or arrests, or open disturbance and may not have been a fair sample of the whole situation. Here however is a typical item of experience. One of the lady members of our committee, going to a shop for the purpose of investigation, asked a question of one of the pickets in front of the shop and then walked up to the entrance. Here she hesitated for a moment, debating in her own mind whether to enter or go on to another shop. Scarcely had she come to a stop, in fact she was still turning toward the entrance, when a six-foot

representative of the outraged majesty of the law rushed forward, seized her roughly by the shoulder and gave her a violent shove down the street, at the same time shouting, "Get right out o' this. You ain't got no business stoppin' here. Move right down the block, quick." She hesitated just long enough to take his number, which was 727, and then obeyed his polite request. Before some ten or twelve shops picketed, which we passed and where we made inquiries of the pickets, there were on duty apparently constantly during the hours of our visits, from 2:30 to 6 p.m. from one to three policemen, usually supported or accompanied by two or three roughly dressed, surly-looking fellows of the familiar "bar-room fighter," or dance-hall "bouncer" type. Both they and their comrades in uniform struck us as distinctly disgusted with their job, and ready to vent their internal irritation on any passerby who loitered or gave them a fair excuse for an explosion.

• • •

Just how much of the taxpayers money has been expended in protecting ten-story buildings from the attack of girl pickets is difficult to determine. Nominally the police are on duty only for an hour in the morning, another at noon and one in the evening, when the workers are entering or leaving the building. Practically in the shops which we visited or passed we saw them standing in front of or in the hallways of the building through all the hours of the afternoon from two to five.

• • •

As to the outcome of the strike, it is impossible to express any opinion of value. Both sides claim that they will win. On the one hand the strikers declare, and so far as we are able to judge, fairly correctly, that whereas before the strike less than five per cent of the workers were members of the union, now some seventy to eighty per cent are enrolled; that of the 30,000 workers who at different times in the past twenty weeks have been on strike, some twenty-three to twenty-five thousand have been taken back to work on their own terms, including recognition of the Union, leaving only about 5,000 still out on strike.

On the other hand the manufacturers declare that they have got from sixty to seventy-five per cent of the workers that they need; that their shops are all running, and they are able to take care of all the work that they have. They point with pride to the fact that whereas before the strike there was no combination or organization of manufacturers, now some 160 to 170 firms "controlling two-thirds of the cream of the shirtwaist business" are united in an association to work together both in peace

(continued)

and in war. They express themselves as willing to grant all the demands of the strikers, as to wages, shop conditions, holidays, and to a certain extent the inside contractor system and proportional employment distributed over the whole year.

• • •

It would certainly seem as if a community whose opportunities, whose prosperity and whose laws have permitted the building up in so short a time of these large and remunerative businesses, by those who have sought refuge here from other and less favorable conditions, should have some voice in the distribution of their profits and a right to decide whether their real earners have been fairly paid and so treated as to promote the public health and the general weal. It certainly strikes strangely upon the ear to hear denounced in broken English as "un-American," "un-democratic," "despotic," any attempts to "interfere in my business," or "between me and my employes," by any public authority or any organization permitted to exist by the laws of the land. Such an attitude is only a belated echo of the defiance of the slave-owners or of the head of the family in the days when he had power of life and death over his wife and children against anyone who attempted to interfere between him and his chattels. It would appear to the unprejudiced observer as if the worker had just as much right to bargain collectively as the employer had, and that any manufacturer who absolutely declines to deal on any terms with an organization of his employes, large or small, is out of place and out of date here in this twentieth century.

An "Ally" Views the Strike

Helen Marot, author of this "appreciation," was secretary of the Women's Trade Union League of New York. When the strike began, she and other league members volunteered their services to the union. Marot helped organize the strike headquarters in Clinton Hall on the Lower East Side. She oversaw the process of enrolling new members in the union, helped administer the payment of benefits to strikers, and organized much of the picketing. So central was her participation that a number of upper- and middle-class women saw Marot as the real leader of the strike. Rheta Childe Dorr, for example, commented that, after the crowd at Cooper Union stood up and took the "old Jewish oath," "Clara Lemlich's part in the work was accomplished. . . . The Women's Trade Union League, under the direction of Miss Helen Marot, secretary, at once took hold of the strike."[1] Marot made no such claim. Although she acknowledged the importance of "the wide range of sympathy which it drew from women outside the ranks of labor" even as she deplored the "sensational snobbery" of the press accounts that highlighted the role played by "society ladies," her account stressed the qualities of the strikers themselves and of the members of the union's executive committee. She also emphasized the importance of gender and

---

[1] Rheta Childe Dorr, *What Eight Million Women Want* (Boston: Small, Maynard & Co., 1910), 170–171. See also her "Battle between Manufacturers and Women Workers," *Hampton's Magazine* 24 (March 1910): 424.

ethnicity. Given that the league would soon find itself divided over the issue of whether to continue to fund organizing efforts among immigrant women or instead to concentrate upon those born in the United States, and given that historians would struggle to understand why the coalition that came together to support the strike did not last, her not altogether complimentary comments about the "Russian [Jewish] element" in the union are particularly interesting. Rheta Chide Dorr to the contrary notwithstanding, the real question was not whether the Clara Lemlichs would step aside and let the Helen Marots lead the way but whether the Helen Marots, Anne Morgans, and Mrs. Belmonts could accept the determination of the Clara Lemlichs, Rose Perrs, and Rose Schneidermans to control their own destinies.[2]

---

[2] The WTUL and the leaders of the International Ladies Garment Workers Union soon found themselves at odds over the future of the union. Union officials, although continuing to express gratitude for the WTUL's assistance during the strike, did not wish to consult with the league over future strategy. Instead they insisted on their right to make their own decisions. The WTUL leaders saw this as worse than ungrateful. They saw it as unwise. They came to view the union leadership as high-handed and unrepresentative of the rank and file. Marot indicted them as manipulative and despotic—characteristics she attributed to their Russian Jewish heritage—in "Revolution and the Garment Trade," *The Masses* (August 1916): 29.

A WOMAN'S STRIKE—AN APPRECIATION OF THE SHIRTWAIST MAKERS OF NEW YORK

BY HELEN MAROT

Women's Trade Union League, New York City.

The usual object of monographs on strikes which appear in economic journals is to state impartially both sides of the controversy, so that students and a public more or less remote from labor struggles may estimate their merits.

• • •

The present article does not attempt to estimate either the moral or the economic factors in the recent shirtwaist-makers' strike of New York, but to lay before the reader some of those motive forces which may be counted upon in strikes

Helen Marot, "A Woman's Strike—An Appreciation of the Shirt-waist Makers of New York," *Proceedings of the Academy of Political Science of the City of New York* 1 (October 1910), 119-28.

composed of like elements, especially in strikes of women in unorganized trades.

The shirtwaist-makers' "general strike," as it is called, followed an eleven years' attempt to organize the trade. The union had been unable during this time to affect to any appreciable extent the conditions of work. In its efforts during 1908-9 to maintain the union in the various shops and to prevent the discharge of members who were active union workers, it lost heavily. The effort resolved itself in 1909 into the establishment of the right to organize. The strike in the Triangle Waist Company turned on this issue.

(continued)

The story of the events leading up to the Triangle strike as told by a leading member of the firm partially agrees with the story told by the strikers. The company had undertaken to organize its employes into a club, with benefits attached. The good faith of the company as well as the working-out of the benefit was questioned by the workers. The scheme failed and the workers joined the waistmakers' union. One day without warning a few weeks later one hundred and fifty of the employes were dropped, the explanation being given by the employers that there was no work. The following day the company advertised for workers. In telling the story later they said that they had received an unexpected order, but admitted their refusal to re-employ the workers discharged the day previous. The union then declared a strike, or acknowledged a lockout, and picketing began.

The strike or lockout occurred out of the busy season, with a large supply at hand of workers unorganized and unemployed. Practical trade unionists believed that the manufacturers felt certain of success on account of their ability to draw to an unlimited extent from an unorganized labor market and to employ a guard sufficiently strong to prevent the strikers from reaching the workers with their appeals to join them. But the ninety girls and sixty men strikers were not practical; they were Russian Jews who saw in the lockout an attempt at oppression. In their resistance, which was instinctive, they did not count their chances of winning; they felt that they had been wronged and they rebelled. This quick resentment is characteristic of the Russian Jewish factory worker. The men strikers were intimidated and lost heart, but the women carried on the picketing, suffering arrest and abuse from the police and the guards employed by the manufacturers. At the end of the third week they appealed to the women's trade union league to protect them, if they could, against false arrest.

The league is organized to promote trade unions among women, and its membership is composed of people of leisure as well as of workers. A brief inspection by the league of the action of the pickets, the police, the strike breakers and the workers in the factory showed that the pickets had been intimidated, that the attitude of the police was aggressive and that the guards employed by the firm were insolent. The league acted as complainant at police headquarters and cross-examined the arrested strikers; it served as witness for the strikers in the magistrates' court and became convinced of official prejudice in the police department against the strikers and a strong partisan attitude in favor of the manufacturers. The activity and interest of women, some of whom were plainly women of leisure, was curiously disconcerting to the manufacturers and every effort was used to divert them. At last a young woman prominent in public affairs in New York and a member of the league, was arrested while acting as volunteer picket. Here at last was "copy" for the press.

During the five weeks of the strike, previous to the publicity, the forty thousand waist makers employed in the several hundred shops in New York were with a few exceptions here and there unconscious of the struggle of their fellow workers in the Triangle. There was no means of communication among them, as the labor press reached comparatively few. In the weeks before the general strike was called the forty thousand shirtwaist makers were forty thousand separate individuals. So far were they from being conscious of their similarity that they might have been as many individual workers employed in ways as widely separated as people of different trades, or as members of different social groups.

The arrests of sympathizers aroused sufficient public interest for the press to continue the story for ten days, including in the reports the treatment of the strikers. This furnished the union its opportunity. It knew the temper of the workers and pushed the story still further through shop propaganda. After three weeks of newspaper publicity and shop propaganda the reports came back to the union that the workers were aroused. It was alarming to the friends of the union to see the confidence of the union officers before issuing the call to strike. Trade unionists reminded the officers that the history of general strikers in unorganized trades was the history of failure. They invariably answered with a smile of assurance, "Wait and see."

The call was issued Monday night, November 22nd, at a great mass meeting in Cooper Union addressed by the president of the American Federation of Labor. "I did not go to bed Monday night," said the secretary of the union, "our Executive Board was in session from midnight until six a.m. I left the meeting and went out to Broadway near Bleecker street. I shall never again see such a sight. Out of every shirtwaist factory, in answer to the call, the workers poured and the halls which had been engaged for them were quickly filled." In some of these halls the girls were buoyant, confident; in others there were girls who were frightened at what they had done. When the latter were asked why they had come out in sympathy, they said, "How could you help it when a girl in your shop gets up and says, 'Come girls, come, all the shirtwaist makers are going out'?"

(continued)

As nearly as can be estimated, thirty thousand workers answered the call, or seventy-five per cent of the trade. Of these six thousand were Russian men; two thousand Italian women; possibly one thousand American women and about twenty or twenty-one thousand Russian Jewish girls. The Italians throughout the strike were a constantly appearing and disappearing factor but the part played by the American girls was clearly defined.

The American girls who struck came out in sympathy for the "foreigners" who struck for a principle, but the former were not in sympathy with the principle; they did not want a union; they imagined that the conditions in the factories where the Russian and Italian girls worked were worse than their own. They are in the habit of thinking that the employers treat foreign girls with less consideration, and they are sorry for them. In striking they were self-conscious philanthropists. They were honestly disinterested and as genuinely sympathetic as were the women of leisure who later took an active part in helping the strike. They acknowledged no interests in common with the others, but if necessary they were prepared to sacrifice a week or two of work. Unfortunately the sacrifice required of them was greater than they had counted on. The "foreigners" regarded them as just fellow workers and insisted on their joining the union, in spite of their constant protestation, "We have no grievance; we only struck in sympathy." But the Russians failed to be grateful, took for granted a common cause and demanded that all shirtwaist makers, regardless of race or creed, continue the strike until they were recognized by the employers as a part of the union. This difference in attitude and understanding was a heavy strain on the generosity of the American girls. It is believed, however, that the latter would have been equal to what their fellow workers expected, if their meetings had been left to the guidance of American men and women who understood their prejudices. But the Russian men trusted no one entirely to impart the enthusiasm necessary for the cause. It was the daily, almost hourly, tutelage which the Russian men insisted on the American girls' accepting, rather than the prolongation of the strike beyond the time they had expected, that sent the American girls back as "scabs." There were several signs that the two or three weeks' experience as strikers was having its effect on them, and that with proper care this difficult group of workers might have been organized. For instance, "scab" had become an opprobious term to them during their short strike period, and on returning to work they accepted the epithet from their fellow workers with great

reluctance and even protestation. Their sense of superiority also had received a severe shock; they could never again be quite so confident that they did not in the nature of things belong to the labor group.

If the shirtwaist trade in New York had been dominated by any other nationality than the Russian, it is possible that other methods of organizing the trade would have been adopted rather than the general strike. The Russian workers who fill New York factories are ever ready to rebel against suggestion of oppression and are of all people the most responsive to an idea to which is attached an ideal. The union officers understood this and it was because they understood the Russian element in the trade that they answered, "Wait and see," when their friends urged caution before calling a general strike in an unorganized trade. They knew their people and others did not.

The feature of the strike which was as noteworthy as the response of thirty thousand unorganized workers, was the unyielding and uncompromising temper of the strikers. This was due not to the influence of nationality, but to the dominant sex. The same temper displayed in the shirtwaist strike is found in other strikes of women, until we have now a trade-union truism, that "women make the best strikers." Women's economic position furnishes two reasons for their being the best strikers; one is their less permanent attitude toward their trade, and the other their lighter financial burdens. While these economic factors help to make women good strikers, the genius for sacrifice and the ability to sustain, over prolonged periods, response to emotional appeals are also important causes. Working women have been less ready than men to make the initial sacrifice that trade-union membership calls for, but when they reach the point of striking they give themselves as fully and as instinctively to the cause as they give themselves in their personal relationships. It is important, therefore, in following the action of the shirtwaist makers, to remember that eighty per cent were women, and women without trade-union experience.

When the shirtwaist strikers were gathered in separate groups, according to their factories, in almost every available hall on the East Side, the great majority of them received their first instruction in the principles of unionism and learned the necessity of organization in their own trade. The quick response of women to the new doctrine gave to the meetings a spirit of revival. Like new converts they accepted the new doctrine in its entirety and insisted to the last on the "closed shop." But is was not only the enthusiasm

(continued)

of new converts which made them refuse to accept anything short of the closed shop. In embracing the idea of solidarity they realized their own weakness as individual bargainers. "How long," the one-week or two-weeks-old union girls said, "do you think we could keep what the employer says he will give us without the union? Just as soon as the busy season is over it would be the same as before."

Instructions were given to each separate group of strikers to make out a wage scale if they thought they should be paid an increase, or to make out other specific demands before conferring with their employers on terms of settlement. The uniform contract drawn up by the union, beside requiring a union shop, required also the abolition of the sub-contract system; payment of wages once a week; a fifty-two-hour week; limitation of overtime in any one day to two hours and to not later than 9 p.m.; also payment for all material and implements by employers. Important as were the specific demands, they were lightly regarded in comparison with the issue of a union shop.

Nothing can illustrate this better than the strikers' treatment of the arbitration proposal which was the outcome of a conference between their representatives and the employers. In December word came to the union secretary that the manufacturers would probably consider arbitration if the union was ready to submit its differences to a board. The officers made reply in the affirmative and communicated their action at once to the strikers. Many of the strikers had no idea what arbitration meant, but as it became clear to them they asked, some of them menacingly, "Do you mean to arbitrate the recognition of the union?" It took courage to answer these inexperienced unionists and uncompromising girls that arbitration would include the question of the union as well as other matters. The proposition was met with a storm of opposition. When the strikers at last discovered that all their representatives counseled arbitration, with great reluctance they gave way, but at no time was the body of strikers in favor of it. A few days later, when the arbitrators who represented them reported that the manufacturers on their side refused to arbitrate the question of the union, they resumed their strike with an apparent feeling of security and relief. Again later they showed the same uncompromising attitude when their representatives in the conference reported back that the manufacturers would concede important points in regard to wage and factory conditions, but would not recognize the union. The recommendations of the conference were rejected without reservation by the whole body.

The strikers at this time lost some of their sympathizers. An uncompromising attitude is good trade-union tactics up to a certain point, but the shirtwaist makers were violating all traditions. Their refusal to accept anything short of the closed shop indicated to many a state of mind which was as irresponsible as it was reckless. Their position may have been reckless, but it was not irresponsible. Their sometime sympathizers did not realize the endurance of the women or the force of their enthusiasm, but insisted on the twenty to thirty thousand raw recruits becoming sophisticated unionists in thirteen short weeks.

It was after the new year that the endurance of the girls was put to the test. During the thirteen weeks benefits were paid out averaging less than $2 for each striker. Many of them refused to accept benefits, so that the married men could be paid more. The complaints of hardships came almost without exception from the men. Occasionally it was discovered that a girl was having one meal a day and even at times none at all.

In spite of being underfed and often thinly clad, the girls took upon themselves the duty of picketing, believing that the men would be more severely handled. Picketing is a physical and nervous strain under the best conditions, but it is the spirit of martyrdom that sends young girls of their own volition, often insufficiently clad and fed, to patrol the streets in mid-winter with the temperature low and with snow on the ground, some days freezing and some days melting. After two or three hours of such exposure, often ill from cold, they returned to headquarters, which were held for the majority in rooms dark and unheated, to await further orders.

It takes uncommon courage to endure such physical exposure, but these striking girls underwent as well the nervous strain of imminent arrest, the harsh treatment of the police, insults, threats and even actual assaults from the rough men who stood around the factory doors. During the thirteen weeks over six hundred girls were arrested; thirteen were sentenced to five days in the workhouse and several were detained a week or ten days in the Tombs.

The pickets, with strangely few exceptions, during the first few weeks showed remarkable self-control. They had been cautioned from the first hour of the strike to insist on their legal rights as pickets, but to give no excuse for arrest. Like all other instructions, they accepted this literally. They desired to be good soldiers and every nerve was strained to obey orders. But for many the provocations were too great and retaliation began after the fifth week. It occurred around the

(continued)

factories where the strikers were losing, where peace methods were failing and where the passivity of the pickets was taunted as cowardice. But curiously enough, during this time the arrests in proportion to the number still on strike were fewer than during the earlier period and the sentences in the courts were lighter. The change in the treatment of pickets came with the change in the city administration. Apparently, peaceful picketing during the first two months of the strike had been treated as an unlawful act.

The difficulty throughout the strike of inducing the strikers to accept compromise measures increased as the weeks wore on. However, seventeen contracts were signed in these latter weeks which did not give the union a voice in determining conditions of work of all workers in the factory. During the ten weeks previous, contracts were signed which covered all the workers in three hundred and twelve factories. Before the strike every shop was "open" and in most of them there was not a union worker. In thirteen short weeks three hundred and twelve shops had been converted into "closed" or full union contract shops.

But the significance of the strike is not in the actual gain to the shirtwaist makers of three hundred union shops, for there was great weakness in the ranks of the opposition. Trade-union gains, moreover, are measured by what an organization can hold rather than by what it can immediately gain. The shirt-waist makers' strike was characteristic of all strikes in which women play an active part. It was marked by complete self-surrender to a cause, emotional endurance, fearlessness and entire willingness to face danger and suffering. The strike at times seemed to be an expression of the woman's movement rather than the labor movement. This phase was emphasized by the wide expression of sympathy which it drew from women outside the ranks of labor.

It was fortunate for strike purposes but otherwise unfortunate that the press, in publishing accounts of the strike, treated the active public expression of interest of a large body of women sympathizers with sensational snobbery. It was a matter of wide public comment that women of wealth should contribute sums of money to the strike, that they should admit factory girls to exclusive club rooms, and should hold mass meetings in their behalf. If, as was charged, any of the women who entered the strike did so from sensational or personal motives, they were disarmed when they came into contact with the strikers. Their earnestness of purpose, their complete abandon to their cause, their simple acceptance of outside interest and sympathy as though their cause were the cause of all, was a bid for kinship that broke down all barriers. Women who came to act as witnesses of the arrests around the factories ended by picketing side by side with the strikers. These volunteer pickets accepted, moreover, whatever rough treatment was offered, and when arrested, asked for no favors that were not given the strikers themselves.

The strike brought about adjustments in values as well as in relationships. Before the strike was over federations of professional women and women of leisure were endorsing organization for working women, and individually these women were acknowledging the truth of such observations as that made by one of the strikers on her return from a visit to a private school where she had been invited to tell about the strike. Her story of the strike led to questions in regard to trade unions. On her return her comment was, "Oh they are lovely girls, they are so kind—but I didn't believe any girls could be so ignorant."

The strike was an awakening for working women in many industries, and it did more to give the women of the professions and the women of leisure a new point of view and a realization of the necessity for organization among working women than any other single event in the history of the labor movement in this country.

The Triangle Fire

John Sloan, one of the most influential American artists of the first half of the twentieth century, drew the untitled cartoon about the Triangle fire for the *New York Call*, the city's socialist newspaper. Sloan kept a diary at the time.[1] On March 25, 1911, he wrote: "Over one hundred and forty shirtwaist workers were burned to death in the Triangle Factory. These girls made the successful strike of the last year! This is a sort of holocaustic celebration in honor of the fact that the Supreme Court of N.Y. yesterday declared the employers Liability Act of last session unconstitutional. It wasn't much of an act but it was a move in the right direction!" On the 26th he added: "After breakfast I got at a cartoon idea in regards to the frightful fire of last evening in the Triangle Shirtwaist Factory. A black triangle each side marked ('Rents,' 'Interest,' 'Profit') death on one side, a fat capitalist on the other and the charred body of a girl in the center." The entry for September 21, 1909, gives a fair view of Sloan's political sympathies at this time: "Went out proposing to vote at the primaries but found I was enrolled as a Democrat—so did not ratify the Socialist ticket. 'Might as well vote Democratic!' said the lame man in charge, 'no thanks, Socialist or nothing,' my reply."

In New York City, where space was always at a premium, real estate developers sought to increase the value of their holdings by building taller and taller structures. The Asch Building, home to the Triangle Shirtwaist Factory, was one of the new high-rises that shot up

---

[1] Published as *John Sloan's New York Scene* from diaries, notes and correspondence, 1906–1913, edited by Bruce St. John (New York: Harper & Row, 1965).

CORNER OF THE WORK-ROOM ON THE NINTH FLOOR OF THE
THESE WINDOWS THAT MANY OF THE GIRLS JUMPED
UNTIL THEIR CLOTHING WAS ON FIRE

RENT PROFIT INTEREST

THE HERO OF THE FACTORY FIRE
"His Heart was True to Pol"

WATER-TOWER EXTENDED TO ITS FULL HEIGHT, PLAYING ON THE ASCH BUILDING, WAT
CAN FIGHT FIRE SUCCESSFULLY ONLY AS HIGH AS THE SEVENTH STORY
WATER REACHED THE EIGHTH AND NINTH FLOORS IT WAS

around the turn of the century. As one can see in this photograph from the September 1911 issue of *McClure's*, firefighting equipment did not keep pace. Ladders did not reach to the upper stories, and New York's "water towers" could effectively shoot water only up to the seventh floor.

Catastrophic fires were supposed to be impossible in modern factory buildings like the Asch. Such buildings were "fireproof." And, in fact, the Triangle fire did little structural damage to the building. What burned were the cotton textiles, the wooden tables and floors saturated with oil from the sewing machines, and the hair and clothing of the workers. The photograph, taken several days after the fire, shows a portion of the ninth-floor-interior, including the windows from which many of the victims jumped. The *McClure's* caption noted that "few jumped until their clothing was on fire," a detail John Sloan incorporated in his 1911 cartoon as well as in this 1913 drawing for *The Masses*, the leading radical magazine of the day.

Arthur E. McFarlane's muckraking article, "The Triangle Fire—The Story of a 'Rotten Risk,'" in *Collier's* of May 17, 1913 may have inspired the cartoon, "This heart was true to Pol." McFarlane reported that Triangle's owners collected some $200,000 in insurance compensation for losses in the fire, "more than $70,000 in excess of any claim for which they could furnish a legal or convincing proof of loss." In stark contrast to his pitiable Triangle victims, Sloan drew *Pol* as a voluptuary with money bags for breasts. And he again portrayed her rescuer as a bloated plutocrat. Max Blanck and Isaac Harris, however, were quite ordinary in appearance, as the photograph from the September 1911 issue of *McClure's* makes evident.

CHRONOLOGY OF THE FIRE

1911

January —: Fire in Newark, New Jersey, muslin underwear factory; eight "girls" jumped to their deaths from fourth story.

March 22–24: Owners of warehouses and other business properties below 14th Street in Manhattan formed association to fight Fire Commissioner Waldo's order requiring the installation of automatic sprinklers.

March 25: Fire in Asch Building kills more than 140 workers, most young women, in Triangle Shirtwaist Company factory.

March 26: Eighty-six bodies identified; Red Cross organized fund to aid survivors and families; clergymen held memorial services, preached on disaster.

March 27: Death toll at 142; District Attorney Whitman opened investigation; other government agencies began probes; twenty-seven more victims identified.

March 28: Women's Trade Union League conducted inquiry into working conditions in factories—more than one thousand workers gave secret testimony; ten more victims identified; Local 25 announced funeral march for unidentified victims; bill introduced in legislature calling for investigation of fire.

March 29: Two thousand jammed memorial meeting of Local 25; WTUL and ILGWU in dispute on organization of march to Mount Zion Cemetery for burial of unknowns; three more bodies identified.

March 30: The 143rd victim died; Mayor Gaynor ordered city to bury unidentified victims to end dispute between ILGWU and WTUL.

March 31: Three more bodies recovered at scene; contributions to relief fund over $65,000; Collegiate Equal Suffrage League held mass meeting to protest dangerous factory conditions.

April 1: Three more bodies identified.

April 2: Meeting at Metropolitan Opera House; speakers called for creation of state commission to design fire protection laws; Rose Schneiderman told overflow crowd that workers had tested the public's goodwill and found it wanting.

April 4: Additional victim identified.

April 5: More than 120,000 marched in silent funeral parade for unidentified; march led by WTUL and ILGWU officials; relief fund over $80,000.

April 7: The 144th victim died; District Attorney Whitman presented case to grand jury.

April 11: Triangle co-owners Harris and Blanck indicted for manslaughter.

April 17: Coroner's jury found Harris and Blanck responsible for death of fire victim because of failure to leave door unlocked.

April 26: Mass for Triangle victims at Madonna di Pompeii Roman Catholic Church in Manhattan.

October 10: New York State Factory Investigating Commission hearings opened, chaired by state Senate President Wagner and Assembly Speaker Smith.

October 17: Harris and Blanck sued Royal Insurance Company over nonpayment of fire claim.

November 3: Harris and Blanck pled not guilty to seven manslaughter indictments; A. Rosen, rescued from Triangle fire, burned to death in fire at home in Pittsburgh.

November 10: New York City fire department successfully tested new high-pressure hoses.

November 13: Triangle fire survivors marched through Lower East Side to protest dangerous conditions in factories.

December 5: Three hundred women attacked Harris and Blanck as the two men entered court on first day of trial; called them "murderers!"

December 6: Harris and Blanck given police protection; prosecution opened.

December 27: Harris and Blanck found not guilty; smuggled out of court under police guard as crowd hissed verdict.

1912

February 1: At mass meeting WTUL and Mrs. O. H. P. Belmont called for second trial of Harris and Blanck on remaining manslaughter indictments.

March 25: Relatives and friends of victims held memorial service on anniversary of fire.

March 27: New York State Superior Court dismissed remaining indictments against Harris and Blanck on ground that first trial covered alleged conduct and new trial would constitute double jeopardy.

1913

February 8: Bills to improve factory safety introduced in New York State legislature.

April 4: Governor Sulzer signed factory safety bills.

May 10: Sulzer signed four more factory safety bills.

July 31: Bureau of Fire Prevention cited Asch Building for violations.

August 2: Factory Investigating Commission issued fire safety recommendations.

December 1: Triangle Shirtwaist Company fined for violations of labor law.

1914

March 11: Claims against owner of building in Triangle fire settled for $75 per victim.

March 28: Additional factory protection legislation passed.

June 30: Governor Glynn accepted protests of real estate owners; blocked additional changes in factory laws.

THE FIRE AND ITS IMMEDIATE AFTERMATH

"The Washington Place Fire"

In keeping with editor-publisher Hamilton Holt's long-standing interest in the stories of "undistinguished Americans," *The Independent* interviewed one of the Triangle workers "shortly after the disastrous fire." In the course of it Rosey Safran, a young Jewish immigrant from Galicia in what was then the Austro-Hungarian Empire, told of her almost miraculous escape. She also attempted to describe what it was like to stand outside the Asch Building watching her co-workers jump. Safran had played an active role in the great shirtwaist strike of the year before, and, like many others, she saw a direct connection between the outcome of the strike and the fire.

Holt noted in an editor's note that Triangle co-owners Isaac Harris and Max Blanck had been indicted on manslaughter charges and were awaiting trial when this article appeared. The indictment alleged that they knowingly kept one of the two doors on each floor locked to prevent workers from stealing material. Fire laws required all doors to be unlocked during working hours. Noncompliance was a misdemeanor. But, and this was the key to the prosecution's case, if someone died as a result of the commission of a misdemeanor, the person committing it was guilty of manslaughter. As a result, much of the testimony at the trial would turn on whether the doors were locked, on whether Harris and Blanck knew whether or not they were locked, and on whether any specific individual died because the door was locked. Safran's story, published eight months before the trial, supported key points of the prosecution's case.

THE WASHINGTON PLACE FIRE

BY ROSEY SAFRAN

I, with a number of other girls, was in the dressing room on the eighth floor of the Asch Building, in Washington place, at 4.40 o'clock on the afternoon of Saturday, March 25, when I heard somebody cry "Fire!" I left everything and ran for the door on the Washington place side. The door was locked and immediately there was a great jam of girls before it. The fire was on the other side, driving us away from the only door that the bosses had left open for us to use in going in or out. They had the doors locked all the time for fear that some of the girls might steal something. At the one open door there was always a watchman who could see if any one carried out a bundle or if there was a suspicious lump in any one's clothing.

The fire had started on our floor and quick as I had been in getting to the Washington place door the flames were already blazing fiercely and spreading fast. If we couldn't get out we would all be roasted alive. The locked door that blocked us was half of wood; the upper half was thick glass. Some girls were screaming, some were beating the door with their fists, some were trying to tear it open. There were seven hundred of us girls employed by the Triangle Waist Company, which had three floors, the eighth, ninth and tenth, in the Asch Building. On our floor alone were two hundred and thirty. Most of us were crazy with fear and there was great confusion. Some one broke out the glass part of the door with something hard and heavy—I suppose the head of a machine—and I climbed or was pulled thru the broken glass and ran downstairs to the sixth floor, where some one took me down to the street.

I got out to the street and watched the upper floors burning, and the girls hanging by their hands and then dropping as the fire reached up to them. There they were dead on the sidewalk. It was an awful, awful sight, especially to me who had so many friends among the girls and young men who were being roasted alive or dashed to death. I can't describe how I felt as I stood there watching. I could see the figures, but not the faces—the police kept us all too far back. We hoped that the fire nets would save some, but they were no good for persons falling so far. One girl broke thru the thick glass in the sidewalk and fell

Rosey Safran, "The Washington Place Fire," *The Independent* 70 (April 20, 1911), 840–41.

(continued)

down into a cellar. That shows with what force they came down from the ninth floor.

One girl jumped from the ninth floor and her clothing caught on a hook that stuck out from the wall on the eighth. The fire burned thru her clothing and she fell to the sidewalk and was killed. Another girl fell from the eighth to the sixth floor, when a hook supporting a sign caught her clothes and held her. She smashed the window of the sixth floor with her fist and got in the shop and went down to the street, saving herself. One of my friends, Annie Rosen, was an examiner on the ninth floor. She was near a window when the cry of fire was raised. She tried to open the window to get out. It stuck, but she got it open and climbed on a little fire escape. The fire was coming up from the eighth floor and in getting from the ninth to the eighth her hat and her hair were burned. She doesn't know how she got to the eighth; maybe she fell. She was going to jump to the ground, but the people who were watching her from the street shouted not to do it, and somehow she got thru the flames. She fell from the eighth to the sixth floor on the fire escape and then she was carried down to the street and taken to Bellevue Hospital, where there were many of her companions. She is out now, but pale as a ghost; she does not think that she will ever be strong again. She has lost her nerve and is afraid all the time.

I was on the street with other girls watching. We were screaming for about twenty minutes and then some one took me home. I don't know who it was. Afterward I went to the Morgue and saw my friends there, Ida Jacobowski, Rosey Sorkin, Bennie Sklawer, Jacob Klein, Sam Lehrer and others.

• • •

I was in the great shirtwaist strike that lasted thirteen weeks. I was one of the pickets and was arrested and fined several times. The union paid my fines. Our bosses won and we went back to the Triangle Waist Company as an open shop having nothing to do with the union. But we strikers who were taken back stayed in the union, for it is our friend. If the union had had its way we would have been safe in spite of the fire, for two of the union's demands were adequate fire escapes on factory buildings and open doors giving free access from factories to the street. The bosses defeated us and we didn't get the open doors or the large fire escapes, and so our friends are dead and relatives are tearing their hair.

• • •

I averaged about $14 a week. I worked overtime at that. Sometimes I made $18 a week. That is the most earned by the smartest girl and that means working from 7.30 in the morning till 9 o'clock at night and Sundays too.

I learned to operate a machine in Chlebowice, Galicia, Austria, where I was born. Chlebowice is a little country village. I came to this country three years ago, and for the last two and a half years till the date of the fire I worked for the Triangle Waist Company. The wages were not so bad, tho many of the girls only made $6 and $8 a week, but they should have had some regard for our lives.

"Partners' Account of the Disaster"
New York Times, March 26, 1911

Max Blanck and Isaac Harris, co-owners of the Triangle Shirtwaist Company, were among those who survived the fire. They told their story that same evening to a *Times* reporter. The fact that the interview occurred so soon after the event makes it an important document, particularly because Blanck and Harris soon found themselves the targets of a grand jury probe into the fire and then defendants in the ensuing manslaughter trial. As a result, this turned out to be the only occasion on which they discussed the disaster without the advice of their attorney, Max D. Steuer. Blanck, according to the reporter, was still badly shaken by the ordeal and "told his story in disconnected sentences."

Harris, although injured in the fire, was more composed and "most interested in explaining the precautions which the partners had taken to avoid just what had happened." For his part Blanck, perhaps with some prodding from his partner, insisted that "the doors into the hallways were always unlocked."

However calculated to head off liability for the disaster some of their answers may have been, their account makes clear that several of their employees owed their lives to the quick thinking and level-headedness of the partners. This fact was quickly lost sight of in the rush to determine who was to blame for the fire. Historians have also tended to ignore it. Yet, whatever their responsibility for the conditions that led to the fire and for the locked doors that allegedly cost some workers their lives, Isaac Harris and, to a lesser extent, Max Blanck behaved like heroes that Saturday afternoon.

PARTNERS' ACCOUNT OF THE DISASTER

Blanck and Harris Tell of Their Escape in the Maddened Throng of Employes.

Children of One There

Max Blanck went to the home of his partner, Isaac Harris, at 324 West 101st Street, last night, and there told his story of what happened.

Two of his six children and their governess had come to visit him at the factory yesterday afternoon, and he was so shaken with the terror of the moments when it looked as if he and they would share the fate of the screaming hundreds he knew were perishing on the lower floors that it was only a fragmentary account he could give of the minutes before he and the children found their way to safety.

Mr. Blanck is an average type of the successful business man—short, stocky, and unemotional; but he sat in the reception room of his partner's home last night barely able to hold himself together while he answered questions. His partner, Harris, with his right hand bandaged from injuries received while he was helping some of his employes to safety, paced the room and occasionally interjected facts.

Mr. Blanck's six children are all under 13 years of age. His wife and four of the children went to Florida for their health some weeks ago. Yesterday Henrietta, the oldest, and Mildred, 5 years old, went with their French governess, Mlle. Ehresmann, to their father's office, and were waiting to accompany him home when the fire began. Mr. Blanck said that he was waiting for a taxicab when he heard first a rumble of voices, and then shrill screams, which seemed to come from the street.

Panic Soon Began.

He ran to the front windows, looked out, and saw upturned faces through a haze of smoke drifting out from the second floor below. He threw open the door to the front stairway and met one of his employes running up yelling, "Fire!" His voice was almost drowned in a roar from the hundreds of girls and men, who were already beginning to pile into the stairway.

"Partners' Account of the Disaster," *New York Times*, March 26, 1911. Reprinted by permission.

(continued)

Fearing that it would not be possible to take his children out that way, Mr. Blanck ran for the rear, but as soon as the rear doors to the stairway were opened the rush of heat and smoke drove back the throng of thirty bookkeepers, clerks, and operators who shared the tenth floor with the offices of the partners. It was then that the first elevator which had answered the frantic pushing of the tenth floor button appeared at that level.

Mr. Blanck had marshaled his children and the governess in the private office, and he and his partner were endeavoring to get the panic-stricken operators into some order. They had separated the men and women, and with the help of the bookkeepers managed to squeeze about ten women into the passenger elevator and get the door closed.

The elevator never came up again as far as Mr. Blanck could tell last night. The smoke and heat were becoming suffocating on the tenth floor by that time, and Mr. Blanck turned to his office, to find his two children and the governess out on the window sill.

He was about to join them when he heard the voice of his partner Harris shouting from the rear.

"The roof! Follow me to the roof!"

Blanck and the office force who were gathered in the private office with the children and the governess groped their way north through the smoke-filled sample room to a stairway boxed off near the centre of the building. The door was open and Harris had gone through pushing a group of the frightened operators before him.

Guarded His Children.

Blanck kept his children out of the crush and sent the remaining office force and clerks up a stairway before he went himself. A salesman, E. T. Tischner, who was about to start on a trip and had come to the office to pack his sample cases was in a state of collapse from panic and Blanck and his bookkeeper stopped to help him up the stairway. The smoke and heat were so great behind them that it seemed the fire had finally burst into the tenth floor.

On the roof Harris took the lead and marshaled the women, pushing them toward the northeast corner of the building, where it joins a factory building at Wooster Street and Waverly Place. This building adjoins the rear of the Triangle Waist Company's factory for only about one-quarter of its length. The rest of the way to the westward the two buildings are separated from each other by a narrow well, for part of its length, only ten feet wide. This was spouting flames and embers, which rained on the roof, and swirling eddies of hot gases added to the peril.

* * *

Harris, who is a small man, and frail, as were most of his male operators and bookkeepers, had great difficulty in getting the women out. The two daughters of his partner and the governess had been passed to safety, but the remaining forty or fifty operators and girls were running wildly about in the smoke, and for a few minutes it seemed as if some would jump to the street.

Some of the men had managed to clamber up on the roof of the American Book Company, which joins the Triangle Waist factory building on the west side of Washington Place, and extends along the block front of East Washington Place. This building houses on its upper floors the law department of New York University and is amply equipped with fire apparatus.

Ladders were let down from its roof to the roof of the Triangle Waist Building and many of the girls and men were carried up. It was about fifteen feet higher, and the ladders were crowded with fighting, jostling girls and men, who most of the time were showered with sparks and choked with hot gases, but it is believed all escaped. . . .

Blanck told his story in disconnected sentences, chiefly in response to questions and was hazy as to who had escaped with him, except his children and their governess. He remembered that his niece, Esther Harris, 18 years old, a bookkeeper on the ninth floor, had been badly burned, and sent to one of the hospitals, but was not sure how she escaped.

. . . He remembered, too, that a shipping clerk named Smith had been one of those who got up to the roof, but in his state of nervous collapse could not name any others of the eighty who were waiting for the machinery to stop when the fire began.

Harris, who was pacing up and down with his wife during most of the interview, nursing his injured hand, told something of the escape, but was most interested in explaining the precautions which the partners had taken to avoid just what had happened.

Harris Led Them to the Roof.

He had nothing to say of his own part in leading his partner and the rest to the roof stairway which had at first been forgotten, and it was only when he was questioned that he remembered that he had cut his hand breaking in the skylight of the Waverly Place Building.

He said that when he and Smith climbed up the eight-foot separating wall and saw that the last of those waiting below had been pulled to safety they found the doorway leading into the Waverly Place factory building locked. There was a

(continued)

big skylight close at hand, and while Smith kicked frantically at the locked door he beat on the skylight with his fists. His right hand crashed through and was severely cut. Through the jagged hole he and the girls screamed for help and eventually those inside opened the door and led downstairs those who were on the roof half choked with smoke.

Blanck was asked what precautions he had taken about fire and what were the means of escape. He said the Building Department and factory Inspectors had all passed his lofts, and the only requirements in recent years had been certain guards ordered by the Building Department on the machines on the eighth and ninth floors, and an additional window in the woman's dressing room. He said he had already installed the guards and other safety devices before the orders came from the authorities.

The extra window to the dressing room was put in for light and air and was incidental to the increase in accommodations made after the strike of last Summer. He explained that he and his partner had been tenants in the building for twelve years. It was looked upon as a model building for loft purposes when they began manufacturing there. He had kept pace with improvements ever since and in many respects, he said, had gone ahead of the requirements.

Second Fire in the Building.

Nine years ago, while the factory occupied but one floor of the building, there was a fire at night. Since then, Blanck said, he had employed a watchman night and day to look out for violations of the rules.

• • •

The eighth floor is the main cutting room, and Mr. Blanck, in answer to questions, seemed to think that it was here that the fire might easily have started. He said that there was a large stock of material on this floor, most of it cut into shapes and piled up in stacks ready for the machines.

He also admitted that this material, being mostly lawns and other light cotton goods, was of a highly inflammable nature, and in the sewing rooms, where the flimsy stuff was being basted together and made ready for the operators, there must have been great stacks of fluffy material lying about on the machines.

Neither Mr. Blanck nor Mr. Harris could tell anything definite about the origin of the fire.

• • •

The rear stairway was cut off at the tenth floor by smoke and flame, while the front stairway and front elevator were still running. Both partners agreed that they saw no elevators reach the tenth floor.

Fire Escapes Cut Off.

As for the fire escapes, which were on the rear of the building and in a narrow well, there was never any time after the partners left their private office when escape was possible that way. Mr. Blanck said that when he reached the roof the entire well between his premises and the rear of the Waverly Place buildings seemed a roaring furnace with flames and glowing embers leaping high above the roof. He did not think that any one on either the eighth, ninth or tenth floors could have escaped that way.

Mr. Blanck was asked about the elevator service and the stairways. He said that as nearly as he could calculate the two front elevators, which were used all day long for passengers, easily carried ten passengers each. The two freight elevators in the rear were of iron construction and were also used as passenger elevators morning and evening when work began and ended. These, he said, would carry twenty persons each. The elevator boys on the freight elevators were accustomed to carry passengers during the rush period morning and evening each day.

The halls were fireproof, Mr. Blanck said, and the stairways iron and stone. The elevator shafts were cut off from the factory premises by fireproof wire glass partitions, and the doors leading into the halls were sheathed with iron. He repeated over and over again that he knew the doors into the hallway were always unlocked. He said that the keys were tied to the knobs and that he made it his personal duty every morning to go to each door and see that it was open.

"Scenes at the Morgue"
New York Times, March 26, 1911

An enormous crowd had gathered to see the fire. At first it consisted of passersby. But, as word spread, family and friends of Triangle workers rushed to the scene. Some were reunited with loved ones who had managed to escape. Others rushed off to hospitals where the injured had been taken. And still others, later joined by those unable to find those they sought among the hospitalized, headed for the morgue at Bellevue Hospital, where the first bodies were taken.

Almost as nightmarish as the fire itself was the work of identifying the victims. On the night of the fire virtually all who gathered to view the bodies were friends, relatives, or fellow workers. Fifty-six of the victims were so badly burned that the police doubted they would ever be identified. In the end, all but seven would be, although the process would take almost two weeks.

By the next morning, the bereaved, joined by the merely curious, flocked by the thousands to the Department of Charities pier, next to the city morgue, where the dead were temporarily kept. A circus atmosphere developed, much to the disgust of the police and the dismay of those desperately seeking to find a missing loved one. The following story from the *Times* describes that first night.

SCENES AT THE MORGUE.

Men and Women Gather in a Frantic Throng in Quest of Loved Ones.

A few minutes after the first load of fire victims was received at the Bellevue Hospital Morgue the streets were filled with a clamoring throng, which struggled with the reserves stationed about the building in an effort to gain entrance to view the bodies of the dead in the hope of identifying loved ones.

The frantic mob was reinforced as the hospital wagon brought more of the dead to the institution. The sobbing and shrieking mothers and wives, and frantic fathers and husbands of those who had not been accounted for struggled with the police and tried to stop the wagon that was bearing the dead on its trips to the Morgue. Mothers and wives ran frantically through the street in front of the hospital, pulling their hair from their heads and calling the names of their dear ones.

"Scenes at the Morgue," *New York Times,* March 26, 1911. Reprinted by permission.

(continued)

A few of the surging mob who viewed the situation in a calmer manner attempted to calm the excited ones, but in vain. The police were abused because they would not allow the surging mob in the Morgue, and in many instances they were threatened and had to resort to the use of their nightsticks to keep the struggling mass from breaking in.

• • •

POLICE WORK DESPERATELY.

A hundred policemen, most of them ashen and with trembling lips, worked at the heart-rending task of keeping back, without undue roughness, the maddened thousands.

"For God's sake," one cried to a reporter, who was wedging his way out of the mob, "get me a drink!"

The poor bluecoat needed it.

Every few minutes a patrol wagon or a hastily improvised morgue wagon that had done duty as an auto truck earlier in the day appeared at the head of the mob at First Avenue and Twenty-sixth Street, and the reserves of six precincts had to force open a narrow path through the crowd for it. As soon as the path was opened in front, however, the crowd surged in behind it. At the sight of the bodies the crowd broke into fresh weeping and screaming, each seeming to see in the charred and often unrecognizable remains a loved one.

Twelve patrol wagons from as many stations, besides dozens of hastily impressed dispensary wagons of the Police Department and the Department of Public Charities and a few auto trucks were used in transporting the dead from the fire to the Morgue. The Morgue itself became too crowded, early in the evening, for further storage of bodies, and the Charities Department decided to throw open the long public dock adjoining it. Here, as night settled over the city, the bodies were taken from the wagons and laid out, side by side, in double rows along either side of the long docks.

Besides the thirty attendants regularly at the pier, twenty derelicts who had applied at the Municipal Lodging House in East Twenty-sixth Street for a night's rest, were pressed into service for the ghastly work.

In the narrow lane left between the double rows of the dead on the dark pier, the patrol wagons and rude dead wagons crept slowly to where the lines had freshly ended. They deposited their freight, backed slowly out, and returned to the scene of the fire for more bodies. As fast as the dead were brought to the pier the grimy panhandlers and derelicts were set to work arranging them in rows, and later putting them in the rough wooden boxes that serve as coffins nightly at the Morgue. But the supply of boxes was soon exhausted, and Commissioner Drummond of the Department of Charities was obliged to send over to the storage warehouse on Blackwell's Island for more. Presently there steamed up to the pier from the island a large double-decked launch, bringing stacked up on its deck 100 more boxes.

• • •

At 11:30 o'clock, with the mob still storming more and more outside, the police had counted in the Morgue and on the pier 136 bodies—thirteen men and 123 women. Fifty-six of these were burned beyond all but human semblance and may never be identified. The thousands of clamorers outside could not have identified them, even if the police had let them swarm in on the pier.

As the maddened throng swarmed around the ghastly laden patrol wagons and improvised hearses their misery wrung even the hardened habitual handlers of the dead in the Morgue, making them frequently turn away from their work. There were hundreds scantily clad and shivering, despite their raving, in the cold night air. Many of them had no money. Their week's funds were in the pay envelopes, found in dozens, on the scorched and irrecognizable bodies on the pier. One woman, her head charred to a mere twisted blur of black, carried in her stocking $600 in tightly crumpled bills. Dozens of the girls whose bodies were laid out on the pier were found to have carried their scant savings in this way.

CLUNG TOGETHER IN DEATH.

Two girls, charred beyond all hope of identification, and found in the smoking ruins with their arms clasped around each other's necks, were conveyed to the pier, still together, and placed in one box.

Horrible cries had burst from the misery stricken mob outside when these two were carried through the narrow lane in the street, and a few of the clamorous throng had forced their way to the wagon and lifted the dark tarpaulin. Everywhere burst anguished cries for sister, mother, and wife, a dozen pet names in Italian and Yiddish rising in shrill agony above the deeper moan of the throng.

Now and then a reporter, the way cleared before him by a broad, white-faced policeman, forced his way to the nearest telephone, to send to his office a report of what was happening there. Each time a hundred faces were turned up to him imploringly, and a hundred anguished voices begged of him tidings of those within. Had he seen a little girl with black hair and dark-brown cheeks? Had he seen a tall, thin man, with stooped shoulders?

(continued)

Could he describe any one of the many he had seen in there? The poor wretches were hunting for a "story," too.

Piteously they pleaded with the policemen to let them—only them—past, so that they might see whether their loved ones were on the pier. They would only look around, one short glance, and come straight out. The policemen, struggling with their own emotions more roughly than with the crowd could only put them off. Presently, they said, in a very little while now, they would let them all in.

• • •

"Fifty-six!" muttered Inspector Walsh, turning his face away. They call him "Smiling Dick" Walsh, but his averted face was not smiling. He meant the fifty-six bodies that were burnt or crushed beyond recognition; fifty-six that would certainly be buried in unnamed graves. Dozens of them had every stitch of clothing burned off them. One body—that of a young girl—was headless and burned to a crisp.

Commissioner Drummond realized that when the mad throng was let into the Morgue and on the pier, many of them, already crazed by uncertainty concerning their loved ones, might at the sight of the dead throw themselves into the river. He therefore ordered that every opening in the Morgue building and on the covered pier be boarded up at once, and that no space should be left which would permit of the passage of a body.

At midnight, . . . the door of the Morgue was opened for a brief moment, and the foremost of the surging mob outside, to the number of fifteen, was allowed to enter. The police squad at the doors could hardly keep the rest back, with promises of letting them, too, presently enter in groups of fifteen.

Each group, shivering and clamoring and weeping, was lined up at the door and allowed slowly to file between the rows of boxes. Two policemen accompanied each of them, ready to support them if they should faint. And more than half of them did. They looked around with an air of frightened bewilderment at the ghastly array of dead, and then, one by one, looking down at the nearest box at their feet, where the mangled bodies lay, with heads propped up on boards for the light of the attendant beside the box, they collapsed with cries of terror. Such were carried to one side and revived by physicians from Bellevue, and later warmed with coffee handed to them by attendants and panhandlers at the pier.

Scores of men and women thought they saw in the ghastly bodies propped up in the boxes the relatives they were looking for, but could not identify them positively.

Around several bodies gathered men and women in small knots, each insisting pitifully that what was propped up there belonged to them, and calling the unrecognizable mass with tender pet names.

• • •

At 1 A.M. eight bodies had been identified by relatives and set aside in sealed boxes. The relatives filed into the improvised Coroner's office in the morgue and tearfully stood in line for their slips permitting them to have the bodies removed. There was a competitive mob of undertakers with their wagons at the outskirts of the crowd ready to do that.

Shirtwaist Makers' Union Memorial Meeting

As the initial shock of the tragedy wore off, a rising tide of anger mixed with grief swept through the Lower East Side of Manhattan and other immigrant neighborhoods. The following account of a memorial meeting held by the Shirtwaist and Dress Makers' Union eight days after the fire captures something of that tide of feeling. The *Times* reporter likened the "frenzy" to "an old-time Southern camp meeting" as people cried out, fainted, and almost rioted.

Relatives, neighbors, and co-workers of the victims demanded that something be done to punish those responsible. The question of *who* that might be was the central topic of conversation across kitchen

tables and in union halls and coffee shops. It was the central preoccupation of the memorial meeting as well. The simplest answer was that
Triangle's co-owners were to blame. Union officials and workers alike,
however, knew that Blanck and Harris were not much different from
other employers in the industry. They knew, too, that other work-
places were just as vulnerable to fire. In fact, many were more so. Further, the popularity of radical political ideas among the immigrant
Jewish community meant that speakers at the meeting would seek to
make sense of the fire in the context of class warfare. The Rumanian-
born garment worker Marcus Ravage characterized the Lower East
Side as divided into "atheists," who were either socialists or anarchists, on one side, and "clodpates," who were actual or potential capitalists on the other.[1]

The possibility of a revolution on the Lower East Side, complete
with the sorts of terrorist acts, such as bombing City Hall, that anarchists described as "propaganda of the deed," struck many observers
as quite real. The "frenzy" described here fueled concern elsewhere
and led, as the subsequent meeting at the Metropolitan Opera recounted here demonstrates, to efforts to find more moderate solutions
to the problems dramatized by the fire.

Abraham Cahan, described in the story as "editor of a Jewish
newspaper," *The Forward,* was the most influential Yiddish-language
journalist in the city. A socialist, albeit a nonrevolutionary one, he had
strongly backed the strike. The other featured speaker mentioned,
Leonora O'Reilly, did not lead "a strike last year in the Triangle Waist
Company." The story is correct in identifying her as a member of the
Women's Trade Union League, however, and she did play an active if
supporting role in the "Uprising." O'Reilly had begun her career as a
garment worker, became a union activist, and then took a paid position with the WTUL. She was renowned for her speaking abilities.

---

[1] Marcus E. Ravage, *An American in the Making: The Life Story of an Immigrant* (New York: Dover,
1971; originally published in 1917 by Harper and Brothers), especially Chapter xiii, "The Soul of
the Ghetto." Ravage recalled realizing "that everybody I knew was either a socialist or an anarchist" and wrote (p. 157):

> I have often since looked back with a melancholy regret to those splendid days, and have
> tried to reconstruct them in my memory and to find a parallel for them somewhere. From
> this distance [i.e., from the perspective of 1917] they seem to me comparable to nothing
> else so much as to those early times when Christianity was still the faith of the despised
> and the lowly. There was in us that apostolic simplicity of speech and manners, that disre-
> gard of externals, that contempt of the world and its prizes, that hatred of shams, that love
> of the essential, that intolerance for the unbeliever, which only they who feed on a living
> ideal can know.

FAINT IN A FRENZY OVER TALES OF FIRE

Fifty Shirt Waist Girls, Upset by Socialist Oratory, Carried Out of Central Palace Meeting

The Mayor's Name Hissed

Hysteria Piled on Hysteria, with Police Trying to Calm Gallery of 2,000

Socialist speakers, who told over and over again of the horrors of the factory fire of last Saturday, who drew pictures of the scenes in the temporary morgue on the Charities pier, and who finally called on their hearers to put an end to such conditions by their own efforts, stampeded what was to have been a memorial meeting over the Washington Place fire last night. The meeting was held in the Grand Central Palace under the auspices of the Shirtwaist and Dressmakers' Union. From the moment the first speaker stepped to the front of the platform there could be felt a growing tension among the 2,000 present, most of them relatives of victims of the fire, some of them survivors, who thronged the hall. Four of every five were women.

Presently, as the meeting went on, Chairman Penkin rapped loudly for order and when he could make his voice heard asked that every one join in a silent prayer for the dead. Those in the audience and on the stage bowed their heads. There arose a confused murmur of voices as fathers, mothers, sisters, and brothers who had found their dead almost unrecognizable in the Morgue muttered words in Yiddish, German, and English.

And then the voice of a girl, seated well down in front, failed her. She struggled to continue the prayer which came from her trembling lips and her voice broke in a deep sob. In an instant a woman further back in the hall sobbed, too. The sounds acted on the throng like an electric current. There were sounds of convulsive weeping throughout the hall and then a woman screamed.

Instantly the tension under which the mourners had labored snapped like a broken wire. Cry after cry rang through the hall. Men and women sprang to their feet, wailing out their grief. They waved their arms above their heads. Those on the stage tried for an instant to check the panic, which was spreading like a fire over the hall. The Chairman's lips could be seen moving, but his voice could not be heard. And then behind him, where many of the survivors sat, the cries which resounded from the front of the hall were taken up. In an instant there was scarcely a man or woman among the 2,000-odd who retained his composure.

In the hall women fell, fainting in the midst of companions too excited to do more than gaze on them as they toppled from their feet to crumple up on the floor. It was as though an old-time Southern camp meeting had been overtaken with religious fervor.

In the hall were sixty policemen, however, under Capt. O'Connor of the East Fifty-first Street station. The Captain had expected the very trouble that had arisen, and he and his men sped through the hall, trying to calm those who had not fainted, and to drag from the danger of being trampled on, those whose emotions had overcome them. In a few minutes more than fifty women had been carried to the entrance, where a sort of field hospital was established under doctors from the Flower Hospital. Restoratives were administered to the women as fast as the doctors could reach the sufferers. After a few minutes, when quiet had been restored in the hall, it was found that only one woman was seriously enough hurt to be taken to the hospital. She was hurried to Flower Hospital in an ambulance.

It was Abraham Cahan, editor of a Jewish newspaper, who worked the audience up to the final pitch of excitement. He had tried to praise Mayor Gaynor for having headed a relief contribution list.

Mention of the Mayor's name was the signal for a chorus of hisses throughout the hall. Mr. Cahan strove to make himself heard against the uproar. Finally he managed to tell how an Anarchist had visited him in his office to protest

"Faint in a Frenzy Over Tales of Fire," *New York Times*, March 30, 1911. Reprinted by permission.

(continued)

against such conditions as would permit a fire such as that of Saturday.

"He told me that only the placing of a few bombs in the camp of the capitalists would bring redress to the working classes," cried Mr. Cahan, and his words were taken up by the crowd.

"Pitch a bomb under the City Hall," they cried. "Blow the place up!"

● ● ●

With excitement raised to the pitch, which it attained while Mr. Cahan was speaking, it took only the quiet request for a moment of silent prayer to throw the audience into a frenzy, and once partial quiet had been restored, it remained for Miss Leonora O'Reilly, who led a strike last year in the Triangle Waist Company, the scene of Saturday's fire, to bring the audience back to its usual composure.

Miss O'Reilly, who is the executive member of the Women's Trade Union League, affiliated with the Central Federated Union, spoke feelingly of the 142 victims of the fire. She referred to them as "the martyrs, who died that we may live." The phrase rang loudly through the hall, the speaker's voice carrying beyond the portals even to the hall outside, and instantly there was a commotion there.

A girl survivor of the fire who had been carried out of the hall earlier, caught Miss O'Reilly's words, and crying aloud again in another attack of hysteria, tried to force her way back. Several girls sprang from seats in the rear and tried to keep the half-crazed girl from entering. Policemen ran toward her, fearing that her presence would occasion a scene similar to that which had just been enacted.

In the struggle the girl's shirt waist was torn from her back and she was carried, screaming, out of earshot of the hall. Throughout the commotion, however, Miss O'Reilly continued speaking in a calm and quiet tone and the outbreak which the police feared was averted.

A. L. Simon, editor of a Chicago socialist publication, told the meeting that he was in the city to organize a great demonstration against conditions which allowed capital "to force labor to work in death traps like that in which 142 men and girls lost their lives." He declared that labor should be empowered to care for its own safety; that labor inspectors should see that buildings were made safe and that work was not allowed in factories which did not wholly meet their approval.

"We have the votes," he declared, "why should we not have the power? Your future lies in unionism. Your union should have the right to decide questions which are of most concern to working people, and it can get this right only by organization and combination. These 142 deaths resulted because capital begrudged the price of another fire escape."

It was a thoughtful throng, little like the excited one that had filled the hall a few moments before, that trailed out of Grand Central Palace. . . .

Rose Schneiderman's Speech at the Metropolitan Opera

Even as family members and friends continued the grim business of attempting to identify the remains of the victims, and as socialists and anarchists called upon the working class to organize and take power away from their "capitalist oppressors," more moderate groups were demanding that the government—state as well as city—do something to make sure that such a tragedy could never happen again. Speakers at the City Club, a bastion of prominent New Yorkers, called for new building codes. The Collegiate Equal Suffrage League protested working conditions in factories. And the Women's Trade Union League held a well-publicized series of hearings during which more than one thousand workers testified, on condition of anonymity, about hazards in the workplace. The WTUL also sponsored the largest, and most influential, of the meetings held to protest the fire.[1] It was held on Sunday, April 3, 1911, at the Metropolitan Opera House, which Anne Morgan had rented on behalf of the league. It was, as the *New York Times* account excerpted here makes plain, a tumultuous gathering. Many in attendance openly derided the resolutions ultimately adopted. Yet the meeting proved, in the long run, to have a tremendous influence. Out of it came the Factory Investigating Commission, co-chaired by Robert Wagner and Al Smith and employing a host of WTUL and National Consumers League activists as staff investigators. The league published a "white list" of manufacturers whose working conditions met its standards, and its hundreds of thousands of members were pledged to boycott companies not on the list.

The commission would draft a host of "protective" laws that were adopted not only in New York but in many other states as well. The Metropolitan Opera House meeting thus marked the beginnings of the political partnership between urban Democrats like Smith and progressive reformers and "new women" like Frances Perkins that would form the heart of the New Deal coalition of Franklin Delano Roosevelt. Part of the reason why the resolutions adopted at the Metropolitan Opera meeting had such striking effect was Rose Schneiderman's speech. In it she castigated the "good people" who called for "reform" but refused to support the workers when they went on strike for higher wages and better conditions.

---

[1] For a detailed account of the planning, see *New York Times*, March 26, 1911.

MASS MEETING CALLS FOR NEW FIRE LAWS

❦

Metropolitan Opera House Gathering Decides to Name a Standing Committee on Protection.

❦

Workers Not in Accord

❦

Woman Union Leader Says They Have Lost Faith in the Public and Must Rely on Themselves.

❦

More people went to the Metropolitan Opera House yesterday to participate in the council on the Asch Building fire disaster than could find seats in the grand tier, where the boxes were reserved, or in the orchestra and galleries, where they were open to all. Those in the grand tier came in automobiles, and were admitted at a special side entrance opened thirty minutes before the other doors. Those in the orchestra floor for the main part were from the upper west side, while the east siders overflowed one gallery after another until they had packed the house.

The meeting, which lasted from 3 o'clock until 5:20, proved to be more cosmopolitan than harmonious. The men in the upper galleries, instead of applauding the programme brought forward by the leaders to obtain better fire protection laws, reserved their loudest cheers for those who dissented from the programme, on the ground that citizens' committees were incapable of doing any real good and had always proved a failure.

The outcome of the meeting was the adoption of resolutions by a partial vote calling for the creation of a permanent committee to advocate new legislation and see that there is no official neglect to enforce such laws as now exist.

"Mass Meeting Calls for New Fire Laws," *New York Times,* April 4, 1911. Reprinted by permission.

The dissenters from this programme held that there would be no improvement for the working classes until in class solidarity they demanded it at the polls and through committees of their own. They advocated the organization of working people into Assembly district committees and the giving of fire inspectorship privileges to labor union officials.

THE SPEAKERS INTERRUPTED.

Every little while from the topmost gallery shouts from Socialists interrupted the speakers, and once the meeting got away from the Chairman's control while those upstairs cheered for the interrupters and those below attempted to hiss them down. There was one moment when feeling grew tense to a snapping point, and the audience was held too closely by the speaker's words to interrupt or applaud as the girl who had been speaking went back up the stage to her seat.

Rose Schneiderman, who led the workers out of the Triangle factory in their strike two years ago and bailed them out after being arrested, found words difficult when she tried to speak. She stood silent for a moment, and then began to speak hardly above a whisper. But the silence was such that everywhere they carried clearly.

The first speakers were Jacob H. Schiff, Bishop Greer, Eugene Philbin, and Rabbi Stephen S. Wise, all of whom had advocated a permanent citizen's committee on fire protection.

"I would be a traitor to these poor burned bodies," began Miss Schneiderman after she had gained possession of her voice, "if I came here to talk good fellowship. We have tried you good people of the public and we have found you wanting. The old Inquisition had its rack and its thumbscrews and its instruments of torture with iron teeth. We know what these things are to-day: the iron teeth are our necessities, the thumbscrews the high-powered and swift machinery close to which we must work, and the rack is here in the firetrap structures that will destroy us the minute they catch on fire.

"This is not the first time girls have been burned alive in the city. Every week I must learn of the untimely death of one of my sister workers. Every year thousands of us are maimed. The life of men and women is so cheap and property is so sacred. There are so many of us for one job it matters little if 143 of us are burned to death.

(continued)

"We have tried you citizens; we are trying you now, and you have a couple of dollars for the sorrowing mothers and brothers and sisters by way of a charity gift. But every time the workers come out in the only way they know to protest against conditions which are unbearable the strong hand of the law is allowed to press down heavily upon us.

"Public officials have only words of warning to us—warning that we must be intensely orderly and must be intensely peaceable, and they have the workhouse just back of all their warnings. The strong hand of the law beats us back when we rise into the conditions that make life unbearable.

THE WORKER'S VIEW OF IT.

"I can't talk fellowship to you who are gathered here. Too much blood has been spilled. I know from my experience it is up to the working people to save themselves. The only way they can save themselves is by a strong working-class movement."

"120,000 Pay Tribute to the Fire Victims"

Two days after the Metropolitan Opera House meeting an enormous crowd gathered for the funeral of the last victims of the fire. Although more than fifty had been burned virtually beyond recognition, all but seven were identified by authorities and relatives. Often a ring or other piece of jewelry found on the body provided the needed clue. One woman's relatives recognized a peculiar stitch on a shoe she had recently had repaired. Joseph Wilson's body was identified by his fiancée, Rosie Solomon. According to the *Times* for March 27, 1911, she and her mother

> passed down the line of charred bodies, her attention directed to the hands. Finally she reached the body numbered 34. She asked if there was a watch on the body. There was. The girl looked inside and saw her picture. She gave a shriek, and fell to the floor. Her mother also became hysterical, and it required the attention of several nurses to quiet them.

Similar scenes played out again and again in the days following the fire. Finally, on April 5, the unidentified victims were buried. The Hebrew Free Burial Society and the Shirtwaist Workers' Union had quarreled over who should arrange the funerals, and the city took charge as a way of both settling the argument and placating those in the Italian-American community concerned that some of their co-nationals might be buried in a Jewish ceremony.

Even as the grisly task of identifying the dead had been going on, the Women's Trade Union League had launched a series of public hearings into the issue of worker safety with the active cooperation of the Shirtwaist Workers' Union. The two organizations, however, had squabbled over the line of march in the funeral procession. Finally it was agreed that Rose Schneiderman of the WTUL would lead the mourners, perhaps in recognition of the moral position her speech at the Metropolitan Opera House meeting had given her. The procession began at Washington Square, site of the Asch Building, and proceeded up Fifth Avenue. It required four hours for the more than 120,000 mourners to pass under the arch at the square.

120,000 PAY TRIBUTE TO THE FIRE VICTIMS

Army of Workers, Most of Them Women, March Through the Downpour of Rain

Throngs Along the Line

Leaders in the Suffrage Movement, Undismayed by the Weather, Join in the Line of March.

Rose Schneiderman, the slip of a girl whose eloquence stirred the Metropolitan Opera House mass meeting on Sunday, brought tears to the eyes of thousands yesterday as they stood along Fifth Avenue in a drifting rain, watching the funeral parade for the shirtwaist workers who perished in the Washington Place fire.

Little Miss Schneiderman had made many speeches since the Asch Building fire: workers everywhere had become acquainted with her. Hatless and without raincoat she tried to trudge along in the dripping procession, near its head. But long before it had reached its uptown destination at Thirty-fifth Street her feet began to falter.

Mary Dreier, President of the Women's Trade Union League, noticed that the girl was lagging behind her comrades in a line of eight, and took hold of her arm. Helen Marot, Secretary of the league, grasped her by the other arm, and the three, who more than any others have been in the limelight since the Ash Building fire, trudged on. None had umbrellas, and only one a raincoat. In front of them was a platoon of police, a funeral car laden with floral wreaths, with six white horses to draw it, and a score of fire survivors, one of whom carried a waistmakers' banner.

The crowds, which numbered, the police estimated, about 400,000, while a third of that number were in the line of march, everywhere recognized the girl who was being helped along. Her name ran from lip to lip along the curb lines. Men pressed close to catch a glimpse of her, and among the women, who outnumbered the men on the sidewalks as they did in the line of march, there were few dry eyes.

The parade, declared by the leaders to be the largest demonstration ever made here by working people, practically emptied the downtown and Brooklyn lofts and factories.

• • •

Once in Washington Square, the consolidated columns began the march up Fifth Avenue at 3:40 o'clock, and it required four hours after the first file of eight had left for the last file to pass under the Washington Arch.

There were no propagandist banners and no bands. The intention of the leaders to make the occasion one for the expression of the working people's grief was complied with, but only by the rigid censorship of banners which some had brought to the line of procession. The National colors, draped in mourning, and union banners similarly draped, marked the headquarters of the various divisions. Girls, where the unions were composed of women, carried their banners

"120,000 Pay Tribute to the Fire Victims," *New York Times*, April 6, 1911. Reprinted by permission.

(continued)

throughout the line of march, and then would not admit that they were exhausted. On their hats and around their arms many wore bands of black ribbon.

• • •

While the parade was in progress a funeral procession, consisting of eight black hearses, with white trimmings, carrying the bodies of six unidentified women and a man, left the Morgue, at the foot of East Twenty-sixth Street. Thousands of people who had been attracted by the funeral notice watched the procession on its way to the Twenty-third Street ferries, and thousands more from Brownsville lined the streets through which the procession passed from the Brooklyn ferry slip to the Cypress Hills Cemetery.

Red Cross Relief Efforts

Despite Rose Schneiderman's scorn for the "good people" who found "a few dollars" to give to the victims' families and thereby reassured themselves that they had done their best to help, the Red Cross and Local 25, which had called the strike of the year before, actively appealed for such contributions. They netted record sums. The following two documents disclose how that money was allocated. The first is the official Red Cross report and affords a good example of what contemporaries called "scientific philanthropy." The basic idea was to help without encouraging dependence, and case workers prided themselves on their ability to determine the "true" needs of the families with whom they dealt. This translated into pride in their ability to provide the minimal amount of assistance needed because "scientific philanthropy" postulated that any giving beyond that actually required would encourage the recipient to slacken his or her own efforts. As a result, although the Red Cross and the union together raised over $120,000, they gave only $80,556.16 to the families. The report includes excerpts from the case workers' reports on individual families, several of which are reprinted here. The Charity Organization Society referred to in this document coordinated the activities of several private agencies with a view to preventing duplication of efforts and, especially, the practice of those in need receiving aid from multiple sources.

Elizabeth Dutcher, author of the second document, was a member of the Women's Trade Union League and served on both the union and the Red Cross relief committees. She emphasized the degree to which the fire's victims were responsible for the financial security of their families and used the data collected by the Red Cross to argue that the victims and their families had already demonstrated their willingness and ability to take responsibility for their own lives. Her article appeared first in *The Woman Voter* and then was reprinted in *Life and Labor*, a monthly published by the WTUL. Both documents described the family of "Annie S" (number 168 in the Red Cross report). The differences in the way the two treat the facts in this case are instructive.

THE FACTORY FIRE AND THE RED CROSS

Adapted from the report just issued by the Red Cross Emergency Relief Committee of the charity organization society of the city of New York.

On March 25, 1911, a fire in the premises of the Triangle Shirt Waist Company at 23 Washington Place, New York, resulted in the death of 146 persons, principally women and girls, and the injury of about as many more.

The families affected were for the most part recent Jewish and Italian immigrants; dependent largely on seasonal occupations or work irregular for other reasons; dependent largely, too, on the earnings of girls and women. They were for the most part families who had never received charitable assistance. In only a few cases, moreover, would they have become dependent on charity as a result of this accident if there had been no special fund for their benefit. Around most of them there was a circle of relatives and friends who might have prevented this, if there were not sufficient potential resources in the immediate family. On the other hand, in nearly every case the accident caused, aside from grievous personal bereavement, an economic loss which would have involved a definite lowering of the standard of living of one or more families if there had not been resources in addition to those of the charitable agencies.

The emergency relief fund was perhaps unprecedented in liberality. The total amount contributed to the Red Cross was $103,899.38, and the union fund[1] brought the grand total to about $120,000, a larger amount, in proportion to the number of families and the situation caused by the fire, than has generally, if ever, been available for emergency relief. It seemed to be essentially an expression of sympathy: not so much carefully considered contributions to supply the necessities of life, as impulsive gifts, from a passionate desire to do what was possible to compensate for the horrible event. There was sufficient money to do whatever seemed wise. The principle on which the Red Cross Committee acted in the distribution of the fund was that it is the function of emergency relief not to reimburse financial losses as such, but to restore the victims of the disaster, as quickly as possible and as completely as may be, to their accustomed standard of living, or to prevent a serious lowering of that standard. This involved a consideration of the factor which the killed or injured person played in maintaining the old standard. No schedule of appropriations for different types of cases was worked out on the basis of relationship to the deceased and number of dependents. . . . What was done was to consider each case individually, as is done in ordinary relief work, and on the basis of all the information at command, considering all the elements in the situation, to grant an appropriation which should obviate an otherwise inevitable lowering of the standard of living in that particular family. In not a few cases it was found even easier to facilitate an actual improvement: to grant a lump sum which would set a father up in business, for example, rather than merely to continue, in the form of a pension, his daughter's accustomed contribution.

•　•　•

The total amount spent for relief was $80,556.16. The appropriations range in size from $10 to

(continued)

"The Factory Fire and the Red Cross," *The Survey* 28 (May 25, 1912), 339–45.

[1] The Ladies' Dress and Waistmakers' Union quite properly felt that the relief of its members should be given from its own fund, and arrangements to that effect were made with the union on the first day of the emergency work. The relations between the two offices were absolutely satisfactory and the cases were handled on the same principles.

$1,000 in the families in which no death had occurred; and from $50 to $5,167.20 in the families which had lost one or more of their members. Three-fifths of the appropriations to families in which there was a death were of $500 or over, one-fifth of $1,000 and over; in only one case of injury was the amount over $500, and that one appropriation was of $1,000. About 90 per cent of the expenditure was for families in which there had been a death.

The purposes for which the appropriations were made are shown in the following table:

Emergent and temporary relief
  To families in which
    there was no death .. $7,842.35[1]
  To families in which
    there was a death ... 4,688.66
  To families in charge
    of the union committee   287.00
                           $12,818.01
Funeral expenses . . . . 6,167.10[2]
Permanent provision for relatives
  of those who were killed:
    In the United States . . . . 44,672.15[3]
    In Europe, Palestine, and the
      West Indies 16,898.90
    Total $80,556.16

Emergent relief was given freely throughout the first few days, in the office as well as in the homes; and liberal temporary assistance, pending a final decision or a re-adjustment of family arrangements, was given to families who had lost one or more of their members, and to persons who had been injured or were incapacitated by the shock.

In all of the Jewish families in which there seemed to be any need twenty-five or fifty dollars was given for the expenses of Passover week, and a similar gift for Easter was made in a number of Italian families. Modest amounts were granted to replace clothing that had been lost when it seemed to be really needed. The largest part of this sum, however, was given to enable those who had been injured to regain their health and to do so without unreasonable sacrifice on the part of other members of the family. A few stories may give an idea of the variety of circumstances in these families.

• • •

---

[1] This represents the total expenditures in these cases.
[2] This includes $1,000 to the Hebrew Free Burial Society, to reimburse it for its expenditures in connection with thirty funerals.
[3] $16,500 of this represents trust funds for sixteen children in seven families.

No. 187. (Italian.) Two girls, 20 and 16, uninjured, but hysterical and nervous. They live in Hoboken with their mother and brother, who has a small store. Their father is in Italy, ill with tuberculosis. $50 was given on April 10 for medicine, clothing, and other incidental expenses. When a visit was made in November it was found that the girls were still in a nervous condition and under a physician's care. One of them had married: her family urging it because she could not work; her suitor, because he expected she would receive a large appropriation from the Red Cross fund. He is able to support her, however. It seemed advisable to make a further grant to the unmarried girl, since at present she is dependent on her brother, who has also his mother to support. ($100.00)

• • •

No. 142. (Russian.) A girl of 19, seriously injured: left arm and leg paralyzed and no hope of recovery. She was a favorite niece of one of the proprietors, who made a liberal weekly allowance for her care, but could not meet the expense of all her needs. Her father is comparatively well-to-do and has a small store. $1,000 was sent to the girl through the Brooklyn Bureau of Charities on November 10, to enable her to have the care which her condition requires. ($1,000.00)

• • •

In most of the families in which a death had occurred it seemed necessary, or at least proper, to make provision of a more permanent nature for surviving relatives. The appropriations for this purpose account for over three-fourths of the total disbursements. Of this, $44,672.15 was for the benefit of relatives in the United States, and $16,898.90 for the benefit of relatives in other countries—Russia, Austria, Hungary, Roumania, England, Jamaica, and Palestine. In all of these cases the family had been dependent, in some degree, on the one who had been killed.

• • •

No. 168. (Russian.) A girl of 19 was killed, the chief support of the family of five. Her father, though only 55, looked very old, and earned a very little by teaching Hebrew; her mother did not work; her older brother was about to be married and only paid board; the other brother, 16 years old, had left high school and started to work because of his sister's death. After giving temporary assistance for current expenses a grant of $700 in all was made to enable the father to establish himself in a delicatessen shop, which he opened on May 20. Within a month he came back to say that he had used all the money and could not make expenses, but an interview at the shop did not confirm this nor did it reveal any reason for making a further appropriation. In October it was found that the man had sold his business in July and moved away. His successor was making it pay.

(continued)

He had bought it for $175 and thought the old man had not lost money on the sale. ($830.00)

The most serious situations in the Italian families were caused by the death of girls or young women who had supported and cared for aged or infirm parents. In the case which received the largest appropriation there were also little children who were left orphans by the fire.

No. 85. A widow 33 years old and her sister of 18 were killed, leaving their old father and mother, a brother of 16, and the five little children of the widow, three of whom were already in an institution. The old mother was almost crazed with grief. She did nothing but moan and weep for weeks, and has not yet recovered. There was a married daughter in the same house who undertook responsibility for the little girl, and later combined her household with that of the old people. The other child who was at home at the time of the disaster was placed in the institution with his brothers. The boy of 16 shows a disposition to do all he can for his parents. He is a plume-maker, earning $6 a week. After giving emergent relief and help in paying the funeral expenses, a pension of $25 a month was paid to the father and mother until November. $600 was then placed with the Charity Organization Society to continue this pension for two years;

and a trust fund of $2,500 for the benefit of the five children ($500 for each) was also placed with the Charity Organization Society. ($3,510.00)

• • •

The advantage of a lump sum over a monthly allowance was urged by nearly all the friends who were consulted about families in Europe, and by the beneficiaries themselves from whom word was had directly. In most cases the amounts they suggested did not exceed those granted.

• • •

No. 163. (Russian.) A girl of 18 was killed. She lived with a cousin here and had a brother in the city. Her mother, a widow, and four younger children were in Russia, dependent on the two children here. The girl had sent 20 roubles a month and had also been in the habit of making up deficiencies in her brother's contribution, though he was older than she, when he did not send a similar amount. After the fire he showed a disposition to drop his responsibility entirely, but it was made clear to him that the committee assumed that he would continue his usual contributions. $35 was given him in April and May to send to Russia, and 500 roubles ($257.75) was sent on June 22 to the mother through the American consul-general in Moscow. $80 was given to the cousin to reimburse her for funeral expenses. ($372.75)

BUDGETS OF THE TRIANGLE FIRE VICTIMS

BY ELIZABETH DUTCHER

Agent, Joint Relief Committee, Ladies' Waist and Dressmakers' Union No. 25, and Member of the Red Cross Emergency Relief Case Committee

. . . The women who jumped from the tenth story of the Ashe Building were self-reliant working women, who had never asked for charitable assistance,* and who were making their way in the average fashion—or a little above the average, for the strain of work in this particular factory was very great, and capable women, of good physique, who could be speeded up, and work overtime during the busy season, were sought after by the employers.

. . . They were working in a seasonal industry where there was no work for four months, light work for about three months, and very heavy work with a great deal of overtime* during the remaining five months. The fire occurred late one Saturday afternoon in March, at the close of the busy season, when overtime was still being worked, and the pay-envelopes for that week ranged from $4.50 to $14, with an exceptional few still higher.

What is the first statement made in the report of the Red Cross Committee? Says that report:

(continued)

Elizabeth Dutcher, "Budgets of the Triangle Fire Victims," *Life and Labor* (September 1912), 265–67.

* P. 7 Report of the Red Cross Emergency Relief Committee: "These were for the most part families who had never received charitable assistance." This is the more remarkable because one in every nine families in New York receives some form of charity every year. Only one of the sixty-five union families had so received aid.

* Overtime is legal three nights in the week, but the charge has been made that four nights were commonly worked in this shop, and even Sundays and holidays in time of stress.

"The families affected by the Washington Place fire were for the most part Jewish and Italian immigrants . . . dependent largely on the earnings of girls and women."

These girls, then, just at the age when clothes and good times make their greatest appeal, were not working at a power machine in a high loft building for nothing. They were there because they were the support of a great number of people.

The Red Cross Committee, with its 166 cases makes the statement we have just quoted. I want to illustrate just how this support was given by giving you some figures from the union records, partly because I am more familiar with them, and partly because they are the families where such heavy responsibilities seem most improbable. One would not expect one girl whose young shoulders carried such heavy burdens to run the risk of a long strike, or to make the sacrifices necessary for paying her union dues and assessments, particularly when she was working in a non-union shop, where organization was discouraged in every possible way.*

Sixty-five cases were taken for continued care by the Joint Relief Committee. These included families where one or more members had been killed or injured in the disaster, and there was some union connection.

Of these sixty-five Jewish and Italian families sixty-two of the victims were girls or women (four families having two women victims each; seven families having men victims only):

(a) Fifteen gave practically all their salary toward the support of families living in America.

(b) †Nineteen were the whole or main support (that is, providing more than one-half of the weekly income) of families living in America. Of these three were married, and supported idle husbands, as well as their children, and partly supported aged parents, and ‡ four were the heads of families, in the sense that they had younger brothers and sisters living with them as dependents, and no older people.

(c) Twenty-one sent sums ranging from $5 to $20 per month (verified in all cases by money order receipts), to dependents living in Russia, Austria, Italy and Palestine.

(d) Twenty-one were either alone in New York (without any member of their immediate family in the city), or two sisters were alone and lived and worked together.§

The average age was about nineteen years.

• • •

During the strike of 1909–10 the most frequent complaints were of excessive overtime (of which the greatest grievance was that it precluded night school), excessive speeding up, heavy fines, a subcontracting system which amounted to sweating within the factory, and low wages. It was the revolt of one of the sub-contractors that started the strike. Once it was under way, the girls began to realize their disabilities to the full. They received no protection from their natural protectors, those enforcing the laws or the city.

Special officers were placed at the doors of the factory to insult them as they picketed, and no policeman interfered; the picketing itself was declared illegal, and girls of fifteen were sent to the workhouse for picketing and shut up in the same cells with thieves and prostitutes. Magistrate Cornell's contemptuous pronouncement, "You have no right to picket, you have no right to be on Washington Place, if you go there you will get what is coming to you and I won't interfere," rang out as an expression of the law's typical attitude. It was not until a large number of the so-called "influential women," in other words, women who had assets of wealth and education, and therefore were least in need of such influence, came and picketed morning and night with the girls that there was any change in the law's attitude to these defenseless women.

. . . But the true significance of a five-months' strike comes with new force to the readers of these Fire Disaster reports.* . . .

Annie S., nineteen years old, was the chief support of a family of five. Her father, though only fifty-five, looked very old, and earned a very little by teaching Hebrew; her mother did not work; her oldest brother was about to be married and only paid board, the other brother was in high school.

Sabina A. was the oldest of six children, and had an epileptic father. Lucia D. had three clean little children and a handsome idle husband who complained of a mysterious arm ailment that prevented his working. Every morning Lucia left the

(continued)

---

* This was of course the shop where the trouble started, and which was out the longest in the shirtwaist strike of 1909–10. The strikers were out five months, and were then compelled to settle on an open shop basis. Most of the union girls who went back were discharged shortly thereafter, and only three of the union cases were girls who had been in the strike.

† In two instances two girls were together the main support of a household.

‡ Of these one had an older brother who had never helped her in any way, living in another part of the city.

§ Of course there is considerable duplication in the above list, many girls under (d) coming also under (c). But note, there is no duplication between (a) and (b).

* The cases given are from both the Red Cross and Union reports. In no instance is the real name given.

babies at a day nursery and went forth to earn the family living, and evenings and Sundays she did the cleaning, sewing and washing for the family. Little Dora T. went to the factory the morning of the fire without any breakfast. She had only seven dollars a week, her father, a tailor, was chronically out of work, and there were four young children. Breakfast was a luxury.

• • •

This, then, is the stuff out of which the great strikes of the last few years have been made—the shirtwaist strike, the cloak-makers' strike, the laundry workers' strike, the neckwear makers' strike—the public has grown weary of strikes, and yet the situation must be desperate indeed that forces women with such heavy responsibilities to face not just their own suffering, but that of those dearest to them through a long period.

"Lives at $75"
The Literary Digest 48, March 28, 1914

Relief efforts saw the families of the victims through the initial crisis. Some of them sought financial compensation for their losses, something the Red Cross had—on principle—refused to provide despite the cash surplus left in the relief fund, by suing the insurance company that underwrote the Triangle Shirtwaist Company. For three years the case dragged on until the families, without the money to continue the case, settled for $75 each. Triangle co-owners Isaac Harris and Max Blanck had recovered over $200,000 for their losses from the same carrier. The contrast was sufficiently sharp to provoke a number of critical newspaper editorials, which are described in the following from *The Literary Digest*, a weekly magazine that printed synopses of press coverage of the big stories of the day.

LIVES AT $75

Three years after the Triangle fire in New York, in which, as one writer puts it, "148 lives were sacrificed to greed that violated law," the families of twenty-three girl victims agree to accept $75 as the price of human life, settling at that figure their claims against the liability company which covered the factory. "It seemed little enough, but, to be sure," remarks the New York *Evening Post* with grim irony, "they could console themselves with the thought that it was nearly four times as much as the $20 fine which Chief Justice Russell, of the Court of General Sessions, imposed upon Max Blanck, one of the partners of the fire, two and a half years after the fire, for keeping the door of another factory locked." Twenty-three settlements made on this paltry basis, and more, declares *The*

"Lives at $75," *The Literary Digest* 48 (March 28, 1914), 685.

(continued)

World, are to follow. Why, it asks, and ventures this answer:

"Because the criminal laws were not enforced against those who for profit ignored them.

"Because the criminal laws were not enforced against public officers who neglected their duty to compel obedience to them.

"Because civil law and civil procedure are too slow and too costly for the poor.

"The claimants have been tired out. Their money and their patience have been exhausted. So far as personal guilt is concerned, the men whose methods made everything ready for the tragedy have gone free. So far as financial liability is concerned, the whole affair is in the hands of an insurance company, and stricken families are not well equipped to carry on expensive litigations with corporations."

And the Socialist New York *Call,* remembering that "the troubles of to-day crowd out the memories of yesterday," would recall to our minds how these 148 young lives "were destroyed in the most shocking manner, because their place of work was unsafe in construction, made still more unsafe by the action of their bosses in blocking their exit from the furnace." For this destruction, continues *The Call,* righteously indignant, "nobody was punished, neither Asch, the owner of the building, nor Harris and Blanck, the lessees. There were loopholes in the laws through which they escaped, one and all."

ASSAYING RESPONSIBILITY

Trial Accounts

Were Triangle co-owners Max Blanck and Isaac Harris responsible for the deaths of some or all of the fire's victims? Certainly union activists thought so. They were not alone. Editorial writers in leading newspapers and magazines demanded that Blanck and Harris be prosecuted to the full extent of the law. And, with the entire Lower East Side seething, as evidenced in the various memorial and protest meetings, the New York district attorney's office moved rapidly to indict the owners. The indictment alleged that some of the victims died because a ninth-floor door on the Washington Place side of the Asch building was locked. Sections 80 and 94 of the state labor law required that all factory doors be kept unlocked during working hours. This violation, if the allegation were true, was only a misdemeanor, not a felony, and was punishable by a small fine. But, New York law also stipulated that if someone committed a crime, even a misdemeanor, that led to another person's death, that person was guilty of manslaughter. The indictment invoked this stipulation.

In order to prove manslaughter the prosecution had to show not only that the door was indeed locked, and that it was locked at the behest of Blanck and Harris, but also that a specific person died as a result. The person named in the indictment was Margaret Swartz (sometimes spelled *Schwartz*). Prosecutors chose her, out of the twenty or so victims whose bodies were recovered near the door, because they had two witnesses who could testify to seeing Swartz attempting to open the door. One, Kate Alterman, could also testify to seeing Swartz's dress and hair catch fire as she crouched next to the door and to hearing her cry out that the door was locked. The crucial moment in the trial, as a result, was the cross-examination of Alterman by Max D. Steuer, the defense attorney. That cross-examination is included next.

The trial did not examine other conditions—such as the large quantities of highly flammable waste materials scattered about, the crowding of machines that made passing between work tables difficult—that helped turn the Asch Building into an inferno precisely because those conditions did not involve violations of the law. All agreed that the building itself met the relevant fire codes and other regulations. State factory inspectors had passed the Triangle company just two weeks before. The jury's task, in other words, was not to determine if working conditions contributed to the loss of life, but to decide the narrow question of whether Margaret Swartz had died because Blanck and Harris had ordered the door on the Washington Place side of the ninth floor be kept locked.

Jury selection began on December 4, 1911, and was completed the next day. All were men because women could not serve on juries in New York. Also on the second day spectators crowding the hall of the courthouse, some of them apparently relatives of the victims, attempted to take matters into their own hands.

ENRAGED WOMEN MOB TRIANGLE WAIST MEN

Attack Harris and Blanck as They Enter the Trial Room, Shouting "Murderers!"

Aim Vain Blows at Them

Accused Men Finally Get Into the Courtroom with the Aid of a Squad of Police.

Some 300 women and girls attacked Isaac Harris and Max Blanck, owners of the Triangle Waist Company, when they appeared yesterday at the Criminal Court Building for trial before Judge Crain in General Sessions for the fire in their factory last March, in which 147 persons lost their lives. The two are charged with manslaughter in the first and second degrees for causing the death of Margaret Schwartz of 745 Brook Avenue, the Bronx, who died in the fire.

• • •

Assistant District Attorneys Bostwick and Rubin were the first to arrive in the courtroom. They were greeted with smiles and good wishes from those in the throng that was striving to get in. Harris and Blanck and their counsel, Max D. Steuer, arrived a few minutes later and started toward the courtroom. A young girl spied them. Taking hold of her mother, she shouted:

"Oh, mamma! Look! Here they come! Here are the murderers of poor Stella. Hit them, mamma, for killing my poor little sister!"

The woman turned around, and with a scream of rage rushed toward the two men and their counsel, drawing a black-bordered photograph from under her ragged shawl and waving it in front of the faces of the two men. Immediately there was a rush in the direction where the two white-faced, trembling men and their lawyer were standing. Three hundred voices shouted:

"Murderers, murderers! Kill the murderers!"

Throngs came on the run from other courtrooms and court attendants ran in to stop the disorder and get the screeching women out of the way. . . .

The defendants were shut off from both the elevators and courtroom and stood huddled together, while their lawyer shoved the struggling women back. He managed to clear a little opening and made a rush for the courtroom, followed by Harris and Blanck. Women grabbed their coattails and struck madly at them as they passed, but they stood so close together that the blows were ineffectual. The guard posted at the door of the courtroom slammed it shut when the three men got inside and locked it just in time to stop the rush of infuriated women. They beat on the doors and continued shouting:

"Murderers! Murderers!"

Defense attorney Max D. Steuer immediately requested police protection for his clients, and the trial began with Assistant District Attorney Charles F. Bostwick's opening statement.

JURY HEARS OF LOCKED DOOR

⟨ornament⟩

And That Girl for Whose Death the Men Are on Trial Was Among 20 Bodies Piled Against It.

⟨ornament⟩

• • •

The work of selecting a jury was completed quickly. . . . Assistant District Attorney Bostwick then opened his case for the prosecution. He described the Washington Place building and the fire, and told of the dark stairways leading from the lofts occupied by Harris and Blanck.

"Jury Hears of Locked Door," *New York Times*, December 7, 1911. Reprinted by permission.

"It is the contention of the prosecution," he declared, "that these defendants here are guilty of manslaughter in that they caused the death of Margaret Schwartz, a young girl employed by them on the ninth floor. It was the custom of these two men to keep the door leading from the exit on the Washington Place side of the building locked at all times, except in the dead of Summer, when the door was opened during working hours to create a draft. None of their employes was allowed to leave by this entrance, but all were forced to leave by the Greene Street entrance, where they were met by a watchman, who searched them in order to see that no goods had been stolen.

"When the fire started there was a rush toward these doors, which opened inwardly. . . . Some rushed toward the Washington Place exit, but the door was locked, as usual, and twenty bodies were found there by the firemen, among others that of Margaret Schwartz. It is a misdemeanor to keep the doors in any factory locked during working hours, and therefore these defendants are guilty if I am able to prove these facts to you."

Prosecutor Bostwick first produced witnesses who testified that Margaret Swartz was one of the twenty victims whose bodies were discovered by the door on the Washington Place side of the ninth floor and that she had in fact died as a result of the fire. Next came Carmella Ingenego, the first of a parade of witnesses, all former workers at Triangle, who testified that she had tried to escape the fire via the Washington Place door but found it locked. She was followed by Felix Reinhardt of Hook and Ladder Company 20, who told of having to break in the door and then of finding the twenty bodies.

Reinhardt's testimony clearly helped the prosecution, but it did not establish that the door was locked at the outbreak of the fire. Defense attorney Steuer suggested, in cross-examining Samuel Bernstein, who also testified that he had found the door locked when he tried to escape, that "a number of persons got out of the Washington Place door on the ninth floor and that in their excitement they locked the door." Bernstein claimed that he got to the door immediately after he heard the cry of "Fire!" and that it was already locked.

Because the prosecution suspected that Steuer would be unable to produce a witness who actually did escape through that door, it piled up testimony by former Triangle employees who tried to get out that way but found the door locked. Damaging as this appeared to be, the defense would later introduce witnesses of its own, including co-owner Isaac Harris, who would claim that they used this door throughout the course of their ordinary activities, that it was always left open, and that, in any case, there was a key attached to a string always hanging from the knob. Either the door was unlocked or else someone inadvertently locked it in the panic of the fire, the defense would claim. Its strategy, that is, would be to make the case a matter of one set of witnesses offsetting the testimony of another. If the jury did not know whom to believe, it would be required to acquit based on the principle of "reasonable doubt."

This made it crucial for the prosecution to find some physical evidence that would prove the door had indeed been locked. Finally, after several days of legal wrangling, it succeeded in introducing into evidence the charred remains of part of the door frame containing the lock.

FATAL LOCK LET IN TRIANGLE FIRE CASE

After a two days' struggle Assistant District Attorney Charles F. Bostwick succeeded yesterday in General Sessions in getting into evidence the rusty, fire-blackened lock, which formerly reposed in the woodwork of the Washington Place door of the Triangle Waist Company's loft on the ninth floor, and which the prosecution declares is responsible for the death of Margaret Schwartz and nineteen others on March 25, when 147 of the employes of Harris & Blanck lost their lives in the fire.

The lock is the link connecting the manslaughter charge against Harris & Blanck with the death of Margaret Schwartz, as it is said that it was by their orders that the Washington Place door was locked. This exhibit was twice before offered and ruled out by Judge Crain, but yesterday Mr. Bostwick succeeded in tracing the lock to the man who put it in the door on the ninth floor of the building, and when the District Attorney again asked Judge Crain to receive it the Judge said:

"In view of the evidence now before me, I will receive it in evidence and overrule the objection of the counsel for the defense."

"Fatal Lock Let in Triangle Fire Case," *New York Times*, December 16, 1911. Reprinted by permission.

The door, the physical evidence seemed to prove, had been locked. Now it devolved on Assistant District Attorney Charles F. Bostwick to prove that Margaret Swartz died because it was. Defense attorney Max Steuer later recalled in a speech before the Missouri Bar Association that he and the defendants had been "in hope, in high hope," that the prosecution intended to rest its case on the circumstantial evidence—the position of the body, the locked door.[1] None of the more than one hundred previous witnesses had testified to seeing Margaret Swartz die. But Bostwick had saved his most important witness for last. What follows is his questioning of Kate Alterman, the one person who claimed to have seen Swartz's clothing catch fire as she frantically struggled to get the door open.

---

[1] Max D. Steuer, "Cross-Examination," in *America Speaks: A Library of the Best Spoken Thought in Business and the Professions*, edited by Basil Gordon Byron and Frederic René Coudert (New York: Modern Eloquence Corporation, 1928), 433. Steuer never wrote out his speeches, he claimed, but relied upon the inspiration of the moment. This may explain why he misstated several facts about the trial, including the name of the witness in this speech.

CROSS EXAMINATION OF KATE ALTERMAN BY DEFENSE ATTORNEY, MAX D. STEUER

KATE ALTERMAN, called as a witness on behalf of the People, being first duly sworn, testifies as follows: (The witness states that she resides at 1023 East Susquehanna Avenue, Philadelphia, Pa.)

Direct Examination by Mr. Bostwick:

Q. On the 25th day of March, 1911, were you employed by the defendants Harris and Blanck? A. Yes, sir.
Q. And on what floor did you work? A. On the ninth floor.
Q. What kind of work did you do? A. Dresses.
Q. Were you an operator? A. Yes, sir.
Q. And for how many months had you been working for Harris and Blanck? A. Four months.
Q. In what part of the shop on the ninth floor did you have your machine? A. On the Washington Place side.
Q. And worked opposite to you? A. On the opposite? A small Italian woman.
Q. Did you know Margaret Swartz? A. Yes, sir.
Q. Did she sit anywhere near you? A. Right near me.
Q. In what part of the loft were you when you first knew that there was a fire? A. In the dressing room.

Max D. Steuer's cross-examination of Kate Alterman (*The People v. Harris & Blanck*, 1911).

Q. And how did you first know there was a fire? **A.** I heard a cry of fire from some girl.

Q. As soon as you heard the cry, where did you go? **A.** I went right to the window to look for the fire escapes.

Q. What part of the building was that? **A.** Waverly Place.

Q. Then where did you go after that? **A.** After that I went into—Margaret Swartz was with me.

Q. Margaret Swartz was with you at this time? **A.** At this time, yes, sir.

Q. Then where did you go? **A.** Then I went to the toilet room, Margaret disappeared from me, and I wanted to go up Greene Street side, but the whole door was in flames, so I went and hide [sic] myself in the toilet rooms, and then I went out right away from the toilet rooms and bent my face over the sink, and then I ran to the Washington side elevator, but there was a big crowd and I couldn't pass through there. Then I noticed some one, a whole crowd, around the door, and I saw Bernstein, the manager's brother trying to open the door, and there was Margaret near him. Bernstein tried the door, he couldn't open it, and then Margaret began to open that door. I take her on one side—I pushed her on the side and I said, "Wait, I will open that door." I tried, pulled the handle in and out, all ways, and I couldn't open it. She pushed me on the other side, got hold of the handle and then she tried. And then I saw her bending down on her knees, and her hair was loose, and the trail of her dress was a little far from her, and then a big smoke came, and I couldn't see, I just know it was Margaret, and I said, "Margaret," and she didn't reply. I left Margaret, I turned my head on the side, and I noticed the trail of her dress and the ends of her hair begin to burn. Then I ran in, in a small dressing room that was on the Washington side, there was a big crowd and I went out from there, stood in the center of the room between the machines and between the examining tables. I noticed afterwards on the other side, near the Washington side windows, Bernstein, the manager's brother throwing around like a wild cat on the windows, and he was chasing his head out of the window, and pull himself back—he wanted to jump, I suppose, but he was afraid. And then I saw the flames cover him. I noticed on the Greene Street side some one else fall down on the floor and the flames cover him. And then I stood in the center of the room, and I just turned my coat on the left side with the fur to my face, the lining on the outside, got hold of a bunch of dresses that was lying on the examining table not burned yet, covered up my head and I tried to run through the flames on the Greene Street side. The whole door was a red curtain of fire, but a young lady came and she began to pull me in the back of my dress and she wouldn't let me. I kicked her with my foot and I don't know what became of her, and I ran out through the Greene Street side door, right through the flames, on to the roof.

Q. When you were standing toward the middle of the floor had you your pocketbook with you? A. Yes, sir, my pocketbook began to burn already, but I pressed it to my heart to extinguish the fire.

Q. And you put the fire out on your pocketbook? A. Yes, sir.

Q. So the last time you saw Margaret Swartz? A. Was at the door.

Q. She was at the Washington Place door on the ninth floor? A. Yes, sir.

Q. And she had her hands on the knob of the door? A. Yes, sir.

Q. When she tried to turn the knob of that door before you had tried it what did she do while she was trying the knob of that door? A. She screamed at the top of her voice, "My God, I am lost! The door is locked! Open the door!"

Q. And that is the last you ever saw of Margaret Swartz? A. That is the last I ever saw of Margaret Swartz.

Q. Now, in your last statement you said that Margaret began to open the door, what did you mean by that? A. She tried to open it.

Q. Do you mean she ever got it open? A. No, sir.

Alterman's testimony, Steuer recalled in 1928, created a sensation:

> I cannot describe to you, gentlemen of the Missouri Bar, the pathetic picture made by that little girl. I cannot reproduce the tears that were running down her cheeks, nor can I tell you how the eyes of the twelve jurors were riveted on her and how they sat craning forward, thrilled by this girl's story and how they wept while she told it. Then, after a long, dramatic pause, looking in silence at her, the District Attorney turned and said, "You may [pausing slightly] cross-examine.[2]

No amount of legal training or experience can prepare you for such a moment, Steuer noted, before describing the cross-examination that would make him one of the most celebrated and highly paid defense attorneys in the nation.

> There are many times, many times when a witness had given evidence very hurtful to your cause and you say, "No questions," and dismiss him or her in the hope that the jury will dismiss the evidence too. [Laughter.] But can you do that when the jury is weeping, and the little girl witness is weeping too? [Laughter.] That is the question. While there is no rule of conduct which tells you what to do, there is one that commands what not to do. Do not attack the witness. Suavely, politely, genially, toy with the story.[3]

---

[2] *Ibid.*, 435.

[3] *Ibid.*, 435–436.

Toying with Alterman's story meant suggesting that it was not hers at all but one taught to her by the prosecution. Before doing that, however, Steuer recalled that he spent some time asking questions about the witness's family, living arrangements, and other extraneous matters. ". . . very little progress was made; but the tears had stopped."[4] It was a tactic he would return to throughout the cross-examination.

Cross Examination by Mr. Steuer:

Q. Did you have a sister working in the place? A. No, sir.

Q. When did you come from Philadelphia? A. I came about the 20th of November, the 18th or 20th of November, I do not remember the date.

Q. And you have been here ever since? A. No, sir, I left after the fire.

Q. Oh, you mean that you came about the 18th or 20th of November before the fire? A. Yes, sir.

Q. I mean when did you come here to testify? A. The day of the trial.

Q. When was that? A. On two weeks ago Monday.

Q. And you came from Philadelphia? A. Yes, sir.

Q. And you were not put on the stand here until you are the last, is that the idea? A. I don't know whether I was kept to the last, or first, but I was not on the witness stand.

Q. You know you have been kept for over two weeks from Philadelphia? A. Yes, sir.

Q. Where have you been living? A. In the Bronx.

Q. And your home is in Philadelphia? A. Yes, sir.

Q. With whom? A. With my parents, now.

Q. And your parents reside there in Philadelphia and you have been away from your parents for two weeks now? A. Yes, sir.

Q. You have been willing to go on the witness stand every day since you have been here, haven't you? A. Yes, sir.

Q. And you have been down to Court here, have you? A. Yes, sir.

Q. And you went away from Court each afternoon and came down next morning? A. Yes, sir.

Q. Spent the day down here in one of the offices in the building? A. Yes, sir.

Q. Before you came down here this last time, to come down every day for two weeks, when did you see anybody from the District Attorney's office before that? A. Saturday.

Q. Do you mean the Saturday before you came from Philadelphia to New York? A. It was the last Saturday.

---

[4] *Ibid.*, 436.

Q. How? A. It was the last Saturday.

Q. You mean you came down here this Saturday, the day before yesterday? A. The day before yesterday.

Q. You were down here Saturday, too, were you? A. Yes, sir.

Q. And did you go anywhere with Mr. Rubin and Mr. Bostwick? A. Yes, sir.

Q. They took you up to the building, did they? A. Yes, sir.

Q. And they went along? A. Yes, sir.

Q. And they pointed out to you where the Washington Place door is? A. I had to point it out to them.

Q. You were taken right over to the Washington Place door, weren't you? A. I took them to the Washington Place door.

Q. They didn't know where it was? A. I don't know whether they knew or not, but they asked me to show it to them.

Q. Well, they took you all around the floor, didn't they? A. I took them all around the floor, I.

Q. You took Mr. Bostwick and Mr. Rubin all around the floor? A. Yes, sir.

Q. You had never gone there before in all the two weeks you were in New York, had you? A. No, sir.

Q. With anybody? A. No, sir.

Q. And how was the appointment made for Saturday? A. Mr. Rubin told me to come, he wants to see me. He showed me the plan and asked me to show on the plan where I saw Margaret last; I couldn't show him very well on the plan for I picked it in my mind the place as it was before the fire, and he couldn't make out very well with me there, and he took me to the place and he told me to show him exactly the place.

Q. All that you have told us about that, was that she was right up against the door, isn't that so? A. She was right near the door.

Q. Well, now, that was right alongside of the Washington Place door? A. She was right near the door with her hands at the knob.

Q. With her hands at the knob? A. At the knob.

Q. But you couldn't tell him that before you went up to the loft? A. Well, I don't believe I told him—I think I told him, I am not sure, though, for when I gave my statement first I was sick that time.

Q. And so you did not make it the same way as you are making it now? A. I made it the same way, just the same way.

Q. Did you tell then that she was with her hand on the knob? A. I don't re-member exactly whether I told the knob, or not, for it was nine months ago.

Q. Did you ever have a sister that visited you at that place? A. Never did.

Q. Have you got a sister at all? A. I have sisters, yes, sir.

Q. How many? A. I have five sisters.

Q. Does one of your sisters live in New York? A. No, sir, they never did.

Q. Are you the only one that was working in New York? A. Yes, sir.

Q. Now, I want you to tell me your story over again just as you told it before? A. What kind of a story do you mean?

Q. You told us before that you had gone to the dressing room do you remember that? A. Yes, sir, before I heard the cry of fire.

Q. And then it was in the dressing room that you heard the cry of fire? A. Yes, sir.

Q. Now you tell us what you did then when you heard the cry of fire? A. I went out from the dressing room, went to the Waverly side windows to look for fire escapes, I didn't find any. Margaret Swartz was with me, afterwards she disappeared. I turned away to get to Greene Street side, but she disappeared, she disappeared from me. I went into the toilet rooms, I went out from the toilet rooms, bent my face over the sink, and then I went to the Washington side to the elevators, but there was a big crowd, and I saw a crowd around the door, trying to open the door, there I saw Bernstein, the manager's brother, trying to open the door but he couldn't; he left; and Margaret was there, too, and she tried to open the door and she could not. I pushed her on a side, I tried to open the door, and I could not, and then she pushed me on the side, and she said, "I will open the door," and she tried to open the door, and then the big smoke came and Margaret Swartz I saw bending down on her knees, her hair was loose and her dress was on the floor a little far from her, and then she screamed at the top of her voice, "Open the door! Fire! I am lost! My God, I am lost, there is fire!" And I went away from Margaret. I left, stood in the middle of the room. That is, I went in the dressing room, first, there was a big crowd, I went out of the dressing room, went in the middle of the room between the machines and examining tables, and then I went in; I saw Bernstein, the manager's brother, throwing around the windows, putting his head from the window—he wanted to jump, I suppose, but he was afraid—he drawed himself back, and then I saw the flames cover him, and some other man on Greene Street, the flames covered him, too, and then I turned my coat on the wrong side and put it on my head with the fur to my face, the lining on the outside, and I got hold of a bunch of dresses and covered up the top of my head. I just got ready to go and somebody came and began to chase me back, pulled my dress back, and I kicked her with the foot and she disappeared. I tried to make my escape. I had a pocketbook on me, and that pocketbook began to burn, I pressed it to my heart to extinguish the fire, and I made my escape right through the flames—the whole door was a flame, right to the roof.

Q. It looked like a wall of flame? A. Like a red curtain of fire.

Q. Now, there was something in that that you left out, I think, Miss Alterman. When Bernstein was jumping around, do you remember what that was like? Like a wildcat, wasn't it? A. Like a wildcat.

Q. You left that out the second time. How long have you lived in Philadelphia?

MR. BOSTWICK: There being no question predicated upon that, I move that that statement be stricken out.

THE COURT: Yes, I will strike it out.

MR. STEUER: I except.

Q. You did leave that out, didn't you, just now, when you told us about Bernstein, that he jumped around like a wildcat? A. Well, I didn't imagine whether a wild cat or a wild dog; I just speak to imagine just exactly.

Q. How long have you lived in Philadelphia? A. Before?

Q. Yes? A. For nine years.

Q. Was that the only time you were in New York? A. Yes, sir.

Q. Altogether you spent in New York how many months? A. Four months.

Q. And during all those four months were you working in this same place? A. Yes, sir.

Q. Was that the only time you worked in New York? A. The only time, yes, sir.

Q. When you were at work where did you sit? A. At work? On the Washington side, the third table.

Q. You mean the third table from the Washington Place side? A. Yes, sir.

Q. And about where on that table did you sit? A. About where? Well, how many machines from the end?

Q. Yes. A. I couldn't tell you exactly.

Q. I don't want to be exact. Just give us an idea so that we can picture it here. A. Well, about six machines, probably, or five machines—I don't know exactly.

Q. From the Washington Place windows? A. No, sir, from the other side. From the Washington Place side was about seven or eight machines.

Q. Well, at any rate that would put you pretty near to the middle of the table, wouldn't it? A. Yes, sir, pretty near, crossing the door.

Q. Now, you heard the signal or bell for the shutting off of the power, didn't you? A. Yes, sir.

Q. Then you got up and left your table, is that it? A. Yes, sir.

Q. And was it at that time that you went into the dressing room? A. Yes, sir.

Q. That was the only time you went to the dressing room, was it? A. Yes, sir.

Q. And of course I am speaking of that afternoon—I meant that afternoon? A. Of that day, yes, sir.

Q. Now, could you tell us again what you did after that time? A. After going out from the dressing room?

Q. Yes? A. I went to the Waverly side windows to look for fire escapes. Margaret Swartz was with me, and then Margaret disappeared. I called her to Greene Street, she disappeared, and I went into the toilet room, went out, bent my face over the sink, and then I wanted to go to the

Washington side, to the elevator. I saw there a big crowd, I couldn't push through. I saw around the Washington side door a whole lot of people standing; I pushed through there and I saw Bernstein, the manager's brother, trying to open the door; he could not, and he left. Margaret Swartz was there, she tried to open the door and she could not. I pushed Margaret on the side, tried to open the door, I could not, and then Margaret pushed me on the other side, and she tried to open the door. Big smoke came and Margaret bent on her knees; her trail was a little far from her, just spreading on the floor far from her, and her hair was loose, and I saw the ends of her dress and the ends of her hair begin to burn. I went into the small dressing room, there was a big crowd, and I tried—I stood there and I went out right away, pushed through and went out and then I stood in the center of the room between the examining tables and the machines. There I noticed the Washington side windows—Bernstein, the manager's brother trying to jump from the window; he stuck his head out—he wanted to jump, I suppose, but he was afraid—then he would draw himself back, then I saw the flames cover him. He jumped like a wildcat on the walls. And then I stood, took my coat, covered my head, turning the fur to my head, the lining to the outside, got hold of a bunch of dresses that was lying on the table, and covered it up over my head, and I just wanted to go and some lady came and she began to pull the back of my dress; I kicked her with the foot and I don't know where she got to. And then I had a purse with me, and that purse begin to burn, I pressed it to my heart to extinguish the fire, and I ran through the fire. The whole door was a flame, it was a red curtain of fire, and I went right on to the roof.

THE COURT: Gentlemen of the jury, you are admonished not to converse among yourselves on any subject connected with this trial, or to form or express any opinion there-on until the same is submitted to you. Recess until two o'clock.

(Recess until 2 P.M.)

After recess. Trial resumed.

KATE ALTERMAN, resumes the stand and further testifies.

Cross Examination by Mr. Steuer, Cont'd:

Q. You never spoke to anybody about what you were going to tell us when you came here, did you? A. No, sir.

Q. You have got a father and a mother and four sisters? A. Five sisters. I have a father, I have no mother—I have a stepmother.

Q. And you never spoke to them about it? A. No, sir, I never did.

Q. They never asked you about it? A. They asked me and I told her once, and then they stopped me, they didn't want me to talk any more about it.

Q. You told them once and then they stopped you and you never talked about it again? A. I never did.

Q. And you never talked to anybody else about it? A. No, sir.

Q. And what you told us here to-day you didn't study that and tell it that way, did you? A. No, sir.

Q. You didn't study the words in which you would tell it? A. No, sir.

Q. Do you remember that you got out to the center of the floor—you remember that? A. I remember I got out through the Greene Street side door.

Q. You remember that you did get to the center of the floor, don't you? A. Between the tables, between the machines, and examining table, in the center.

Q. Now, tell us from there on what you did; start at that point now instead of at the beginning? A. In the beginning I saw Bernstein on the Washington side, Bernstein's brother throwing around like a wildcat; he wanted to jump out from the window, I suppose, but he was afraid; and then he drawed himself back and the flames covered him up; and I took my coat, turned it on the wrong side with the fur to my face, and the lining on the outside, got hold of a bunch of dresses from the examining table covered up my head, and I wanted to run, and then a lady came along, she begin to pull my dress back, she wanted to pull me back, and I kicked her with my foot—I don't know where she got to—and I ran out through the Greene Street side door, which was in flames; it was a red curtain of fire on that door; to the roof.

Q. You never studied those words, did you? A. No, sir.

It wasn't until Steuer's final question that he openly raised the suggestion of Alterman having memorized a story prepared by the prosecution. Prosecutor Bostwick immediately sought to discredit the suggestion.

Re-Direct Examination by Mr. Bostwick:

Q. Now, Miss Alterman, each time that you have answered Mr. Steuer's question you have tried to repeat it in the same language that you first told it here in court, have you not? A. Yes, sir.

Q. And you remember every detail of that story as well today as if it happened yesterday? A. Yes, sir.

Q. And it is all true? A. All true, yes, sir.

Re-Cross Examination by Mr. Steuer:

Q. Can you tell that story in any other words than those you have told it in? A. In any other words? I remember it this way, just exactly how it was done.

Q. Will you please answer my question. Could you tell it in any other words than the words you have told it in here three and one half times? A. Probably I can.

By Mr. Bostwick:

Q. As a matter of fact you did on Saturday, didn't you? A. Yes, sir.

Q. And as matter of fact you did in that statement use different words than you have stated now? A. Yes, sir.

Q. And you could repeat over whatever you told me on Saturday, in those other words? A. Yes, sir.

Q. And you could repeat over your statement that you made, in other words? A. Yes, sir.

Q. And the reason you have repeated—

MR. STEUER: You make a mighty good witness, but please answer one question.

THE COURT: I am waiting to hear objections.

MR. BOSTWICK: I withdraw the question.

Q. Will you state to the jury why you tried to repeat the last time what you told Mr. Steuer in the same language that you used the first time you told Mr. Steuer? A. Because he asked me the very same story over and over, and I tried to tell him the very same thing, because he asked me the very same thing over and over.

Q. And did you think you had to tell it in the same words? A. No, I didn't think, I just told the way he asked me to say it over and over, and I told him in the same words.

Q. I have not spoken to you since recess, have I? A. No, sir.

Q. Not a word? A. No, sir.

By Mr. Steuer:

Q. You say you can tell the jury the same words you used in your written statement? A. Probably I can. My written statement was nine months ago.

MR. BOSTWICK: I offer the statement to the jury.

Q. Tell us the words in the statement, please now?

THE COURT: Answer the question.

A.   Shall I tell you just as in the statement?

Q.   Yes, the words in the statement. A. Well, I gave a very long statement, I believe, to Mr. Rubin.

Q.   Now, start with the words in the statement, please, and not an explanation, Miss, if you can. Tell us just how you started the statement, and then give us the words that are in the statement? A. Well, it would be 4:45 on Saturday, I think that I started this way, I am not quite sure, I don't remember just how I started the beginning of the statement, I can't do it to you.

Q.   Do you remember the words of the statement now, or don't you? A. I don't remember the beginning of the statement, how I began it.

Q.   Mr. Bostwick asked you before whether you could tell again in the same words of the statement, and you said yes. Now I suppose you did not understand that question that way, did you? A. No, sir, I did not.

Steuer recalled that, as Alterman left the witness box, "the jurymen were not weeping." She "had not hurt the case." Further "there was not a word of reflection at any time during that trial upon poor little [Kate]." He concluded:

> I just hold that out to you not because I recognize any art in it, but to suggest when there comes a critical situation, and you don't know what to do, why, just do anything [laughter], because the situation is so bad it can hardly be made worse. [Laughter.] You may attack the story in any way that occurs to you. To attack the witness will likely prove disastrous.[5]

---

[4] *Ibid.,* 436–437.

TRIANGLE OWNERS ACQUITTED BY JURY

<hr>

Harris and Blanck Leave Court with a Strong Police Guard to Protect Them.

<hr>

The Jurors Smuggled Out

<hr>

Throng in the Street Hisses and Reviles the Defendants—To be Tried on Another Indictment.

<hr>

New York Times, December 28, 1911

The jury in the case of Isaac Harris and Max Blanck, owners of the Triangle Waist Company at Washington Place and Greene Street, where 147 persons lost their lives in a fire on March 25 last, who have been on trial in General Sessions for manslaughter in the first and second degrees, brought in a verdict of not guilty yesterday after being out an hour and forty-five minutes.

Judge Crain praised the jurors for the close attention they had given to the case, and then gave orders that they be smuggled out of the courtroom by a rear entrance. Harris and Blanck were taken into the Judge's chambers, where a squad of policemen led them through a maze of courtrooms to the Tombs Court, through which they finally left the building, surrounded by a guard of policemen and detectives. They were escorted to the Worth Street Subway station amid the hissing and reviling of relatives of victims of the fire, who were kept out of the courtroom by order of Judge Crain.

The scene in the courtroom when the jury announced its verdict was commonplace enough, and no demonstration was made. Outside, however, there was excitement and confusion. Men rushed about shouting: "Harris and Blanck are acquitted!" while lawyers gathered in groups and freely discussed Judge Crain's charge. Many of them commented upon the fact that he had failed to make any mention of the number of lives lost, or of the locked door in the waist factory. One well-known criminal lawyer said it was also strange that no mention was made of the witnesses for the defense, who first made sworn statements to the District Attorney that the door was locked and then testified in court that it was open.

JUDGE CRAIN'S CHARGE.

• • •

The jury retired at 2:50 o'clock and filed in again at 4:30. Before they consented to leave the jury room they made the court attendant step to one side and came into court with blanched faces. After they had taken their places Judge Crain said:

"Before the jury renders its verdict I wish to say that there must not be any demonstration of any kind in this courtroom, and wish to warn all those in the rear of the room that there must be unqualified silence."

Foreman Leo Abrahams then announced the verdict and Jurors Charles Vetter and Abraham Weschler added: "That is right: that is the verdict of all of us."

The jurors were then directed to leave by a rear door, and after being smuggled through the Judge's Chambers they got out by a back entrance. Harris and Blanck went to the Judges' Chambers where Mrs. Blanck joined her husband, and several relatives of Harris joined him also.

HAD POLICE ESCORT.

In the meantime a special squad of policemen detailed from the Elizabeth Street Station, at the request of District Attorney Whitman, attempted to clear the corridor, but were instructed to leave the crowd of sobbing men and women alone, and escort the defendants out of the building. On the White Street side of the Criminal Court Building a throng of excited people had gathered near the door, and so they changed their plans and went to the Tombs Court, and from there to the street, leaving in a taxicab which the two men had ordered waiting at the White Street entrance.

Just as Harris and Blanck stepped out in Franklin Street David Weiner of 1476 Madison Avenue, whose sister Rose was among those lost in the fire on March 25, rushed up to them and shouted:

"Murderers! Murderers! You are acquitted now, but we will get you yet!"

Weiner fell in convulsions, and had to be taken to the Hudson Street Hospital in an ambulance. There it is said he is suffering from a disordered mind.

What had swayed the jury, beyond the discrediting of Alterman? One member of the panel, Victor Steinman, told the New York *Evening Mail* that

> All I felt sure of was that the door had been locked. I believed that piece of charred wood and the lock with the shot bolt that the State put into evidence. But then I believed also the testimony that the key was usually in the door and that it was tied to it with a piece of string.
>
> So there was the thought in my mind that during the first rush for that door some panic-stricken girl might have turned the key in an effort to open it.[6]

---

[6] Quoted in "147 Dead, Nobody Guilty," *Literary Digest* 44 (January 6, 1912): 7.

"One of Them"

Grief and rage over the fire did not abate in the weeks and months after the trial. Both remained fresh for years after. In part this was due to the uproar that followed the acquittal of Triangle co-owners Isaac Harris and Max Blanck. To an even greater extent, however, it was due to the determination of the shirtwaist workers themselves never to forget their comrades. They had no doubts about whom to hold responsible for the deaths. And they told the story of the fire again and again as newcomers came to the East Side and found work in the needle trades. Such was Elizabeth Hasanovitz, a young Jewish immigrant from Russia who became a union militant and wrote an autobiography in 1918, only five years after immigrating. She recounted the story of the strike and fire as she received it in 1914 from an unnamed union official (probably S. S. Polokoff, himself a Russian Jewish immigrant and an International Ladies Garment Workers Union organizer). Hasanovitz first had heard of the fire while still in Russia and remembered "what a panic that news caused in our town when it first came" because many families had daughters in America and "each of them was almost sure that their daughter was a victim of that terrible catastrophe."

The version of the fire that Hasanovitz heard in 1914, like all folk histories, exaggerated some details and omitted others. So, for example, the Asch Building did have fire escapes; they were simply too narrow to permit more than a handful of workers to use them. And Harris and Blanck did not keep *all* of the factory doors locked. Instead, as prosecutors sought to prove at their trial, they kept one door on each floor locked so that all employees would have to leave by a single exit where a watchman could inspect their bags in an effort to prevent theft. And wages at Triangle were no lower than elsewhere in the industry. Even these errors of fact are important evidence, however. They are part of how the shirtwaist workers remembered their own history and thus disclose something about how they viewed themselves, their union, and their ongoing struggles with their employers.

EXCERPT FROM "ONE OF THEM"

By Elizabeth Hasanovitz

. . . Bundles were flying from hand to hand, waists were slipping from the machines into the baskets, from the baskets to the counter. The girls were bent low over their machines, as if nothing else mattered to them; their talking ceased, only their singing encouragingly speeded the ponderous machines as if driving them quicker. The forelady ran from one table to the other as if in a frenzy—all was rush—and we were in it.

But all that humdrum rush, the buzzing noise, suddenly stopped. I came in to work one morning and found the girls in a peculiarly excited condition. Each looked at the other so strangely. The girls on my table scarcely worked. Some of them were dressed in black. It was unusually quiet: no laughter, no songs to accompany the noisy machinery. The faces of all were so serious and said.

"What happened?" I asked my neighbor.

"Why it's the *25*th of March to-day!"

"The *25*th of March—so what is that?"

Elizabeth Hasanovitz, "One of Them," chapter from *A Passionate Autobiography* (Boston and New York: Houghton Mifflin Co., 1918), 213–19.

She looked at me unpleasantly surprised. I felt very weak that morning and was indifferent to questioning any more. I absorbed myself in the work and I could hardly notice what was going on around me.

Suddenly my neighbor pulled my sleeve. "Why don't you stand up?"

I raised my head. All the people in the shop stood on their feet, mournfully looking at each other. Instinctively I jumped up. We stood that way for a few seconds. Tears were in the people's eyes when they went back to work. I felt ashamed to ask my neighbor again. From the way she looked at me I understood that any waist-maker should know what the 25th of March was. As I sat puzzled, the word "Triangle" was pronounced somewhere behind me. I thrilled with terror! It struck me immediately—the memorial day of the hundred and forty-seven young workers who lost their lives on the 25th of March in the year 1911.

• • •

When that catastrophe occurred I was home in Russia. I still remember what a panic that news caused in our town when it first came. Many a family had their young daughters in all parts of the United States who worked in shops. And as the most of those old parents had an idea of America as one big town, each of them was almost sure that their daughter was a victim of that terrible catastrophe. Their tears never dried until they at last received letters from their children that they were alive. So it was the 25th of March to-day! In the same day three years ago one hundred and forty-seven girls were burned alive! I could work no more. My machine, the work, the shop, and the people all faded, and before me stood out the picture of Waverly Place where the big Ash Building was embraced in fire tongues. Hundreds of people crowded the windows crying piteously for help. The doors were locked, no fire escapes in all the building. Most of the men were quick enough to get into the elevators and were saved. Those girls who could not push themselves through to the elevators jumped through the windows and were killed. The rest were burned.

Impatiently I waited for that evening. . . . our union had a memorial meeting for the hundred and forty-seven innocent victims that evening and [I] was anxious to be present and know more about it. After six o'clock I went to the union office and entered the manager's room. He had his hat and coat on ready to leave. "No complaints to-night, little friend! I must hurry to the meeting," he said.

"Oh, please, just for a few minutes. You are dealing with the Triangle since 1913. You know all about that firm in the past. Will you not tell me about it. I want so much to know of the conditions prevailing there now and before."

I spoke with such urgency that he could not refuse. "Come on for supper with me if you wish. We'll talk while eating," he said.

I gladly consented. In the restaurant in a far corner, at a small table, there we sat silent for a long while until he at last began, his deep, expressive eyes sadly gazing into space while he spoke:—

"For years and years our union had a hard fight with the Triangle Waist Company. The most miserable conditions that could be imagined prevailed in the Triangle shops. Directly the bosses had very little to do with the workers. They kept men inside contractors. Each man had a set of ten or twelve girls, who worked under him. Those men were the actual employees of the Triangle. The people worked the longest hours, getting two and three dollars a week. The discipline there was of the severest. The doors were locked from soon after eight in the morning till lunch hour. If any girl happened to be a few minutes late after lunch, the door was locked against her till the next morning. No one was allowed to leave the shop during working hours.

"The sub-contractors always tried to get in newly arrived immigrants—people without any knowledge of the English language and American life—people who were helpless and lived at the mercy of the bosses, who only gave them enough to keep soul and body together. Their time and freedom belonged to the boss. Like locked-up prisoners they sat working in the shop—a place without the slightest protection for their lives. And when at last the people could not stand any longer such slavery, they went down on strike, demanding a little of their human rights. For twenty weeks the firm fought them bitterly, trying to break the strike. They hired gangsters to make riots and fight the pickets, and when the men gangsters would be afraid to beat girls, the firm went so far as to hire immoral women to beat the pickets. The union, at this time being very small and weak, tried her best to help the strikers. For the first time the union called a general strike, and though many shops were organized, the Triangle remained as it was. The strike was broken, the people returned to work on the previous conditions. Again the people worked for three dollars a week. Again they slaved behind locked doors. The cuttings of the goods were always heaped up around the tables. The smallest spark could inflame all the building in a minute. The people never thought of it. Their

struggle for mere existence could not make them realize in what danger they were every minute of the day in case of fire. While in the
union shops the people worked on Saturday till one o'clock in the afternoon, in the non-union shops, including the Triangle, the people
worked till five. The fire broke out on Saturday between three and
four in the afternoon, and before the people had time to get up from
their machines the house was all in flames. The foremen and contractors, who had the keys of the doors with them, forgot to think of the
people. They hastened to save their own lives, leaving the people to
the mercy of the fire. And oh,—"

Here he stopped for a while, has teeth gnashing, his eyes sparkling
fire.

"Who only saw that panic could never forget it. The heart-breaking
cries of the burning girls! It still rings in my ears. Like wounded ani-
mals they ran from one door to another, knocking, calling for help, but
all in vain.

"Down the street, around the building, thousands of people stood,
but could not help. Women fainted and cried in the streets. The unfortunate parents of the victims ran around in a frenzy.

"Suddenly—a terrible cry—'My child! Oh, my child!' a mother
stood near me clasping her hands in agony, and looking wildly up at
the burning building where her daughter stood near the window, her
hands outstretched.

" 'Mother, mother!' she cried, and jumped out through the window. One instant—and she lay crushed to death on the sidewalk. Her
mother, falling on the body, was immediately stricken with insanity. A
few seconds later four girls clasped their arms and jumped. Their
heads were crushed, their arms still clasped around each other. The
rest of the girls, seeing their co-workers killed on the sidewalk, were
afraid to jump, and they found their death in fire."

He stopped. Tears were in his eyes. He did not touch his supper.
Neither did I.

"To think that the Triangle bosses were so heartless, when only
on Saturday that terrible catastrophe occurred; when all the city
mourned; when the burned and mutilated bodies still lay on the
street,—those bosses were so shameless as to come out with an advertisement the following Monday, notifying the people that they were
ready for business in their new office! Ready for business again, so
soon after the horrible death of a hundred and forty-seven young beings! They could have foreseen the danger in not having fire-escapes,

in not cleaning up the heaped-up scraps of goods. They did not care. They kept the doors closed so that a worker should not be able to leave during working hours—and soon after that fire the Triangle opened that shop again. The factory's contractors got other newly arrived innocent young immigrants. They made these girls work the same long hours, for the same starvation wages, under the same strong discipline as before." . . .

"Fire and the Skyscraper"

". . . after this," one of the jurors in the Blanck-Harris manslaughter trial told the press, "I have no faith in jury trials." Another juror admitted: "I know I didn't do my duty to the people, but the court's charge [i.e., the judge's instructions to the jury] prevented." The judge had instructed the jurors that, because the defendants were charged with a felony, "I charge you that . . . you must find that this door was locked. If it was locked and locked with the knowledge of the defendants, you must also find beyond reasonable doubt that such locking caused the death of Margaret Schwartz." And, as juror Victor Steinman pointed out, he couldn't be sure that Blanck and Harris knew the door was locked. He went on:

> It would have been much easier for me if the State factory inspectors instead of Harris and Blanck had been on trial. For there would have been no doubt in my mind then as to how to vote.
>
> Their duties are clearly outlined by the law. It was up to them, more than to Harris and Blanck, to see that the door was not locked. But they were not on trial. Yet all the time . . . I kept thinking about them.[1]

Many shared Steinman's dissatisfaction with the trial. Legal guilt, it turned out, hinged on a matter—Harris and Blanck's knowledge of the door being locked—about which there was conflicting testimony and thus no final proof. Worse, even if the door had been unlocked, the loss of life in the fire would still have been horrible. Many, like Steinman and several of his fellow jurors, longed for a fuller accounting of the causes of the catastrophe. The newly created Factory Investigating

---

[1] Quoted in "147 Dead, Nobody Guilty," *Literary Digest* 44 (January 6, 1912): 7.

Commission, excerpts of whose hearings are reprinted here, would take this as one of its responsibilities. But the work of the commission went on for several years; its preliminary report was not issued until well into 1912. And its primary concern quickly turned from assaying blame to designing preventive and protective legislation.

It was the press, particularly the so-called muckraking magazines, that offered contemporaries the fullest accounting of what caused the disaster and of where the responsibility for the tragedy lay. The Triangle fire was perhaps the biggest story of 1911. Of the innumerable feature articles it occasioned, Arthur E. McFarlane's piece for *McClure's Magazine* is by far the most carefully researched. *McClure's* was the original home of muckraking journalism, as the investigative reporting pioneered by Lincoln Steffens, Ida Tarbell, and others who wrote for the magazine came to be called. Such writers saw themselves as reformers and their task as educating the public in the underlying causes of the problems they described. If they succeeded in telling their stories vividly enough, they believed that their aroused readers would demand that their elected representatives act.[2] In this instance, at least, the muckrakers' faith in the power of information was justified. The Factory Investigating Commission created by the New York State legislature held its first hearing the month after this article appeared. McFarlane was one of the witnesses who testified before that panel. And the commission followed up many of the issues he raised in this article. In his testimony, he called particularly for reform of the fire insurance industry, a position he elaborated in his "The Triangle Fire—The Story of a 'Rotten Risk,' " *Collier's* 51 (May 17, 1913): 7–8, 28–29.

---

[2] A good recent discussion is Ellen F. Fitzpatrick, "Introduction: Late-Nineteenth-Century America and the Origins of Muckraking," in Fitzpatrick, ed., *Muckraking: Three Landmark Articles* (Boston, New York: Bedford Books of St. Martin's Press, 1994).

FIRE AND THE SKYSCRAPER: THE PROBLEM OF PROTECTING THE WORKERS IN NEW YORK'S TOWER FACTORIES

ARTHUR E. MCFARLANE

• • •

The Asch Building was, and is, safer than most loft buildings. It is a handsome ten-story structure just off Washington Square. It is only a hundred feet by a hundred in area, without irregularities. It has a stairway and two elevators side by side on its Washington Place front, and the same equipment diagonally across the building on its Greene Street side, the latter elevators being used for freight and the operatives. It had a four-inch stand-pipe with hose in racks on every stairway landing, and on every floor there were fire-pails. It had no sprinkler system—without which no cotton mill in New England can buy insurance. But sprinkler systems are not compulsory in New York factories. And the owner, Joseph J. Asch, took a chance on it.

About Fifteen Hundred People at Work on the Afternoon of the Fire

The Triangle Waist Company occupied the eighth, ninth, and tenth floors. It was in this shop that the New York shirtwaist-makers' strike of 1909 first started. The officers of the Women's Trade Union League stated that the proprietors Harris & Blanck, had stood for all the bad conditions which brought this strike about. In the actual matter of danger from fire, the Triangle factory was safer than the average. It had no clotheslines of combustibles, or gas-lights, or electric knives. Its stock- and shipping-rooms were on the tenth floor, where only about sixty people were employed; and its gas-iron pressing was also done there. It had automatic alarms. On the day of the fire fifty or sixty of the employees were at home, because of Saturday being the Jewish holiday; but Max Blanck, the senior partner, estimated that ordinarily there were 225 operatives on the eighth floor

Arthur E. McFarlane, "Fire and the Skyscraper: The Problem of Protecting the Workers in New York's Tower Factories," *McClure's Magazine* 37 (September 1911), 473–80.

and 350 on the ninth, besides the sixty people on the tenth floor. It was the rush season. The factory was under a pressure that kept it working till late Saturday afternoons and even on Sundays. And when the law allows a factory owner to have three hundred and fifty people on the ninth floor, that is exactly how many he is going to have. Many of the girls were constantly in fear. There are stories enough to make that evident. And in 1909 an insurance inspector suggested that it would be the part of safety to arrange fire drills. He had Mr. H. F. J. Porter, the father of factory fire drills, write to Harris & Blanck offering to organize one. His letter was not answered. Of 1,243 cloak and suit factories investigated two years later by the Joint Board of Sanitary Control, a fire drill was found in only one. There might, legally, have been 1,100 people working in the Triangle factory instead of 625; and in the whole building 3,600 instead of the 1,200 or 1,500 that there actually were. Again, the Triangle factory was the only one at work after four o'clock that Saturday afternoon. Throughout this story you are to remember what would have happened had this fire broken out on the second floor or the third when the whole building was full.

The Fire Starts on the Eighth Floor, Just at Closing Hour

There have been various explanations of how the fire started. "A cutter let a match fall on some old waste." "Some one stepped on a match on the floor." "A man was cleaning his coat with gasolene." It really does not make much difference how the fire started, when there are so many ways in which it could have started. On the cutting-tables of the eighth floor the "stretches" of lawn—one hundred and seventy-five or eighty layers of the flimsy stuff to a "stretch," with as many alternating layers of tissue-paper—were waiting ready for the Sunday work. It was a quarter to five. The bell had just rung for "power off," and most of the girls

(continued)

had left the tables for the dressing- and wash-rooms, when one of them, Eva Harris, ran to tell the superintendent, Samuel Bernstein, that the boys were putting out a fire over between two ta-bles on the Greene Street side. (There had been fires before. Blanck had put out one himself with his coat.) Bernstein caught up two fire-pails and went over to put this fire out.

But this was not the fire that was put out. "It was in a rag-bin, and it jumped right up." Some of the girls got pails and tried to help. "But it was like there was kerosene in the water; it just seemed to spread it." Frank Formalek, one of the elevator-men, left his car and ran in to help. Louis Senderman and a boy, Leo Todor, tried to use the stand-pipe hose in the hall. They couldn't turn the valve-wheel. "It was rusted," they said, "and the hose, wherever it was folded, was rot-ten." The whole Greene Street side was burning now, and the fire had begun to come over the ta-bles. Diana Lipschitz, the bookkeeper, sent in an alarm, and then telautographed up to the office staff on the tenth floor to run for their lives. The girl who received the message thought that Diana was "stringing" her. Already the fifty cutters had begun to run for *their* lives. It was what firemen call a "flash fire"; and all such factory fires, when once they get started, are going to be flash fires. Bernstein yelled to Louis Brown, a machin-ist, that they couldn't do anything, to get the girls out.

On the street, a hundred feet below, the fire was heard before it was seen. An Italian named Cardiane, standing at the Greene Street entrance, heard a sound "like a big puff." He saw smoke and flame come out with it, and a noise of falling glass started a horse to running away. The falling glass came from the first eighth-floor windows that blew out.

The Flames Spread to the Ninth and Tenth Floors Inside of Three Minutes

You will be told that when a building is fire-proof the fire can't spread from one floor to another. Foreman Howard Ruch, of Engine Company 18, ar-rived on a high-pressure truck two or three min-utes after the eighth-floor windows blew out. "I saw a sheet of flame come out from the eighth floor," he testified.* "It welled into the street, and then it veiled into the windows of the ninth and tenth floors as if drawn by a magnet." Firemen generally call that "lapping in."

• • •

For all three floors it was now a question of get-ting out.

Triangle Employees Could Not Have Got Down by the Fire-Escape in Less than Three Hours

On the eighth floor the boy Todor and an operative named Starkofsky ran for the fire-escape. For there was a fire-escape—a series of landings, eighteen inches in the clear, leading to stairways little better than ladders. It ended five feet from the ground in a closed court. The court itself was soon to be full of fire, and on some of the landings the fire-escape was blocked by iron shutters which had been fastened open. . . . the employees on those three upper floors could not have got to the ground by such an escape in less than three hours; and the fire allowed them perhaps three minutes.

Yet ten or twelve girls and men threw them-selves out after Todor and Starkofsky, and began to fight their way down, one upon another. Several fell from landing to landing. One man let himself down by knotting two sections of machine belting together. Most of them managed to break their way in through the windows of the sixth floor, where they were found later, bleeding and moaning. But the boy Todor went all the way to the bottom; falling most of the way, he broke the skylight in the court and got out through the cellar. From the *ninth* floor one girl, Comella Vetere, got down the fire-escape, shielding her head from the flame with her big hat. But that belch of smoke and flame from the eighth floor did not let many more get down. Out of nearly six hundred, this "good and sufficient means of egress" (to quote the Building Code again) saved fewer than twenty.

• • •

Girls Testify that the Doors Were Locked

Some of the girls on the eighth floor had followed the fleeing cutters to the Greene Street door. But to get to it they had to go through one of those narrow passages where their handbags were ex-amined at night. The fire was already over the top of it; in another minute it was entirely cut off. Blocked on the Greene Street side, the girls who knew where the Washington Place door and

(continued)

---

* After the fire there were investigations by the Board of Coro-ners, the Fire Marshal, and the Bureau of Buildings. All that ap-pears hereafter in quotation marks comes from the evidence of witnesses and survivors, taken under oath; or, in cases where there was vagueness, of amplifying statements made to the writer.

elevators were ran screaming to them. Downstairs the elevator bells began to ring,—they never stopped ringing,—and then the wire glass of one of the elevator doors was pushed in.

The door into the Washington Place stairway opened inwardly,—that is, toward the girls,—and they testified that it was, as always, locked.* They screamed and beat upon it with their fists, but it would not open. Louis Brown, the machinist, denies that it was fastened. But he "wanted to *see* if it was locked," he says queerly. "I tried to turn the key, and it would not turn. I seen I could not turn the door (*sic*). I pulled the knob open, and the girls rushed out." Behind them the superintendent, Bernstein, kept telling them to "go nice."

There were about a hundred and twenty-five girls to go down by that stairway. It was thirty-three inches wide, and practically a winding stair. According to both the girls and the firemen, no lights were burning in it. Even when people are cool, they can hardly go down a stairway such as that without stumbling. One of the girls fainted or fell at the seventh floor, others fell on top of her, and that "backed them up,"—that, too, when most of the girls were still in the room and the fire rapidly coming nearer.

"There were many girls at the door," says Isaac Szivos, a Hungarian tucker. "They were screaming and crying. There were so many I could not get out. I went on a window and I would like to jump. But on the other side of the street I saw some girls that was working there wave their hands that I must not." "A girl's clothes caught fire, and a man's, and they jumped," says Rose Bernstein; "I seen one girl run to a window, and when I got down to the sidewalk I had to step over her." Brown, and a policeman named Meehan who had run in and up the stairs, managed to break that jam on the seventh floor, and every girl who got into the stairway from the eighth floor got out alive. It must be remembered that below the eighth floor the stairs were empty.

THE RUSH FOR THE ROOF

The tenth floor received the alarm before the ninth. And on the tenth nearly every one escaped, most of them through the Greene Street stairway to the roof. "Never go to the roof," Chief Bonner used to say. But here the roof saved lives. Both partners were on the tenth floor. Blanck had two

of his children with him. That day he was taking a chance, like everybody else. But students of the University of New York climbed over from their roof adjoining and helped. One of them, Frederick Newman, groped his way down into that tenth-floor loft itself. And they thought they had taken out everybody. Four girls, however, had been left behind in the dressing-room. "When I came out," says one of them, Anna Dorrity, an Irish girl, "I saw them all gone, and I didn't know what was the matter." They went to the Greene Street door, and saw the Greene Street stairway below them full of smoke and fire. They didn't know that there were any exits on the Washington Place side, and they didn't know that the Greene Street stairs would take them to the roof. One girl jumped at once. The others started to pile up chairs and tables, in the hope of getting out through the skylight.

WHAT HAPPENED ON THE NINTH FLOOR

On the ninth floor, after that first "lapping in" of the flames from below, there were two or three minutes in which almost every one who was going to escape, escaped. The passage leading to the Greene Street door and to the elevators was just twenty inches wide. The little door in it opened inward, and men and girls tore the clothes from one another, trying to get through. Yet a hundred and fifty or more did get through, and three fourths of that hundred and fifty got down alive.

But on the ninth floor, as on the eighth, it was the Greene Street door, the *open* door, that was cut off first. And nearly two hundred people, most of them girls, remained inside. The thing that was to happen, happened there.

Natie Weiner, a thick-set little Jewish girl, who with eight others worked in one of the aisles cutting out lace, "saw a fellow who knew there was a door on the Washington Place side." And she joined a rush of girls for it. Once more, those girls had no way of knowing for themselves that there were two doors. The partitions hid them, as they do in all such factories. And there were no ruby incandescents and red arrows pointing the way to fire exits, such as you have even on the ground floors of theaters. "We run first to the elevator," says Natie Weiner, "and he was not up. We knocked on the door, and he didn't come." Then they turned to the stairway door. "It was locked and there was no key there. . . . I tried to break it open, and I couldn't. . . . There was a woman forty years old there who was burned—Mary Herman—and Bessie Bischofsky, and there was others, and they were next to me and with me at the door; and I

---

* There were two stairways, one on the Greene Street side and one on the Washington Place side. The charge is that on the ninth floor Harris & Blanck kept the doors on the Washington Place side locked, compelling all the girls to leave the building by the narrow passage on the Greene Street side where the hand-bags were examined.

(continued)

said to the woman, 'You try. You may be stronger.' She said, 'I can't.' So then I said, 'Let us all go at it!' And we did."

By that time, even had they been able to get the door open, could they have got past the fire now pouring itself up that stairway from the eighth floor? However, they never got it open. The lock, with the bolt shot, was found later in the débris, a few paces in front of where the charred remnants of floor-board and paneling still held together till the firemen burst them in.

ELEVATORS RUN UNTIL BROKEN BY THE FALLING BODIES

But why talk of fire-escapes and stairways when there were elevators? Every one knows it is upon their elevators that high buildings depend, just as it is the elevator that has made the high building possible.

On the Greene Street side one of the elevator-men ran away at the first cry of fire. His car stood useless till an elevator-man from the street, a young fellow named John T. Gregory, who happened to be passing, threw himself into the car and made trip after trip in a building that was already a nightmare. He ran the car until he was half dead himself, and until the bodies of those who could not wait and flung themselves down the shaft kept the car from running any longer.

Thomas Horton, a negro porter, helped keep the machines going in the basement. "They ran until they couldn't run," he testified; "we were putting in the switch cables till they were overrun with water. They stuck. The circuit-breakers were blowing out."

On the Washington Place side, to which the hundreds cut off on the eighth and ninth floors were crowding, there were two elevators, measuring five feet by six. They went first to the eighth floor, because it was on that floor that the fire broke out; and then to the tenth, to save the proprietors and staff. One of the elevator-men, Giuseppe Zito, ran his car until he fainted; and he still shows the effects of what he went through. But his companion, Gaspar Mortillaro, tells the story:

"I had too much on the car. The car gave way. They jumped down and everything, on top of me." (Because of the smoke the operators could not see where the floor levels were, and had to open their doors at random.) "They were holding my hands and pulling my hair and jabbing me in the face. I do not know what I hit. The door would not close and all the glass came down on me. They fell on me and I could not stop them. They slid down the ropes." (Many tried to slide down the "ropes." An

Italian woman, Levantina, gave another the center cable "because it would be easier." And when somehow she got to the bottom herself, she found herself putting her foot on a dying girl who said, "Please don't step on me.") "They jumped on the roof of my car. About twenty jumped on top of the roof." Even when the cars were far below them, the girls continued to jump, and their bodies wedged in between car and shaft. Above one elevator on the Greene Street side nineteen bodies were found so. It did not take long to finish with the elevators.

THE FIRE DEPARTMENT HELPLESS

But the New York Fire Department—four thousand men, with aërial trucks and water-towers and a high-pressure system—why wasn't it doing anything?

There was a delay of only two or three minutes in sending in the alarm. The pipemen of Engine Company 72 met the first mob of men and girls at the bottom of the stairs. But some had jumped by then. "They were down quicker one way than the other," said a truckman. And more were crowding out on the sills. Battalion Chief Worth used his first two lines to hose down the building above their heads. "That was the only reassurance we could give," he said. And a minute later, when the wind swung the flames around, that was of no avail. There was hardly time to get the scaling-ladders out of the truck. And when they ran up the extension-ladder, that reached only to the sixth story. High-Pressure Company 18, with some citizens helping, stretched a new fourteen-foot rope net. Three girls jumped together from the ninth—and fireman and citizens together were jerked headlong in upon their mangled bodies. A mathematical calculation made afterward showed that the impact of those three bodies was equal to a dead weight of *sixteen tons*. Within two minutes, so many bodies had piled themselves on top of the first high-pressure line that it had to be left where it was and another was stretched in. Hook and Ladder Company 20 spread its big twenty-foot Browder net. "There were so many bodies hitting the ground," Worth testified, "that it was impossible to see them. You did not see them. You heard the sound of the impact of the body hitting the ground. They came down entwined in bunches and with their arms around each other. It tore the springs out of the canvas of the net and tore open the steel frame." They broke holes that a horse could have fallen into through the glass and concrete vault lights over the cellar. You might as well have sent a fire department to handle a powder-mill explosion. Why talk of
(continued)

fire departments, when fire departments have no power to take those measures that will prevent fires, when the fireman is not called in until the case is hopeless?

STORIES OF THE GIRLS WHO ESCAPED

But the story is still to tell of what was taking place within those ninth- and tenth-floor lofts. It is told by five or six survivors who escaped, they themselves know not how.

The day after the fire there were a great many people who hastened to explain that the loss of life was due almost entirely to panic. Panic has always been a good explanation. When those girls saw themselves trapped a hundred feet above the street, some of them tried to fight the fire with the pails. One little girl was still holding fast to her pail when her body was taken up from the sidewalk. But the flames were coming in from outside, and there wasn't anything to fight. "I broke the window with my pail," says Anna Gullo, of the ninth floor, "and more came in." "We started to run all around," says Yetta Lubitz, "and the flames came out all around." Some of them began to catch fire. Almost none jumped till they were on fire. And those who weren't had to keep away from those who were. "The flames were near me. My mouth was full of smoke," says Natie Weiner; "I wanted to get on a table and jump. But the windows were too crowded, and I seen so many bodies laying dead on the ground that I thought I would be dead, too. . . . But the smoke and flames were terrible, and some of the girls said it was better to be smashed than burned, and they wanted to be identified." "They didn't want to jump," says little Rosie Yusum; "they was afraid. They was saying their prayers first, and putting rags over their eyes so they should not see." Up on the tenth they were jumping, too. "Her name was Clotilde," says the Irish girl, Anna Dorrity. "She was an Italian. She said, 'You jump first.' But when she had said her prayers she said, 'No; let me jump now.' "

On the ninth floor fifty-eight girls crawled into a little corridor or cloak-room. "I saw them *piled*," testified fireman Jacob Wohl, one of the first to enter. "They had their faces toward a little window."

• • •

THE JEWISH GIRL, SALLIE WEINTRAUB, WHO JUMPED FROM THE NINTH STORY

They were still jumping. It was all happening together, it is necessary to remember. A Jewish girl, Sallie Weintraub, had got out on a ledge on the Washington Place side. "For a minute," says an on-looker, "she held her hands rigid, her face upward, looking toward the sky." The fire was coming nearer to her. But, before she jumped, "she began to raise her arms and make gestures, as if she were addressing a crowd above her."

What was she saying? We have all of us a pretty good idea of what she was saying. But it isn't the kind of thing we want to let ourselves think about.

• • •

In New York, two days after the fire, the officials of the Bureau of Buildings posted a notice on the door of the Asch Building to inform its owner, as was their official duty, that, under the requirements of the department, his building could no longer be regarded as safe. It was unsafe, among other reasons, "because the treads on the rear stairs from the tenth floor were cracked and broken"; because "the fire-escape on the rear was warped, twisted, and unsafe"; because "the doors of the elevator shafts were burned, damaged, and in an unsafe condition"; because "*the vault lights on Washington Place and Greene Street, together with the supports for the same, were broken and unsafe.*" These were the vault lights that were broken by the impact of the falling bodies. If those holes had been left open, and any one had fallen into them, the said owner, Joseph J. Asch, would almost certainly have been held to be responsible. Damages might have been collected from him. It is even possible that responsibility might have attached to the great city of New York itself. Therefore, before he could open his building for loft factories again, the said owner must make these detailed and necessary repairs.*

---

* The damage done to the Asch Building amounted to a little more than $10,000. The building was insured for $300,000, and the contents of the Triangle Waist Factory for $200,500. Under an employers' liability law setting a price of only $1,000 upon the life of a worker, the additional loss would have amounted to $146,000. With a law preventing the factory owner from transferring his liability, could any employer afford to take the chance which brought the Triangle fire about?

Abram I. Elkus, Opening Statement

Muckraking accounts like McFarlane's "Fire and the Skyscraper" made it plain that the locked door on the Washington Place side of the ninth floor of the Asch Building, the alleged misdemeanor that enabled the City of New York to indict the Triangle co-owners for manslaughter, was—however culpable one thought Isaac Harris and Max Blanck—hardly the only reason why the fire occasioned such a terrible loss of life. In fact, one of the merits of McFarlane's account was the way it so clearly showed that the number of dead could easily have been much greater had the fire broken out on a lower floor or had the lower floors been occupied with workers also seeking to evacuate the building. What was more, even had the jury found Harris and Blanck guilty, their punishment would not address the fact that factory buildings were not required by law to install sprinkler systems. Nor would it address the inadequate fire escapes or the absence of fire doors or the fact that the city's fire companies could not direct water at fires above the seventh floor because of the limits of the water pressure available. McFarlane's estimate, sustained by expert testimony at the Factory Investigating Commission hearings, that the Triangle workers had perhaps three minutes from the outbreak of the fire during which to get out of the building, meant that, even in the event that all the doors had been open, most of the victims would still have lost their lives. Only changes in the ways factories were regulated and inspected could address the problems he and others pointed out.

The first public hearing held by the Factory Investigating Commission was on October 10, 1911, at City Hall in New York City. Abram I. Elkus served as chief counsel and interrogated the witnesses and organized the testimony; he began the hearing with an opening statement that summed up both the legislature's charge to the commission and the reforming spirit with which it began its work. Of particular note is Elkus's effort to state a rationale for the state to regulate working conditions. This was a crucial issue because the U. S. Supreme Court had previously struck down a number of state efforts to regulate wages and working conditions as violating the "due process" clauses of the Fifth and Fourteenth Amendments and had only recently upheld a state law limiting the working hours of women in *Muller v. Oregon*.[1]

---

[1] Both amendments prohibit a state from interfering with a citizen's exercise of any rights, including property rights, without due process of law. The court had held that laws regulating hours of work, for example, improperly restricted the rights of employers and employees to enter into contracts freely. *Muller v. Oregon*, decided in 1908, represented a retreat from this position and a return to an earlier constitutional doctrine that recognized the broad "police" powers of the states to protect the lives and health of their citizens.

OPENING STATEMENT: ABRAM I. ELKUS, COUNSEL TO THE COMMISSION

Minutes of the Hearing of the New York State Factory Investigating Commission Held in the City Hall at 10.30 A.M.

MR. ELKUS: . . . It is unfortunate that the occurrence of a catastrophe is often necessary to awaken a people to its true sense of responsibility. The Triangle Waist Company fire of March, 1911, with its attendant horrors and loss of life shocked both city and State. The loss of one hundred and forty-three lives in one factory fire brought to the attention of the public with terrible force the dangers that daily threaten the lives of hundreds of thousands of employees in manufacturing establishments in the City of New York and elsewhere throughout the State.

Public attention was directed not only to the dangers which threaten employees because of inadequate fire-escape facilities, and because of the lack of precautions against fire, but also to the less obvious but greater menace of unsanitary conditions.

Minutes of the hearing of the New York State Factory Investigating Commission, opening statement: Abram I. Elkus, counsel to the commission, October 10, 1911 (Preliminary Report II: 5–6, 7, 8, 9).

It has become increasingly clear that it is the duty of the State to safeguard the worker, not only against the occasional accidents, but the daily incidents of industry, not only against the accidents which are extraordinary, but against the incidents which are the ordinary occurrences of industrial life.

• • •

The problem before the Commission which meets to-day, is the problem of human conservation—the conservation of the lives of the toilers who most need protection at toil on the part of the State, and the destruction of whom by accidents, avoidable or unavoidable, constitutes a deadly injury to the State. This Commission must concern itself with the problem of how to meet the evils that have arisen in the development of industry out of human wastage that has not only been needless but often reckless and wanton.

• • •

If it has rightly been said that a man may be killed by a tenement house as truly as by a club or a gun, is it not equally true that a man may be killed by a factory and the unsanitary conditions which obtain therein, as surely as he may be killed by a fire accident. And it is not less true that the slaughter of men and women workers by the slow processes of unsanitary and unhealthful conditions is not only immoral and anti-social, but the state is beginning to declare that it is legally indefensible, and therefore must, through carefully considered legislation, be made virtually impossible.

Apart from the humanitarian aspect of the matter which must appeal strongly to every lover of his kind, to require the establishment and maintenance of safe and hygienic conditions in the places of employment of these hundreds of thousands of operatives so that their industrial efficiency may be unimpaired is of prime economic importance to the state. Sickness due to unwholesome conditions is one of the chief causes of poverty and distress, of the destruction of the lives of men and women whose energy are the sources of the nation's wealth. The economic value of the human life is everywhere being more and more recognized. The proper safeguarding of the health of the employees, the prevention and limitation of industrial or occupational diseases is now one of the most important problems before any industrial community and one which must be solved.

• • •

Under the act creating it, the Commission is charged with the duty of inquiring into the following matters:

1. Hazard to life because of fire: covering such matters as fire prevention, inadequate fire-escapes and exits, number of persons employed in factories and lofts, arrangement of machinery, fire drills, etc.
2. Accident prevention; guarding of machinery, proper and adequate inspection of factories and manufacturing establishments.
3. Danger to life and health because of unsanitary conditions: ventilation, lighting, seating arrangement, hours of labor, etc.
4. Occupational diseases: Industrial consumption, lead poisoning, bone disease, etc.
5. An examination of the present statutes and ordinances that deal with or relate to the foregoing matters, and of the extent to which the present laws are enforced.

The Commission is to recommend such new legislation as may be found necessary to remedy defects in existing legislation and to provide for conditions now unregulated.

The Commission is directed to present its report to the Legislature before the 12th day of February, 1912.

William L. Beers Testimony

What caused the Triangle fire and how it might have been prevented were among the Factory Investigating Commission's initial concerns, and so the testimony of William L. Beers, who was fire marshal of the City of New York at the time of the fire, was particularly important. Beers began by explaining how, in his opinion, the fire started. Virtually all later accounts accept his view, that a male worker on the eighth floor probably carelessly tossed a match too close to the waste material kept under the cutting tables, as the most likely explanation of what happened. This very much complicated the cases of the victims' families who sued the insurance carrier. Under a legal doctrine known as the "fellow servant" rule, employers (and therefore their insurers) were not liable if an employee was injured through the carelessness of a fellow worker. Present-day worker compensation programs explicitly set aside the "fellow servant" rule and so hold employers liable even in cases where their employees are injured through the mistakes of co-workers.

Beers was sure it was a male employee who started the fire because only men, in the early twentieth century, smoked. Later, when he made a series of specific recommendations for changes in state factory legislation, he called for the absolute prohibition of smoking in a number of industries. In the following testimony, unless otherwise indicated, Abram I. Elkus, commission counsel, asked the questions.

TESTIMONY OF WILLIAM L. BEERS

Q. Did you visit the Triangle Waist Company Building immediately after the fire? A. Yes, sir.

Q. Did you make an investigation? A. I was there all during the evening of the fire, and was there on the ground the next morning at nine o'clock.

Q. Tell us what you observed. A. The result of my investigation and the taking of testimony for ten days after the fire was that I was of the opinion that the fire occurred on the eighth floor on the Greene street side, under a cutting table, which table was enclosed, and that contained the waste material as cut from this lawn that was used to make up the waists. They were in the habit of cutting about 160 to 180 thicknesses of lawn at one time; that formed quite a lot of waste, which was placed under the cutting tables, as it had a commercial value of about seven cents a pound.

Q. Was it boxed, or just placed on the floor? A. Well, the boards that were nailed on the legs of the table formed the box or receptacle.

Q. The outside of that receptacle was wood? A. Yes; it was all wood.

Q. How did the fire start there in that stuff? A. Well, we formed the opinion that it started from the careless use of a match from one of the cutters. They were about to leave to go home, and in those factories they are very anxious to get a smoke just as quick as they get through work.

Q. A man simply lighted a match? A. Yes; and carelessly threw it under there; then the attention of the occupants was called to it, and they tried to extinguish it before they rang in a fire alarm.

Q. Did you examine the fire-escapes of that building? A. After the fire.

Q. What did you find? A. I found the fire-escape on the rear of the building, which was the only one, and was entirely inadequate for the number of people employed in that building.

Minutes of the hearing of the New York State Factory Investigating Commission, testimony of William L. Beers, November 17, 1911 (Preliminary Report II: 580–81, 582–83).

Q. Why were they inadequate? A. Too small and too light, and the iron shutters on the outside of the building when opened would have obstructed the egress of the people passing between the stairway and the platform.

Q. How many people were there on the eighth floor? A. Something over 250, as I recall it.

Q. How many sewing machines? A. There was a cutting department, and it was partially used for machines for making fine waists. About 220 persons were on the eighth floor, all of whom escaped.

Q. How did they come to escape? A. They went down the stairway and down the fire-escape, some of them.

Q. How about the ninth floor? A. The loss of life was greatest on the ninth floor. There were about 310 people there.

Q. How many sewing machines? A. Two hundred and eighty-eight.

Q. Now, will you tell the Commission whether or not the place was overcrowded with the machines? A. Yes, sir. All the space that could be utilized there was utilized.

Q. Were any attempts made in that case to extinguish the fire? A. Yes, there were. They used fire pails there, and then attempted to use the fire hose.

Q. What happened to the fire hose? A. Well, they claimed they could not get any water to it.

Q. How about the fire pail, why did not that put out the fire? A. They did not get enough water to put it out. It spread very rapidly. The material is very inflammable, and it travels very fast, and the conditions were there, everything, to build a fire.

• • •

Q. What recommendations have you to make for legislation to the Commission with reference to the prevention of fires and the saving of lives, and also with reference to the spread of fires? . . . A. I think that all manufacturing establishments should have an interior automatic signalling device to call attention to fires when they occur, and they should also have an automatic extinguishing device in the form of sprinklers and of standpipes. Local fire drills should be compulsory and all the exits in factories should be marked, as in theatres, and the factory employees should be drilled the same as the crew of a ship is drilled. The fire stations should be known, and the specific duties of each employee should be known in case of fire. That is, some of the men should be directed to get the female employees out of the building, and the others should be directed to get the male employees together for the purpose of fighting the fire and holding it in check until such time as assistance came. I think that here in the city, all these loft buildings that are used for manufacturing purposes, the equipment should be standardized and should be as nearly fireproof as possible, and no tenant should be permitted to occupy a building of that kind without first filing a plan showing the way in which the manufacturing apparatus is to be installed, and that should be as near fireproof as possible; and he should not be permitted to fill up his building with a lot of combustible material without proper supervision. The number of persons employed in a given area should be specified and approved and the plan of the building, with the exits all marked, should be posted on the walls of the building, so that it would be there and the employees could become familiar with it, and know just where they are to go in case of fire. Smoking should be absolutely prohibited in such industries as shirt-waist making and light lawn dresses, or where any of those light inflammables are used, chiffons and veilings, straw goods, hat factories, or in any factory using a large quantity of material that is inflammable. I think, also, it would be wise to have lectures in the public schools, under the auspices of the Board of Education, instructing these employes what to do in case of fire, especially in schools located in these districts where the factory employees reside.

G. I. Harmon Testimony

At least one of the jurors in the Harris-Blanck trial had wished that the state factory inspector had been on trial instead. It was his responsibility, this juror felt, to make sure that all the doors were kept unlocked. It was G. I. Harmon, a factory inspector with fifteen years' experience with the New York State Department of Labor, whom the juror claimed he would have had no trouble convicting. Harmon inspected the Triangle factory just a month before the fire. He was one of the first witnesses called by the commission. It was the closest thing to a trial that Harmon would encounter, and commission counsel Elkus questioned him closely about what he noticed during his inspection and about how he carried it out. This phase of the interrogation shed considerable light on one of the mysteries of the fire: How did the Triangle Shirtwaist Company lofts pass a state inspection only a month earlier when postfire examinations by the city fire department disclosed several major violations?

TESTIMONY OF G. I. HARMON

G. I. Harmon, called as a witness, and being duly sworn, testified as follows:

• • •

Q. Now, when was it that you examined the Triangle building prior to the fire? A. The 27th of February.

Q. 1911? A. 1911.

• • •

Q. What examination did you make of that building? A. I made a regular inspection of each factory in the building.

Q. What did that consist of? What did you do? A. I first go to the office and introduce myself. I get the data that I have to have—the number of people employed, men and women. If they have children there, I want to get their certificates, see their register, ascertain all the information in the office, then get someone to go with me and go through the factory. If they have machinery, look at the machinery. In the Triangle building underneath the table I found cuttings there, and then I looked into the sanitary conditions, examined the toilets, to see that there are enough of them, and that they are clean, and the number employed there, to see if there are enough of them. I see that they have a dressing room if they have girls employed. If they have a fire-escape, I see that the windows to the fire-escape are open and free, raise them and try them. If there are doors to the halls I open the doors and see that they are unlocked. I look into the general sanitary condition of the entire building, the care of sinks and water, and see that their drinking water is all right.

Q. How long did it take you, for instance, to examine the Triangle Waist building? They have three lofts? A. Yes.

Q. How long did it take you? A. Possibly an hour and a half to two hours.

Q. And were any of aisles which led to the fire-escapes blocked by material? A. No. The aisles that lead to the fire-escape, you mean? Between the machines, you mean?

Q. Yes. A. Not that I recall. . . .

Q. Were any of the doors locked which led to the stairs? A. They were not.

Q. Did they have locks on them? A. Yes.

Q. Before you went around to examine this factory, you went to the office and asked for someone in authority and told them your business and what you were there for? A. Yes.

Minutes of the hearing of the New York State Factory Investigating Commission, testimony of G. I. Harmon, October 13, 1911 (Preliminary Report II: 242, 243–49).

Q. So that they had plenty of time to remedy any defects that existed temporarily while you were there? A. Yes.

Q. So, as far as the locking of the doors was concerned, or even material in the aisles, that might have been hastily cleaned up or remedied for the moment? A. That might have been.

Q. Well, don't you think it would have been a better and a fairer examination if you didn't tell them who you were, and just walked through? A. Well, in the first place, it is sometimes difficult to get into a place of that kind without telling them who you are.

Q. Well, I mean if you had no difficulty in getting in? A. Well, you have to get a certain amount of information.

Q. Do you mean about the number of employees, how many men and how many women and so forth? A. Yes. You go into a perfectly strange shop that you were never in in your life, and you would be pretty near lost unless you asked questions of somebody.

Q. You wouldn't be lost in trying to find where the staircase was, and whether doors were locked or not? A. You have got to find a lot of other things; you have got to find the toilets and the dressing rooms, and you have got to find if they have children employed, you have got to call upon and find the children.

Q. You can ask any employee where they are? A. Sometimes you get an answer and sometimes you don't. Some of them are foreigners.

Q. And it may become necessary to have someone who understood a foreign language with you? A. I do—I take an interpreter very often.

Q. You, of course, could just as well get this information about the number of people in the factory afterwards as you could in the beginning. You see what we are trying to point out, Mr. Harmon, is that these conditions which exist in factories are not discovered because the inspectors inform somebody in authority that they are there, and the persons in authority know what you are looking for. • • •

Q. Well, now, go back to this particular Triangle Waist Company loft. Did you discover any violations of the law when you were there at all? A. Yes, sir, I did.

Q. What did you discover? A. Well, the shafting under the machine tables was not guarded; that is, a portion of it was not guarded, and part of it was. They had no dressing rooms for the girls, that is, that complied with the law, and the lights in the halls were inadequate.

Q. That is, the lights in the hall which went downstairs? A. Yes, the hall should be kept lighted.

Q. Did you find the doors leading to the stairs opening inward? A. They all opened in, every one of them.

Q. Did you report that to the Department? A. I did.

Q. Did you order it remedied? A. I did not. In my judgment it wasn't practicable to open out into the hall because the halls were too narrow, and I so reported.

Q. Did you order sliding doors put in? A. I did not.

Q. Did you order a vestibule door put in? A. I did not.

Q. Do you realize that if those doors had not opened inward there might not have been such a loss of life? A. Well, the idea of sliding doors is new since. Yes, I realize that. I know that. I knew that before. The doors should swing out.

Q. How wide were the spaces between the wall and the end of each row of machines where the employees had to walk in order to get to the doors or fire-escapes? A. Well, you are asking me questions that it is hard for me to answer. The only thing that I can rely on is the record I have in my book, and my book makes no record of anything of that kind at all.

Q. Didn't you bring your report here with you? A. Yes, I have it.

Q. Well, look at it. A. That does not show what you are asking; it doesn't show the space between the end of the tables and the wall.

Q. The space there ought to be wide enough for the employees to pass through easily in case of fire or in ordinary cases of panic? A. Yes.

Q. Isn't it a fact that the space was only eighteen inches? A. Between the end of the table and the wall?

Q. Between the end of the table and the wall. A. Well, between the end of the table and the wall on the Washington Place side that may be possible.

Q. Well, that is where they have to go, these employees had to go? A. I beg your pardon. They had to go the other way to get out, they had to pass between the tables. At the end of the table on the north side of the building, what is known as the north side of the building, there was ample room there, there was no aisle there, and they used the Greene Street stairway, they didn't use the Washington Place stairway.

Q. Couldn't they use the Washington Place stairway in case of fire? A. Yes.

Q. Wasn't it your duty to see that there was adequate space for the employees to reach either staircase, whether Washington or Greene Street in case of fire or other hazardous causes? A. Well, yes, it is my duty, yes.

Q. Well, then, didn't you find that the space leading to the Washington Place stairs between the end of the tables and machines and the wall was only eighteen inches, and that that was inadequate? A. I did not measure the space, but I think that that is about right.

Q. And that was an inadequate space? A. Well, that depends altogether on conditions. That is an adequate space for people not in a hurry.

Q. Well, when there is a fire, people are in a hurry and your duty was to examine this space to find out whether the people could get out in a hurry? A. I know, but there were other ways besides that aisle, that 18-inch aisle.

Q. I know, but doesn't the law require you to find that every way out is a proper way? **A.** If you can show me that in the law, I would be glad to see it.

Q. Doesn't the law require you to inspect and find out that proper space is given to every egress in case of fire, and that the ways are not blocked or impeded? **A.** It doesn't say egress, it says exits. As I understand the meaning of the word "exit," it is a window or door which leads to the fire-escape.

• • •

Q. Understand, I don't want to be in the least unfair to you. I wouldn't for anything. Now, what else did you discover? You started to tell me some violations of the law you discovered there when you examined it. What else did you discover? Was there any dirt on the floor? **A.** No dirt, except the natural refuse from the work that they were doing.

Q. Was there any more than would be there from one day's work? **A.** That is all.

Q. Were the employees smoking? **A.** Well, I saw stains on the table where cigarettes had laid.

Q. The marks of the cigarette? **A.** In that particular case I saw nobody smoking there. I have reported that to the employers time and again, of seeing men smoking in shops, because I know it is a mighty dangerous habit.

Henry Bruere Testimony

As counsel Elkus's questioning of G. I. Harmon indicated, the commission wanted very much to pin down which government agencies were responsible for enforcing safety regulations. The commission requested Henry Bruere, director of the Bureau of Municipal Research in New York City, an organization that specialized in recommending ways of making government more efficient, to make a study of which agencies had jurisdiction in the Triangle case. There were at least ten, Bruere found, and their jurisdictions so overlapped that it was virtually impossible to determine which was responsible for enforcing any given regulation. Clarifying lines of authority became, as a result, one of the chief goals of the commission, and several of its legislative recommendations dealt with consolidating agencies and simplifying the process of enforcing existing regulations. The following excerpt suggests the confusion that Bruere's report documented.

TESTIMONY OF HENRY BRUERE

• • •

THE WITNESS: The Bureau of Buildings has, of course, with respect to all buildings, exclusive jurisdiction over the approval of plans, excepting, of course, tenement house construction.

MR. ELKUS: Of course, we are very much more interested in the factory investigation.

THE WITNESS: In connection with the approval of plans, the Bureau of Buildings has exclusive jurisdiction. With the State Department of Labor it has a concurrent jurisdiction to inspect factories for all violations of the Building Code and to enforce corrections of violations.

With the Fire Department it has concurrent jurisdiction to inspect factories for violations of the Building Code regarding matters relating to fire prevention, and to enforce the corrections of violations.

With the Fire Department it shares jurisdiction for approval of processes of fireproofing.

With the Fire and Health Department it may require the destruction or repair of unsafe buildings.

With the Health and Tenement House Departments it is required to inspect drainage and plumbing in factories and enforce correction of violations.

The Fire Department shares with the Bureau of Buildings those functions which I have just enumerated; has exclusive jurisdiction to inspect factories for violation of all laws and ordinances, except the Building Code as to fire prevention, and to enforce corrections of such violations.

With the Health Department the Fire Department may require the destruction or repair of unsafe factory buildings.

With the Police and Tenement House Departments it may prevent encumbrances of fire-escapes.

With the Department of Water Supply, Gas and Electricity it may inspect electric installation in factories.

The Health Department has concurrent jurisdiction with respect to factories with the Bureau of Buildings and the Fire Department again to require the repair or destruction of unsafe factory buildings.

With the State Department of Labor to inspect buildings as to violations of the laws or ordinances for the preservation of life and health, and to enforce corrections of such violations.

Minutes of the hearing of the New York State Factory Investigating Commission, testimony of Henry Bruere, December 21, 1911 (Preliminary Report III: 1969–70).

With the Fire Department to examine overcrowding in factories, and order those conditions remedied.

With the State Labor Department and Tenement Department to require in factories proper toilet facilities, proper temperature, clean and light walls and ceilings, proper safeguards against accident.

With the Tenement House Department the Health Department may inspect factories and tenement houses where disease is discovered and condemn infectious articles.

Rose Schneiderman Testimony

Despite the welter of government agencies charged with inspecting conditions in New York factories—and Henry Bruere calculated that ten agencies spent more than a million dollars annually just to inspect factories in New York City—or, perhaps because of it, the commission employed its own investigators. Most came from reform organizations, such as the National Consumers League or the Women's Trade Union League, which had long agitated for more stringent regulation of working conditions, especially for women workers. Indeed the commission's work was, in several respects, a continuation of the hearings held in the immediate wake of the fire by the WTUL. Several of its investigators had played prominent roles first in the shirtwaist workers' strike, then in the WTUL hearings, and had then campaigned for the creation of the commission. Rose Schneiderman is the most conspicuous case in point.

It was somewhat surprising that she had joined the commission's staff. She had, in her speech at the Metropolitan Opera House the previous April, expressed doubt that the sorts of reforms the commission would propose would make any difference. Only direct action by the workers themselves, she had said, would avail. Yet she did join the commission. Later, when its co-chair, Al Smith, became governor, she would take a position in his administration as a labor mediator. She stayed on through the governorship of Smith's successor, Franklin D. Roosevelt, and then became part of the New Deal when he became president. Schneiderman's service with the commission, as a result, proved a turning point in her life—and in her politics as she turned from socialism to liberal reform. This did not mean any lessening of her devotion to the interests of working women, however. Toward the end of her testimony, after detailing some of the dangerous conditions she had found, she returned to a key theme of her Metropolitan Opera speech:

> It seems to me that that is a very vital question—the question of wages because we know that people die from other causes besides being burned alive. . . . I think the wages and hours are the most fundamental evils for the people that work. . . . [For] a girl to live decently . . . [she] must start with a certain amount of money. . . .

TESTIMONY OF ROSE SCHNEIDERMAN

• • •

Q. How many of these factories did you personally inspect last week? A. Fourteen.

• • •

Q. Now, will you take one, Miss Schneiderman, and give us the place and location of the factory or of the building it was in—what floor it was on and how many people were employed there, and tell us generally what you found? A. I investigated, first of all, a factory on West Broadway, between Houston and Bleecker, and going into that factory I became interested in the factories on the other block, being that the factory facing the West Broadway factory was so near. There was only a space of about eight or nine feet between them.

Q. You mean the rear of one building was within eight or nine feet of the other? A. Yes.

Q. The fronts being on two different streets? A. Yes; and what interested me most in this West Broadway factory was that the fire-escape led out presumably into a courtyard, which was a blind alley, and once you get down there you could not get out; there was no exit.

Q. The fire-escape from which building? A. From the West Broadway building, as well as the other side.

Q. What street was the other fronting on? A. Wooster.

Q. These two buildings were back to back? A. Yes, sir.

Q. West Broadway and Wooster Street run parallel? A. Yes.

Minutes of the hearing of the New York State Factory Investigating Commission, testimony of Rose Schneiderman, October 11, 1911 (Preliminary Report II: 109–10).

Q. There was an open court way? A. No; just a blind alley.

Q. It is a court way? A. Yes.

Q. That is open at the top? A. Yes.

Q. Between these two buildings? A. Yes, sir.

Q. How large was that court way? A. Well, it went all the way through the block, the length of it, and the width was about eight or nine feet; that is all.

Q. Eight or nine feet wide? A. Yes.

Q. And there was no way of getting out of that courtyard or alley except through one of the buildings? A. Exactly.

Q. If you could get in the building? A. Yes.

Q. Was there a door from one building to this courtyard? A. No, there was not.

Q. Nothing but windows? A. Nothing but windows. In fact there was a sort of a glass roof over an extension from the main floor and it was barred with irons and iron spikes sticking up, so that if you did get down into the alley there were those iron spikes there that would not be very comfortable.

Q. Prevent you from crawling up and getting out? A. Yes; and the alley was terribly dirty. There was all kinds of rubbish in that alley. I don't know how long ago the inspector must have been there. It seemed to me as though he had not been there for years because of the dirt accumulated there.

Q. Now, to inspect that alley all you had to do was to look out of the window of either building? A. You had to get out on the fire-escape.

Q. All you had to do was to walk out on the platform of the fire-escape and look down? A. Yes, sir.

Q. It would not take more than a minute, would it, after you got there? A. No, when you thought of getting there.

Q. The fire-escapes from both buildings ran into this blind alley; the drop ladder at the bottom, if there was one, was that fixed to the ground? A. No; it was up a floor above—I think the second floor.

Q. So that if there was a fire and anybody went down the fire-escape and got the drop ladder down they would land in this blind alley? A. Yes, sir.

Q. And they could not get out? A. No; and I really believe the alley itself would burn because of the papers and shoes and all the kind of things like that.

Q. Also lumber? A. Yes, sir.

Q. Do you mean to say there was so much stuff on the floor of the alley it would burn up of itself? A. Yes.

Alfred R. Conkling Testimony

Women's Trade Union League participation in the work of the commission meant that the public hearings frequently reflected a prounion point of view. Consider the beginning of Leonora O'Reilly's testimony of October 10, 1911, the first day of hearings:

> Q. What is your business or profession? A. My business is shirtwaist maker; my profession, labor agitator.[1]

On the other hand, the commission strove to make good on its promise to listen to all sides of the issue. Alfred R. Conkling was one of several concerned factory and/or building owners to testify. In addition to providing an example of what contemporaries called "enlightened" business opinion, especially on safety issues, Conkling's testimony is interesting for the light it sheds on how factory owners viewed the fire. In this context, his explanation of why so many died stands in stark contrast to that of Elizabeth Hasanovitz, the union militant. Bernard L. Shientag, the commission's assistant counsel, questioned Conkling, as did the chair, state Senator Robert Wagner.

---

[1] O'Reilly, a longtime member of the WTUL, had helped organize the shirtwaist workers' strike. She also spoke at the union memorial service for the fire victims that almost turned into a riot. See the *New York Times* story reprinted earlier.

TESTIMONY OF ALFRED R. CONKLING

• • •

Q. Mr. Conkling, in what capacity do you appear before the Commission this afternoon? A. As the owner of factories . . . in regard to smoking and to fire drills in factories.

Q. The Commission will be very glad to hear your views on those two matters; first, with reference to smoking, do you think that smoking

---

Minutes of the hearing of the New York State Factory Investigating Commission, testimony of Alfred R. Conkling, November 16, 1911 (Preliminary Report II: 516–17, 519–20).

should be made a crime? A. Smoking in factories and manufacturing establishments?

Q. Yes, smoking in factories and manufacturing establishments. A. I do; I think the smoker should be the guilty man, and not the owner or employer.

Q. Not under any circumstances, Mr. Conkling? Suppose the owner or employer sees the smoking and takes no steps to prevent it? A. I will tell you my own experience.

Q. We would be very glad to hear that from you, Mr. Conkling. A. I have a factory about half a mile south of that ill-fated Washington Place building. After the fire I went to my building and had the words "No Smoking" in large letters on the wall of the lower hall and again on the floors, written in black letters on white ground. I asked the tenants to put up the sign "No Smoking" on all floors, which they did. I talked with the tenants about it, speaking about some cigars there, and in spite of that there was a fire there about July 5th, at five minutes past six. The damage was small and no one was injured.

I then went up the fourth floor, the guilty tenant, and scolded him for smoking. He says, "The boys will smoke." Burnt cigarettes on the floor, empty boxes of cigarettes and burnt matches. Now, you ask if I would make the misdemeanor apply to the employer who lets the operatives smoke in his presence. I must take time on that. I cannot decide that with such short notice.

Q. But you do believe in making smoking in a factory or manufacturing establishment a misdemeanor? A. Absolutely.

• • •

Q. We would like to hear your views on the subject of fire drills in manufacturing establishments. A. I got interested in that subject after the Washington Place fire last March. I went through the factories which I owned and put in fire axes on every floor and one of them that I owned, the next building, about thirty feet away, I put in ropes like in the hotels, from the windows. I tried to get a fire drill. I got the names of several principals of the public schools and offered to pay them, with the price of cab, on Saturday, to meet the employees of the buildings which I owned. I could not do it. They were too busy. . . .

I then thought about employing exempt firemen to teach the fire drill, and I think that is practicable, to have a sort of auxiliary force or rather a bureau of fire prevention in the Fire Department, to put on the exempt firemen, experienced men.

THE CHAIRMAN: Retired firemen?

THE WITNESS: . . . I thought it would be wise to have exempt firemen, even old volunteer firemen, to teach the fire drill. They are men of years, they are patient, unlike young men and young women, and I think it would be wise to have them teach the employees at the factories.

But I want to emphasize the fact that all fire drills and fire prevention laws in the world would be of no use if the working men and working women will lose their heads.

I come back and will start with the Washington Street place. Yesterday I talked with a friend of mine who saw the fire. He lives around the corner. He told me that before the smoke came out of the windows about sixty women jumped from the upper floors, the eighth and ninth floors; some before the Fire Department came and some afterwards, when it was not necessary. Now there was no fire-escape there on the front of the building. The firemen came with their nets. They jumped six at a time into the net and the firemen fell forward, and they were killed.

Dr. Antonio Stella Testimony

In addition to government officials, "labor agitators," and factory owners, the commission called upon a number of expert witnesses. One of the more influential, in terms of its final recommendations, was Dr. Antonio Stella. He was a physician with an international reputation for the treatment of tuberculosis. Himself an immigrant from Italy, Stella had long interested himself in the connections between industrial working conditions and the incidence of the disease. So he eagerly cooperated with the commission. His testimony reflected the best medical opinion on not only the causes of tuberculosis but also on women's health issues. His view that women were particularly susceptible to fatigue and that long hours, therefore, contributed "to all the ills woman's flesh is heir to" was important because, under the position adopted by the U.S. Supreme Court in *Muller v. Oregon* (1908), states could regulate working conditions provided they could show that the well-being of women, the future mothers of the "race," was at stake.

TESTIMONY OF DR. ANTONIO STELLA

By Mr. Elkus:

Q. May I direct your attention to what you found to be the causes of tuberculosis in this country among the Italian immigrants and Italian workers in factories? A. The causes are many, but the nature and quality of work are the main factors.

Q. That is the question. Will you answer it in your own way? A. I infer that you have probably this fact in your mind, which is coming to be every day more impressed on physicians, that tuberculosis of the lungs among the workers in factories is really, in two-thirds of the cases an occupational disease. In other words, some occupations so undermine the system that the advent of bacillary invasion must be considered only as a coincidence and a secondary accident. This is especially true of workers who are exposed to dust of different natures. They primarily develop what is called by Oliver, industrial lung disease. Later the Koch bacilli find their way into the damaged tissues and cause tuberculosis of the ordinary type. There is, therefore, a close relation between occupation and tuberculosis, and in two-thirds of the cases the disease might properly be considered as the result of the former, regardless of all other factors (alimentation, home surroundings, etc.). We find this from studying the excessive death rate of certain well-defined occupations, where we observe that the workingmen of that class live as well and comfortably, are as well paid, housed and clothed as men employed in other trades. Yet they develop tuberculosis and the others don't. We are then forced to admit that it is the effect of certain occupations that is the primary factor in the development of the disease.

Q. How about working in homes? A. Just as bad from the viewpoint of health.

Q. Haven't you found that there is a great deal of that, Doctor, among the Italians in this city? A. Yes, the Italian women contribute ninety-four per cent of all the home finishing in New York city.

Q. How about the children? A. The children develop the surgical form of tuberculosis, that is tuberculosis of the glands and bones.

Q. From working too early in life? A. For that reason and from ante-natal causes. The mothers are so exhausted by overwork and fatigue, that they beget weak and feeble children, who are thus predisposed to all sorts of infection and primarily to tuberculosis.

Minutes of the hearing of the New York State Factory Investigating Commission, testimony of Dr. Antonio Stella, December 21, 1911 (Preliminary Report III: 1940–41).

Q. The mother working while she is pregnant works at this very confining work at the house, and I suppose has improper ventilation, and improper or insufficient food, and long hours chiefly? A. They don't know how long they work.

Q. The great trouble, isn't it, with home work is the long hours? A. Yes, the long hours. Long hours are the cause of all the ills woman's flesh is heir to. The sitting posture, to mention one factor, protracted for many hours, for days and weeks, is responsible for many disorders and displacements of the generative organs, the arrest of their development and their faulty function.

Fatigue, considered as a morbid condition of the system, induced by overwork, is in itself the main cause of the entrance of all infectious diseases, and of the diminished resistance to disease in general. I would even say that alcoholism in women of the laboring class very often is the result of long hours of work and the direct consequence of the excessive demands made upon their muscular and nervous system.

Melinda Scott Testimony

Part of the reason why Dr. Stella's testimony resonated so strongly with the commission is that it provided a medical rationale for key planks in the Women's Trade Union League reform platform. Melinda Scott, a WTUL organizer who specialized in working with English-speaking women workers, presented the league's proposals. As already noted, the commission largely continued the investigations initiated by the WTUL and continued to employ WTUL members in key staff positions. And the commission's recommendations closely followed the league's agenda. Even so, as Scott made clear, in the early weeks and months of its work, the WTUL was not yet sure it could trust the politicians on the commission, especially co-chairs Robert Wagner and Al Smith, with their links to Manhattan's notorious Tammany Hall Democratic machine.

When Mary Dreier resigned the New York league presidency, Scott would defeat Rose Schneiderman in the race to succeed her. The central issue in the campaign was whether the league should continue to attempt to organize immigrant women (Schneiderman's belief) or concentrate entirely upon the native-born (Scott's belief). Indications of Scott's despair of organizing the foreign-born, despite the fact that the league's greatest success was with the shirtwaist workers, the overwhelming majority of whom were immigrants, run through her testimony.

TESTIMONY OF MELINDA SCOTT

THE WITNESS: The Women's Trade Union League and the members and representatives of separate unions affiliated believe that much good may come from the investigating work undertaken by this Commission, if the investigation is directed to an effort to obtain facts, opinions and recommendations primarily from the workers instead of the employers. It is the opinion of trade union women, based on past experience, that the efforts of employers are to conceal or deny the dangers and health-destroying conditions under which most business is carried on. This is natural for employers, but that is all the more reason why a Commission such as this should put more faith in the experience of the workers, since the only purpose for the existence of the Commission is to improve working conditions. We therefore recommend, first, prohibition of all work in tenements. Work in tenements is done almost entirely by the lately landed emigrants, Jews and Italians and other nationalities unfamiliar with American conditions and American standards. At present there are 12,000 licensed tenements, with an average of twelve licensed apartments to a tenement, 144,000 apartments in all to be inspected. While this is the case there is not, and cannot be, adequate inspection. The time of the inspectors, which ought to go to the factories, is taken up by the tenement factories in order that unscrupulous employers may escape payment for rental, light, heat and machinery, thus competing unfairly with employers in decent factories which are paying for them. Moreover, this home work is a constant force destroying the efficiency of the laws limiting the hours of working women or forbidding child labor. Since such laws do not and cannot extend to the tenements, women here work ten, fifteen and twenty hours a day, competing with women in the factories.

• • •

There is no justification for these conditions, and no decent wages made. One mother and a child working after school, sometimes as late as 1 A.M., made twenty to fifty cents a day. A mother and five children, making

Minutes of the hearing of the New York State Factory Investigating Commission, testimony of Melinda Scott, December 20, 1911 (Preliminary Report III: 1803–06).

flowers, fifty to seventy-five cents a day. These foolish workers are destroying their own chances of improvement by competing with their own bread earners in the factory.

Second, a pension for pregnant mothers at work. If married women are at work in the factories, they must be protected against the infliction of permanent injury of themselves and their children by working during the time immediately preceding and immediately following the birth of a child.

Merely to prohibit work at such times does not solve the problem. We must have a pension for a period immediately before and immediately after childbirth.

The third recommendation is the bill limiting the working hours of women to forty-eight hours per week. This is the trade union standard, and is recognized by the State in the case of men employed in State work. . . .

Fourth, a bill creating a special Commission to investigate the question of a minimum wage in sweated trades. Such a Commission has been appointed in Massachusetts and a minimum wage is in operation in certain trades in England and also in Australia.

Fifth, an increased number of women inspectors in New York city. This city contains more than one-half of the women workers in the entire State.

Sixth, added inspectors to be permanently in New York city, and the inspection to be done according to trades and not according to districts.

• • •

Seventh, laws protecting workers from danger in case of fire. All the clamor, denunciations, and so-called public interest since the Triangle fire have resulted so far in a bill placing the entire responsibility on the Fire Department, and creating a limited number of inspectors. But no law has been passed defining the requirements for protection of workers in factories. In regard to that the statutes are as vague as formerly. The question of automatic fire alarms, fire walls, exits, number and kind of fire-escapes, and other means of protection is still unsettled. The trade union women, in connection with trade union men, have incorporated their best thought on this subject in a bill which was ignored last year. This Commission could do nothing better than to recommend the passing of this bill. We hope that the Commission will not be persuaded into making unnecessary compromises by the oft-used cry of "expense."

• • •

We also urge that this Commission hold at least one executive session, and make every effort to procure women from unorganized shops and trades to give evidence about their conditions. Fear of dismissal if their names become known prevents them from testifying. This is also a fatal obstacle in procuring evidence for present violations, and some means ought to be devised by law for protecting these girls.

Florence Kelley Testimony

The National Consumers League (NCL), whose hundreds of thousands of members pledged to boycott goods manufactured in substandard conditions, joined the Women's Trade Union League in many of its reform proposals. NCL general secretary Florence Kelley testified in favor of extending maximum hour protection to women over sixteen, lengthening the list of industries in which women could not work until they reached the age of sixteen, and providing thorough annual physical examinations to child workers. The sections of her testimony excerpted here deal with preventing pregnant women and new mothers from working and with the abolition of all tenement house labor, both key demands of the WTUL. Kelley's views typified those of many early supporters of what later became Aid to Families with Dependent Children (AFDC), a program that grew so large in the two decades following Richard Nixon's election in 1968 that it became synonymous in many people's minds with the term "welfare."[1] Present-day "reformers" of the welfare system associate AFDC with the politics of the 1960s and the "Great Society" of Lyndon Johnson. This is not so much incorrect as misleading. Proposals for "widow's pensions" and grants for working mothers date to the end of the nineteenth century; several states adopted versions of them in the years surrounding World War I. Federal programs began with the New Deal. Nor, as Florence Kelley's testimony illustrates, did these early advocates indulge overmuch in "bleeding heart" sentimentality. Instead their attitudes reflected the "scientific" approach to philanthropy that governed the Red Cross's dispersal of relief funds to the Triangle victims' families.

---

[1] The Nixon administration energetically expanded a number of the Johnson administration's "War on Poverty" programs. As Nixon's attorney general, John Mitchell, was wont to admonish the press and other critics, "Watch what we do, not what we say."

TESTIMONY OF FLORENCE KELLEY

• • •

Q. What have you to say with regard to the employment of women who are pregnant, either before or after childbirth? A. I think it a monstrous outrage that a woman should be employed in that condition. . . . It ought not to be tolerated.

Q. Would you obviate it altogether? A. Absolutely.

Q. How long after childbirth? A. At least three months. I do not believe that it is true that the economic conditions in any city in the United States make that necessary. I have lived amongst the poorest of the poor for twenty years.

Q. Why is that done; it is done frequently, not only in the cities but in New England? A. Well, it is done largely through a mistaken idea of thrift on the part of the family, or by the shiftlessness and selfishness of the husband drinking up the family earnings, and largely encouraged by the manufacturers or employers for the purpose of reducing the wages by having both heads of the family and all the children contributing to the family purse. . . . A man who is in the position of the head of a family which is increasing ought to be held up by the community rigidly to his duty in supporting his wife and children.

Q. Suppose he cannot do it? A. I think he ought to go to the workhouse; the responsibility ought to be put on him, and kept on him, unless we are going to accept as an American institution one of the very worst vices of European industries. What have we a protective tariff for if those industries do not pay the heads of families enough to support their families?

Q. Would you be in favor, if it were demonstrated, for instance, that the head of a family was unable to support his wife and family, as is usually the plea, of separating him from his family and making him work out his own salvation, and not increasing the family? A. I do not believe in the continuation of the family relations where the mother is both mother and father.

• • •

Q. Would you suggest anything with reference to the practicability; these women may become charges in some of the cases? A. A community which acquiesces in having the heads of families paid such insufficient wages that their wives have to support the family ought to take its medicine and contribute to the maintenance of widows with children.

Minutes of the hearing of the New York State Factory Investigating Commission, testimony of Florence Kelley, December 19, 1911 (Preliminary Report III: 1599, 1600, 1602).

• • •

Q. Would not your recommendations for the abolishment of all labor in tenement houses work very considerable hardship? A. There is nobody self-
sustaining by tenement-house work now.

Q. What would be their condition if they were deprived of the proceeds of
their labor and were employed directly? A. The work would be taken out
of the tenement houses, and the workers would go into lofts and work
under more sanitary conditions.

• • •

Q. What would happen in these cases? A. The children would go to school;
the sick people would go to the hospitals and the able-bodied would
work in lofts under better conditions. There would be left the little remaining portion of those widows and children who now have to be
partly taken care of by charity. They would have to be taken care of by
charity a little more than they are now; that is all. There would not be
any more paupers than there are now. The mothers could take better
care of their children, and we should not have the invasion of the
kitchen and bedroom, if the tenement house work were abolished.
That is the way it would work, I feel sure, from what I have seen in the
other industries.

TAMMANY HALL AND THE POLITICS OF REFORM

The Roosevelt I Knew

In the years following the publication of the Factory Investigating
Commission's *Preliminary Report* (1912) a number of states placed lim-
itations on the number of hours women might work. In several, such
as Rhode Island and Delaware, the laws covered virtually every industry. In Texas, on the other hand, it covered only workers in the garment trades, one of the state's smallest industries, and exempted
workers in cotton mills, the state's largest industry. New York did more
than limit total hours. It prohibited any employment of women between the hours of 10 P.M. and 6 A.M. Massachusetts already had such

a law.[1] Thus began the wave of "protective" legislation that would both help and hinder women workers until the 1970s.

One of the keys to the success of the Factory Investigating Commission in enacting its recommendations was the decision by New York City's Democratic machine, also known as Tammany Hall, to support reform. Tammany had long opposed measures that restricted the rights of employers, and it had certainly proved itself no friend to the shirtwaist workers or their union during the strike, as evidenced by the behavior of police and police magistrates alike. Many reformers who hoped for substantial reform were disheartened when state Senate President Robert Wagner and state Assembly Speaker Al Smith, both loyal members of Tammany Hall, named themselves chair and co-chair of the commission. To the reformers' great surprise, Wagner and Smith not only supported the entire reform package that the commission's expert staff proposed, but they also worked tirelessly and effectively to pass the legislation. How did this political turnabout happen? There are no records of Tammany meetings on the question. And Al Smith's autobiography is silent on the subject. We do have the shrewd speculations of Frances Perkins.

No one played a greater role in organizing the day-to-day work of the Factory Investigating Commission than Frances Perkins. She came to the commission from the New York branch of the National Consumers League, where she had been working as a factory inspector. Like Rose Schneiderman she later joined the Smith administration and stayed on when Franklin Roosevelt became governor. She then became secretary of labor in 1933, the first woman to hold cabinet rank, and served in that office throughout Roosevelt's presidency. She got her start in Democratic politics as a lobbyist for the commissions' legislative recommendations. This excerpt from her autobiography describes her work with the co-chairs, Robert Wagner and Al Smith, and her initial meeting with the "boss" of the Tammany Hall machine in New York City, Charles D. (Charlie) Murphy.

---

[1] A useful summary is "Some New State Laws Affecting Women's Work," *The Survey* 30 (May 3, 1913): 161–162.

THE ROOSEVELT I KNEW

By Frances Perkins

I was an investigator for the Factory Investigating Commission and we used to make it our business to take Al Smith, the East Side boy who later became New York's Governor and a presidential candidate, to see the women, thousands of them, coming off the ten-hour night-shift on the rope walks in Auburn. We made sure that Robert Wagner personally crawled through the tiny hole in the wall that gave egress to a steep iron ladder covered with ice and ending twelve feet from the ground, which was euphemistically labeled "Fire Escape" in many factories. We saw to it that the austere legislative members of the Commission got up at dawn and drove with us for an unannounced visit to a Cattaraugus County cannery and that they saw with their own eyes the little children, not adolescents, but five-, six-, and seven-year-olds, snipping beans and shelling peas. We made sure that they saw the machinery that would scalp a girl or cut off a man's arm. Hours so long that both men and women were depleted and exhausted became realities to them through seeing for themselves the dirty little factories. These men realized something could be done about it from discussions with New York State employers who had succeeded in remedying adverse working conditions and standards of pay. Such a man was Edward Huyck, a blanket and wool textile manufacturer at Hudson; such businesses were the Carolyn Laundry in the Bronx and a concern in Rochester with the strange name of "Art in Buttons."

It was the experiments of these and other manufacturers (all successful moneymakers) that brought conviction to the members of the Commission that conditions in industry were frequently bad for the workers; that they were correctable by practical means; and that correction by lawful process would benefit industries as well as workers. Production and business would increase and the whole state would profit.

Frances Perkins, *The Roosevelt I Knew* (New York: Harper & Row, 1964 reprint of 1946 Viking Press edition), 16, 17, 22–25. Reprinted by permission of Viking Penguin.

These principles the Commission recommended, and the legislature, over a period of three to five years, put into law the program of compulsory shorter work day and week for women, limitation of age of children at work, prohibition of night work for women, workmen's compensation for industrial accidents, measures to prevent industrial accidents, and elaborate requirements for the construction of factory and mercantile premises in the interests of the health and safety of the people who worked in them.

The extent to which this legislation in New York marked a change in American political attitudes and policies toward social responsibility can scarcely be overrated. It was, I am convinced, a turning point; it was not only successful in effecting practical remedies but, surprisingly, it proved to be successful also in votegetting.

New York was a great industrial state. It had within its borders one huge city, the largest in the United States, and a number of other large cities. This differentiated the influence of this program of labor legislation in New York from that, for example, in the State of Wisconsin. Wisconsin was a small homogeneous community, more agricultural than industrial, with a few large industries and no large cities. The experimental development of legislation to remedy social adversity in Wisconsin was of great value and was quoted in support of the New York legislation, even though in Wisconsin it was of lesser scope. But New York! If it could be done there, it could be done anywhere. The fact that the Democratic party became dominant in New York for many years largely on the basis of this program of legislation (combined with competent, sympathetic administration), riveted in American life the conception that it was the duty and opportunity of people elected to office to develop programs for prevention of poverty and for improving the conditions of life and work of all the people.

As a young, relatively uninfluential social worker, with a beginning acquaintance of Albany politicians and political methods, I was able to have a hand in these programs. I am convinced that the pull of social forces rather than vote-getting considerations moved the politicians in this direction. It was not because some of the Democrats were poor boys and many of the Republicans were well-to-do in their youth that the Democrats were more responsive to social reform. I think it was purely chance that the Democrats were in office when the opportunities and necessities to move in this direction came. Thousands of people became Democrats or voted that ticket when the Democrats espoused these ideas.

There was nothing social minded about the upstate Democrats who boasted they were Jeffersonians, whatever that means. In my experience it meant that they were for the farmers and the canneries and regarded labor laws as interfering with the liberty of individuals.

Certainly there was nothing social minded about the head of Tammany Hall, Charles Murphy, whom I went to see when legislation on factory buildings was before the state legislature. I went to enlist his support for this legislation. I climbed up the stairs of old Tammany Hall on 14th Street in a good deal of trepidation. Tammany Hall had a sinister reputation in New York, and I hardly knew how I would be greeted, but, as I later learned, a lady was invariably treated with respect and gallantry and a poor old woman with infinite kindness and courtesy. Mr. Murphy, solemn dignity itself, received me in a reserved but courteous way. He listened to my story and arguments. Then, leaning forward in his chair, he said quietly, "You are the young lady, aren't you, who managed to get the fifty-four-hour bill passed?"

I admitted I was.

"Well, young lady, I was opposed to that bill."

"Yes, so I gathered, Mr. Murphy."

"It is my observation," he went on, "that that bill made us many votes. I will tell the boys to give all the help they can to this new bill. Good-by."

As I went out of the door, saying "Thank you," he said, "Are you one of these women suffragists?"

Torn between a fear of being faithless to my convictions and losing the so recently gained support of a political boss, I stammered, "Yes, I am."

"Well, I am not," he replied, "but if anybody ever gives them the vote, I hope you will remember that you would make a good Democrat."

EXCERPT FROM "ONE OF THEM"

By Elizabeth Hasanovitz

[In late 1915] our union began to make preparations to improve conditions in our trade. Our board of directors immediately began working on the modifications of the protocol and new demands, so as to present them to the Employers' Association.

Each new demand was carefully discussed and acted upon by special member meetings. Our mass meetings were successful; our workers showed great enthusiasm and understanding of the demands.

We demanded an increase in wages, and a forty-eight-hour week instead of fifty.

We were ready to declare a general strike if our demands were ignored. But the Employers' Association soon met our union in conference to discuss matters.

After many conferences, unable to agree, both parties submitted their disputes to the Board of Arbitration.

The association controlled only half the industry; the rest was in the hands of individual employers, some of whom had individual agreements with our union and some were not unionized at all. To make similar agreements with them and enforce equal standards throughout the industry, we had to call a general strike.

The exciting preparations then began. First, we organized the workers among whom we worked for the coming demonstration. Many of us were discharged from several places for doing it, I among them. But I did not care. I hoped that in the near future, through this new strike, we would gain better conditions, that the new agreement would forbid an employer discharging a worker for union activities, and so I was willing to suffer another few weeks.

The active members were assigned by the union to different committees, each performing an important duty. And we worked very hard. In rain or snow, we did not fail to meet and plan together. We

---

Elizabeth Hasanovitz, "One of Them," chapter from A *Passionate Autobiography* (Boston and New York: Houghton Mifflin Co., 1918), 292–98.

were all anxious to plan right and do our bit for the success of the strike.

At last, on February 9th at two o'clock in the afternoon, a red circular waved by a committee in each shop was the signal to the workers to stop. At the sight of the red circular thousands of workers stood up at the same minute, folded their work, put their aprons into the baskets and peacefully marched down. Crowds of them were pouring out from the different buildings into the streets, mingling together, greeting each other. Their happy cheers loudly echoing in the air were caught and enthusiastically answered by new groups who were constantly joining the crowd from the neighboring streets, and the avenues soon became black with the multitudes of the young toilers. Races, nationalities, were forgotten: Jews, Italians, Americans, Slavs, Germans, colored people—all combined together in one desire, a desire for a better life. On they marched, the crispy frost encouragingly crackling under their swift feet. Their happy cheers were like the remote, sweet bell-ringings of a glorious future, and my heart bubbled with emotion as I watched that live procession on the snow-clad February day.

I compared them with the many processions I witnessed so often in the early morning when the crowds were moving on to the monotonous toiling world. Those were mourning processions, dull, automatic movements of a down-trodden mass who carried all the thorns of life in their ignorant indifference.

But what a different procession I saw now. Multitudes moving on, but moving lively,—pale but happy were those young toilers who clothed the nation and themselves were shabby. Pride and dignity shone in their eyes. . . .

The meeting halls especially provided for the strikers were soon overcrowded. Over thirty thousand workers were on strike, . . .

• • •

In the halls the committees in charge worked hard to keep the strikers enthusiastic and everything was conducted in an orderly manner, but a demoralization arose among the strikers in certain halls due to the misleading of some speakers from the ranks. There were a few members, quite intelligent persons and with good intentions, who caused some trouble with their speeches. Not being present at the special meetings at which our demands were discussed before the strike, they were ignorant of many facts, and, failing to realize that, entrusting our disputes to the Board of Arbitration, we had to accept its decision, unless it is absolutely against us, they appealed to the strikers not to make any compromises, not to accept any decisions from the Board unless all our demands were granted to us.

The Board of Arbitration did not grant us all our demands, but its decision as a whole was favorable, and though a great many of us were not quite pleased we accepted the conditions because we had agreed to arbitrate.

When the decision was brought to the strikers, those who were influenced by the appeals of the few not to compromise refused to accept it. They accused the representatives of the conference as acting autocratically by accepting the decision, but the clearer-thinking workers, who had carefully followed and studied the special meetings and also the sessions of the Board of Arbitration, were in full sympathy with our representatives, for they saw our strenuous efforts to get for the people whatever possible. With great difficulty we succeeded in restoring order among the discontented ones, and after one week, when also a great number of individual agreements were signed, the people gradually returned to work.

By little and little everything smoothed. After such a huge demonstration of over thirty thousand workers, things were slowly coming into shape. The last decision was given out by the Board, and the final modified agreement was drawn up.

The protocol as it read appeared favorable if the employers would only carry out all that is provided for us as stated; and if instead of short seasons we had steady work; but above all, if the workers themselves would stand together, and all like one be on the lookout.

The "General Strike" of 1916

If the chief legacy of the Triangle fire was the "protective" legislation sponsored by the Factory Investigating Commission, the great strike that preceded it left a legacy, too. The "Uprising of the Twenty Thousand" of 1909–1910 was essentially about gaining recognition for the International Ladies Garment Workers Union as the collective bargaining agent in the so-called needle trades. The union's success had been partial; Local 25 went from fewer than one hundred members to more than ten thousand. Many firms signed "closed shop" agreements, under the terms of which they agreed to hire union members and to submit grievances to arbitration. Other firms, including the largest, held out and remained "open shops." Even in the shops that recognized the union the ILGWU found it difficult to enforce the agreements. The arbitration process was very slow. Employers often set up new companies, hired nonunion workers, and closed down their unionized shops. Workers, however, remained determined to hold on to the ground gained and to extend it. Joining the issue of union recognition as central to workers was the principle of arbitration of grievances. Strikes were common. One of the most important was the "general strike" of 1916, recounted here by union activist Elizabeth Hasanovitz. It was, in many ways, a reenactment of the "Uprising," and the moral that Hasanovitz drew, that all would be well if all the workers stood on the lookout "like one," forms a fitting complement to the "protective" legislation and a fitting epilogue to this story of triumph, tragedy, and heroism.

The Strike

The "The Uprising of the Twenty Thousand," the Triangle fire, and the New York Factory Investigating Commission have long fascinated historians. Virtually no one, however, has studied them together, although every study of the fire mentions the strike, and every study of the Factory Investigating Commission contains at least a brief description of the fire.

Louis Levine, *The Women's Garment Workers: A History of the International Ladies' Garment Workers Union* (New York: B. W. Huebsch, Inc., 1924), is both the earliest and the best history of the strike. Levine's was the official union history, and ILGWU officials, many of them participants in the events he described, cooperated not only by giving him interviews but also by granting him access to union records. Despite his declared sympathy for the ILGWU, Levine was a scrupulously careful researcher. Not the least of his work's merits is his detailed description of the nature of work in the needle trades. Also useful are Joel Seidman, *The Needle Trades* (New York: Farrar and Rinehart, 1942), and Hyman Berman, "The Era of the Protocol: A Chapter in the History of the ILGWU, 1910–1916," unpublished Ph.D. dissertation, Columbia University, 1955.

Levine provides a good survey of early organizing efforts before the "uprising." Joan M. Jensen, "The Great Uprisings, 1900–1920," in *A Needle, a Bobbin, a Strike: Women Needleworkers in America*, edited by Jensen and Sue Davidson (Philadelphia: Temple University Press, 1984), pp. 81–93, provides a briefer overview and a more up-to-date set of references, but some of her statistics about the numbers of strikers and the percentage of industrial workers in New York City in the needle trades need to be used with caution. A popular account is Barbara Mayer Wertheimer, *We Were There: The Story of Working Women in America* (New York: Pantheon Books, 1977), pp. 293–317. Her version of the "uprising" is based in large part on the memories of Pauline Newman, an early organizer for the ILGWU. A useful corrective to Wertheimer's hagiographical approach is Anne Schofield, "The

Uprising of the 20,000: The Making of a Labor Legend," in *A Needle, a Bobbin, a Strike: Women Needleworkers in America*, pp. 167–82. Also helpful is Roger Waldinger, "Another Look at the International Ladies' Garment Workers' Union," in *Women, Work, and Protest: A Century of U.S. Women's Labor History*, edited by Ruth Milkman (London and New York: Routledge & Kegan Paul, 1985, 1987), pp. 86–109. Melvyn Dubofsky, *When Workers Organize: New York City in the Progressive Era* (Amherst: University of Massachusetts Press, 1968), places the "uprising" in the context of New York City's many strikes.

The Role of Immigrant Women in Union Radicalism

Although Italians played important roles in the strike and in the organization of the ILGWU, most of the strikers and virtually all of the early leaders of the union were Jewish immigrants from Russia or elsewhere in eastern Europe. As a result, Levine devoted much attention to them. Melech Epstein, *Jewish Labor in the U.S.A.: An Industrial, Political and Cultural History of the Jewish Labor Movement, 1882–1914* (New York: KTAV Publishing, 1969, reprint of the 1950 edition), is largely drawn from *The Women's Garment Workers*. A recent look at the ethnic roots of union radicalism in the garment trades is Daniel Soyer, "Landsmanshaftn and the Jewish Labor Movement: Cooperation, Conflict, and the Building of Community," *Journal of American Ethnic History* (1988), pp. 22–45. A *landsmanshaftn* was an association of immigrants from the same town in Europe who banded together in the United States for mutual protection. Often *landsmanshaftn* began as burial societies. *American Jewish History* devoted its September 1986 issue to them. Gerald Sorin argues that Jewish radicalism, including early trade union activities, derived from traditional Jewish values in his *The Prophetic Minority: American Jewish Immigrant Radicals 1880–1920* (Bloomington: University of Indiana Press, 1985). A more common view is that radicalism represented a departure from traditional Jewish belief. Irving Howe, *World of Our Fathers: The Journey of the East European Jews to America and the Life They Found and Made* (New York: Simon and Schuster, 1976), especially pp. 287–359, states that view with grace and panache. Syndey Stahl

Weinberg, *The World of Our Mothers: The Lives of Jewish Immigrant Women* (Chapel Hill: University of North Carolina Press, 1988), is a reliable introduction to an important topic as well as a corrective to Howe's tendency to focus upon the male experience. More narrowly focused is Elizabeth Ewen, *Immigrant Women in the Land of Dollars: Life and Culture on the Lower East Side, 1890–1925* (New York: Monthly Review Press, 1985).

Rose Schneiderman and Other Union Activists

A good introduction to Rose Schneiderman's union career is Alice Kessler-Harris, "Rose Schneiderman and the Limits of Women's Trade Unionism," in Warren Van Tine and Melvyn Dubofsky, editors, *Labor Leaders in America* (Urbana: University of Illinois Press, 1987). On her role in the Women's Trade Union League, the standard work is Gary Endleman's *Solidarity Forever: Rose Schneiderman and the New York Women's Trade Union League* (New York: Arno Press, 1982). Also useful is Annelise Orleck, "Common Sense and a Little Fire: Working Class Women's Organizing in the United States," unpublished Ph.D. dissertation, Columbia University, 1989, which contains a full account of Schneiderman's union career. Ellen Condliffe Lagemann, *A Generation of Women: Education in the Lives of Progressive Reformers* (Cambridge: Harvard University Press, 1979), devotes an excellent chapter to Schneiderman and another to her mentor, Leonora O'Reilly, who also played an important role both in the "uprising" and in the work of the New York Factory Investigating Commission. Sally M. Miller profiles another immigrant Jewish union activist and radical in "From Sweatshop Worker to Labor Leader: Theresa Malkiel, a Case Study," *American Jewish History* 68 (December 1978), pp. 189–205. Malkiel covered the "uprising" for the socialist *New York Call* and then wrote a novel, *Diary of a Shirtwaist Striker* (Ithaca: Industrial and Labor Relations Press of Cornell University Press, 1990 reprint of 1910 edition). Malkiel made her heroine an "American" rather than an immigrant, presumable to appeal to a wider audience.

The Triangle Fire

Leon Stein, *The Triangle Fire* (Philadelphia: J. B. Lippincott), dominates the literature on the fire. Oddly, despite his years of service to the ILGWU as editor of its paper, Stein made no effort to place the conflagration in the context of the strike. He did devote a final chapter to the legislation sponsored by the New York Factory Investigating Commission but did not discuss the politics of the era. The book's great merit is its meticulous re-creation of the fire itself.

Factory Safety Legislation

Surprisingly little has been written on the history of factory safety legislation. On New York, there are a couple of useful articles: Melvyn Dubofsky, "Organized Labor and the Immigrant in New York City, 1900–1918," *Labor History* (Spring 1961), pp. 182–201; and Thomas J. Kerr, Jr., "The New York Factory Investigating Commission and the Minimum Wage Movement," *Labor History* (Summer 1971), pp. 373–91. Kerr's footnotes are a useful introduction to some of the primary sources for the Progressive Era. Also useful are the notes to Maurine Weiner Greenwald's introductory essay in Elizabeth Beardsley Butler, *Women and the Trades* (University of Pittsburgh Press, 1984 reprint of 1909 original). A helpful survey is Ronnie Steinberg, *Wages and Hours: Labor and Reform in Twentieth-Century America* (Rutgers University Press, 1982). Another useful overview is Alice Kessler-Harris's *Out to Work: A History of Wage-Earning Women in the United States* (Oxford University Press, 1982). There is also Lynn Y. Weiner's *From Working Girl to Working Mother: The Female Labor Force in the United States, 1820–1980* (University of North Carolina Press, 1985).

The Role of the Women's Trade Union League

Although historians have not devoted much attention to factory safety legislation, the literature devoted to the Women's Trade Union League, the organization that did so much to agitate for such laws, is immense. Elizabeth Anne Payne, *Reform, Labor, and Feminism: Margaret Dreier Robbins and the Women's Trade Union League* (Urbana: University of Illinois Press, 1988), is an excellent introduction. Her opening chapter is especially insightful on the sources of the reform ideas of Margaret Dreier and her sister Mary, who together founded the league. Payne's focus is on the Chicago branch of the league. For New York see Nancy Schrom Dye, *As Equals & As Sisters: Feminism, Unionism, and the Women's Trade Union League of New York* (Columbia: University of Missouri Press, 1980), whose title nicely captures the fascination that the league holds for feminist scholars. Dye's account of the WTUL role in the "uprising" is very helpful. Her account of why the league turned from union organizing to campaigning for protective legislation is also of interest, if uneven. She is very good at tracing league members' gradual discouragement with strikes and with union officials but overlooks the positive attraction exerted by the New York Factory Investigating Commission. The Dreier sisters, like many other women reformers of their generation, Ellen Condliffe Lagemann persuasively argues, justified their demands for a more meaningful role in society for themselves in the name of service to others. The league's success in working with the commission stood in stark contract to its inability to organize workers in the paper box, millinery, paper flower, and white goods trades.

For Nancy Schrom Dye, the turn to protective legislation illustrated the division between upper- and upper-middle-class reformers like the Dreier sisters and working-class union activists like Rose Schneiderman and Leonora O'Reilly. See her "Creating a Feminist Alliance: Sisterhood and Class Conflict in the New York Women's Trade Union League, 1903–1914," *Feminist Studies* (Spring 1975), pp. 24–38. Robin Miller Jacoby argues in "The Women's Trade Union League and American Feminism," *Feminist Studies* (Fall 1975), pp. 126–39, that the more important tension in the WTUL was between union organizers and suffrage advocates, It is, however, difficult to avoid judgment that most studies of the WTUL exaggerate its importance.

New York Factory Investigating Commission

Historians of the politics of the period, on the other hand, seriously underestimate the importance of the work of the Factory Investigating Commission. John D. Buenker, in his influential *Urban Liberalism and Progressive Reform* (New York: W. W. Norton, 1978), flatly states that "much of the legislative output [of the urban liberals] began with the work of the famous New York State Factory Investigation Commission" (p. 48), but subsequent scholars have paid little heed. A noteworthy exception is Elizabeth Israels Perry's biography of her grandmother, *Belle Moskowitz: Feminine Politics and the Exercise of Power in the Age of Alfred E. Smith* (New York: Routledge, 1992).

CREDITS AND ACKNOWLEDGMENTS

Text

Excerpt from *The Roosevelt I Knew* by Frances Perkins. Copyright 1946 by
    Frances Perkins, © renewed 1974 by Susanna W. Coggeshall. Used by
    permission of Viking Penguin, a division of Penguin Books USA Inc.

Excerpt from *All for One* © 1967 by Rose Schneiderman (with Lucy Gold-
    thwaite). Published by Paul S. Eriksson. Reprinted by permission of Paul
    S. Eriksson.

Excerpts from, the *New York Times* copyright © by The New York Times Co.
    Reprinted by permission.

Photos

Page 21, Brown Brothers
Page 21, ILGWU Kheel Center, Cornell University
Page 21, ILGWU Kheel Center, Cornell University

A

Aid to Families with Dependent Children
(AFDC), origins of, 161

Alterman, Kate, key witness in manslaughter
trial of Blanck and Harris, 111, 115–125

Arbitration, failure of, 48–49

Asch Building, described, 134; pictured, 85;
site of fire, 84–86

Associated Waist and Dress Manufacturers
[employers' organization], view of strike, 39, 40

B

Barrows, Alice P., investigated strike for *The
Survey,* 75–78

Beers, William, L., N.Y. City fire marshal,
testimony before Factory Investigating
Commission, 142–145

Belmont, Mrs. August, support for strike, 7,
40, 41–42, 45, 46; support for co-operative
factory to aid strike, 51

Blanck, Max, account of fire, 90–93; fined in
unrelated factory safety violation, 109;
portrait, 85; trial for manslaughter, 110–127;
view of origins of strike, 29–30

Bostwick, Charles F., prosecutor in Blanck-
Harris manslaughter trial, 110–127

Bruere, Henry, director, Bureau of Municipal
Research, testimony before Factory
Investigating Commission, 149–151

Butler, Elizabeth Beardsley, quoted, 4

C

Cahan, Abraham (editor of *The Forward),*
speech at union memorial meeting for
strikers, 97, 98–99

Carnegie Hall, meeting at, 49–50

Charity Organization Society, role in
coordinating giving of relief, 104

City Hall, strikers march on, 38–40

Cole, Elsie, role in strike, 28, 72

Colony Club, meeting at, 7, 42–44

Conkling, Alfred R., factory building owner,
testimony before Factory Investigating
Commission, 154–156

Cooper Union [strike] meeting, Nov. 22, 1909,
31–33, 80

D

Dance/reception for strikers released from
prison, 46–47

Darwinism, social and reformed, defined, 9–10n

Dorr, Rheta Childe, quoted, 9n, 78

Dreier, Margaret, role in Women's Trade Union
League (WTUL), 7

Dreier, Mary, arrest in shirtwaist strike,
26–28; at colony Club meeting, 44;
marching in funeral procession for
unidentified fire victims, 103; role in
organizing shirtwaist strike, 34, 39, 72; role
in WTUL, 7

"Double standard" defined, 5; and "social
feminism," 8

Dutcher, Elizabeth, role in providing relief to
fire victims and their families, 104–109; role
in Women's Trade Union League and strike, 72

E

Elkus, Abram I., chief counsel, N.Y. Factory
Investigating Commission, opening
statement, 139–142

Epstein, Jacob, *Intensely Serious,* ii–iii;
Working Girls Returning Home, 1

F

"Fellow servant," rule, defined, 142

Fining system in shirtwaist shops, 54

Frowne, Sadie, "The Story of a Sweatshop
Girl," 13–16

Funeral procession of unidentified fire
victims, 102–104

G

"General Strike" of 1916, 168–171
Gibson, Charles Dana, "Gibson Girl," ii, 1
Goldmark, Fannie, role in strike, 55
Goldstein, Eva, account of strike's beginning, 54–55
Goldthwaite, Lucy, co-wrote *All for One* with Rose Schneiderman, 13, 71
Gompers, Samuel, speech at Cooper Union meeting, 31–33
"Great Society" program of Lyndon Johnson, 161

H

Hapgood, Hutchins, *The Spirit of the Ghetto,* xx
Harmon, G. I., factory inspector, testimony before Factory Investigating Commission, 145–149
Harris, Isaac, account of fire, 90–93; portrait of, 85; trial for manslaughter, 110–127
Hasanovitz, Elizabeth, role in 1916 strike, 168–171
Hayes, Ellen, organized support for strike at Wellesley, 743
Hippodrome Meeting of Dec. 5, 1909, news account of, 41–42
Holt, Hamilton, publisher of *The Independent,* 12
Hutchinson, Woods, investigated strike for *The Survey,* 74–78; quoted, 5
Hyman, I. D., of Associated Waist and Dress Manufacturers, denies use of "toughs" against strikers, 40; on rejection of arbitration agreement by union, 49

I

Independent, life stories of "undistinguished" Americans, 12–19
Insurance settlement with fire victims' families, 109–110
International Ladies Garment Workers Union (ILGWU), formation of, 6; poststrike dispute with Women's Trade Union League, 78–79, 79n, 102; relief efforts for fire victims and families, 104–107

K

Kelley, Florence, president of National Consumers League, 58n; testimony before Factory Investigating Commission, 161–163
Kellogg, Arthur P., investigated strike for *The Survey,* 75–78
Kellogg, Paul U., editor of *The Survey,* 31; quoted on growth of sympathy for strike, 24–25; view of strike, 68

L

Lemlich, Clara, described by brother, 68; portrait, 21; role in strike, 37, 78; "soul" of the strike, 67–68, 69–70; speech at Colony Club meeting, 42–44; speech at Cooper Union meeting, 20, 31, 33, 38

M

Marot, Helen, analysis of strike, 78–83; marching in funeral procession for unidentified fire victims, 103; role in strike, 28, 29, 39, 72; role in Women's Trade Union League, 78
The Masses, 1
McClure's, and muckraking, 3, 133
Metropolitan Opera meeting, account of, 99–102
Mitchell, John, Attorney General in Nixon administration, quoted, 161n
Morgan, Anne, criticism of socialists in strike, 50; organizer of Colony Club meeting, 42–43, 72; organizer of Metropolitan Opera meeting, 100; support for shirtwaist strike, 7, 45
Morgenthau, Mrs. Henry, Sr., deeded property to support strike, 72
"Muckraking" journalism, defined, 133
Mulholland, Inez, support for strike, 45, 46
Muller v. Oregon (1908), cited, 10n, 140n, 156
Murphy, Charles ("Charlie"), Tammany Hall "boss," and reform, 8, 167

N

National Consumer's League, commissioned *Making Both Ends Meet,* 58; factory safety proposals, 161–163; historical sketch of, 58n

"New Woman," defined, 3; compared to "working girl," 5; role in work of Factory Investigating Commission, 8

New York State Factory Investigating Commission, creation of in wake of fire, 7; hearings, 139–163; organized, 100

New York Times, editorial approach to strike, 26

Nixon, Richard, role in expanding welfare programs, 161

O

O'Reilly, Leonora, Carnegie Hall speech, 49–50; role in strike, 42, 47, 72; speech at union memorial meeting for strikers, 97, 99; testimony before Factory Investigating Commission quoted, 154

The Outlook, editorial on strike quoted, 52n

P

Perkins, Frances, role in N.Y. Factory Investigating Commission, 7, 100, 163–167

Perovskaya, Natalyla [pseudonym for Rose Perr], "tale of adventure," 57–67

Perr, Rose [Edith], account of strike, 58–67; fundraising speaking tour with Rose Schneiderman, 53, 73; speech at Carnegie Hall, 50, 52–53; role in strike, 7, 47, 52–53, 56

Pike, Violet, arrest for picketing, 44–45; role in strike, 27, 72

Police harassment of strikers, 24–25, 77

Polokoff, S. S., union official, account of fire by, 127, 129–132

"progressive mentality," defined, 4, 5

R

Ravage, Marcus, quoted on life in Lower East Side community, 97n

Red Cross, relief efforts for fire victims and families, 104–107

S

Safran, Rosey, account of fire, 89–90

scabs, violence against, 37

Schneiderman, Rose, account of strike in autobiography, 70–74; biographical sketch, 12–13, 151–152; "A Cap Maker's Story," 17–19; fundraising speaking tour, 53; portrait, 21; marching at head of funeral procession for unidentified fire victims, 102–103; role in N.Y. Factory Investigating Commission, 7; role in strike, 7; role in Women's Trade Union League, 70–71; speech at Colony Club meeting, 44; speech at Metropolitan Opera, 99–102; on "social evil," 57, 70; testimony before Factory Investigating Commission, 151–153

Schwartz, Margaret, fire victim for whose death Blanck and Harris were charged with manslaughter, 111

"Scientific philanthropy," defined, 104

Scott, Melinda, Women's Trade Union League organizer, testimony before Factory Investigating Commission, 158–161

Scudder, Vida, organized support for strike at Wellesley, 73

Shaw, Josephine Lowell, founder of National Consumers League, 58n

Shaw, Rev. Dr. Anna, speech at Hippodrome meeting, 41, 42

Shepherd, William, eyewitness report of Triangle Fire, iv–v

shirtwaist, *Harper's Bazar* ad for, 1

shirtwaist strike, chronology of, 22–23; news accounts of, 26–52; rules for pickets, 24–25; see also "Uprising of the Twenty Thousand"

Simon, A. L., speech at union memorial meeting for strikers, 99

Sloan, John, cartoon on fire for *New York Call,* 85; drawing, *This heart was true to Pol,* for *McClure's,* 86; diary quoted, 84; *New York Etchings,* quoted, 1; quoted on fire, 5; *The Return from Toil,* 1

Smith, Al, N.Y. state Assembly Speaker, and Factory Investigating Commission, 100, 164, 165; and reform, 8

"social feminism," and reform, 8, 156, 158–161

Steinman, Victor, juror in Blanck-Harris trial, quoted on acquittal, 127, 132

Steuer, Max D., attorney for Blanck and Harris, 90, 111–127; speech before Missouri Bar Association quoted, 114–115, 117, 125

Stella, Dr. Antonio, physician, testimony before Factory Investigation Commission, 156–158

Stokes, Rose Pastor, speech at Hippodrome meeting, 42

Sussman, Minnie, role in strike, 55–56

Swartz, Margaret, see Margaret Schwartz

T

Tammany Hall, Manhattan political machine and reform, 7–8, 164–167

Triangle Fire chronology, 86–88; accounts of, iv–v, 88–93, 134–138

Triangle Shirtwaist Company, fire at, 2; beginning of shirtwaist strike in, 6, 79–80

U

Union memorial meeting [for fire victims], account of, 96–99

union recognition, key demand of strikers, 48–49

"Uprising of the Twenty Thousand," 6; see also shirtwaist strike

Urusova, Natalya [pseudonym for Rose Perr], 57, 58

V

Van Kleeck, Mary, investigated strike for *The Survey,* 75–78

W

Wagner, Robert, president of N.Y. state Senate, and Factory Investigating Commission, 100, 164, 165; and reform, 8

Weyl, Mrs. Walter [of WTUL], view of police harassment, 40

Woerishoffer, Carola, role in Women's Trade Union League and strike, 71–72

Women's Trade Union League (WTUL), and Factory Investigating Commission, 100, 152–153, 158–161; factory safety proposals, 159–161; postfire investigations into factory safety, 99–100; poststrike dispute with International Ladies Garment Workers Union, 78–79, 79n, 102; role in funeral of unidentified fire victims, 102–103; role in strike, 7, 33–34, 71–74

"Working Girl," protection of, 1–9

Y

Younger, Maud, cited, 9n